Pearl Harbor

PROBLEMS IN
AMERICAN CIVILIZATION

Pearl Harbor

Roosevelt and the Coming of the War

Third Edition

Edited and with an introduction by

George M. Waller

Butler University

D. C. HEATH AND COMPANY
Lexington, Massachusetts   Toronto

CONTENTS

INTRODUCTION

Well over a quarter of a century has passed since December 7, 1941, branded by President Franklin D. Roosevelt the "date that will live in infamy," when Japanese bombers struck the United States by surprise at Pearl Harbor and inflicted a disastrous defeat upon the nation. Almost immediately the question was asked: "How could it have happened?" The question was asked and answered—a hundred different ways—with passion.

The war with Japan culminated a decade of mounting concern about Japan's course on the part of many American leaders. In 1931 Japanese military forces had taken over Manchuria, exploiting the "Mukden incident," a mysterious explosion on the Japanese-controlled South Manchurian Railroad. Early in 1932 Henry L. Stimson, President Hoover's Secretary of State, reacted to Japan's seizure of Manchuria by proclaiming what became known as the Stimson doctrine, a policy of nonrecognition of changes forced by aggression. When Japan persisted in establishing a puppet state, Manchukuo, in the area that was formerly Manchuria, the United States applied Stimson's doctrine of nonrecognition. President Hoover rejected more forceful action. Nor did Britain and France respond to Stimson's appeal for action against Japan, although the League of Nations condemned Japan's seizure of Manchuria and endorsed Stimson's doctrine. As a mere moral sanction, nonrecognition proved useless. It was also dangerous. It alienated Japan and showed her and other would-be aggressors that they could defy treaties and the League of Nations with impunity.

Only a few years later fighting broke out between Chinese and Japanese troops at the Marco Polo Bridge near Peking, in July 1937 This "China Incident," as the Japanese euphemistically termed it, rapidly escalated into an undeclared war between China and Japan. Whoever had been at fault in the original incident, Japan's aggressive prosecution of the war convinced President Franklin D. Roosevelt that this was a further example of Japanese aggression. Roosevelt's Quarantine Speech of October 5, 1937 was both a warning to aggressors and an attempt to rally Americans against isolationist impulses and win them to a policy of international cooperation in maintaining world peace.

As the war in China dragged on, divisions between American and Japanese interests became more serious. Meanwhile relations with Germany and Italy—the Axis powers—deteriorated as Hitler and Mussolini followed a course of aggression in Europe. After war broke out on September 3, 1939 between Britain, France, and their allies and the German-Italian Axis, the United States gradually abandoned neutrality and subscribed support to the Western democracies. Japan concluded an alliance on September 27, 1940 with Germany and Italy: the Tripartite Pact. This act entangled Roosevelt's mounting confrontation with the aggressors of Europe with his policies of resistance to Japan's course in China and his fear of further Japanese expansion in Southeast Asia.

By early autumn of 1941 the United States was in an undeclared shooting war against the Axis in the Atlantic and was extending material and monetary aid short of actual military intervention to Great Britain, Russia, and China in their struggles against Germany, Italy, and Japan. Unlike the attitude that preceded our entry into World War I, few in this country expressed any pretension of neutrality toward aggressor nations after Hitler's sweeping victories in Europe in the spring and summer of 1940 and his attack on Russia on June 22, 1941. Roosevelt, in campaigning for his impressive victory at the polls when he was reelected for an unprecedented third term in November 1940, had promised to extend all aid short of war to the victims of Axis power. He had followed this with his speech of December 29, 1940, in which he declared America as "the arsenal of democracy," and then enacted the Lend-Lease Act in March 1941.

But war came in the Pacific. Japan's attack plunged us into World War II, a long-shunned "two-ocean" war. Why did war come? How had our growing involvement in the war in Europe affected our relations with powers across the Pacific? What bearing did it have on the emerging crisis with Japan?

The following selections deal with the general question of whether the United States could or should have avoided war with Japan. Within this general question is a particular one: Why did Japan's attack catch us by surprise?

Historians now tend to regard much that seemed at issue in the years immediately following the war as a stale controversy. Whether the Roosevelt administration is to be blamed for an unnecessary war with Japan or defended in its policies remains a valid question but one that scholars increasingly subordinate in their search for answers to the question of why war came. Where once partisans argued fiercely from positions of loyalty to Roosevelt's administration or opposition to it—finding in the same facts reasons to support or condemn United States policy, rationalizing and justifying on the one hand, criticizing and blaming on the other—scholars now exhibit a readiness to understand the forces at work on both sides, the calculations and miscalculations that led to a war neither side wholly wanted and one that in retrospect failed to attain goals each sought.

The charges made by many of the "revisionists" writing in the decade following the end of the war may now be dismissed on the grounds that the evidence they produced did not support their contentions. Their accusations against Roosevelt betrayed ill-disguised personal hatred, pacifist convictions, concern lest war distract attention from needed domestic reform, and fear of presidential power. Writers like Charles A. Beard, William Henry Chamberlin, John T. Flynn and a number of others (see Suggestions for Additional Reading) held Roosevelt to account both for taking the United States into war and for leaving Hawaii open to attack. They accused him of a secret plot to maneuver the country into war by a "back door," and of being the architect of a policy designed to provoke Japanese attack when American isolationists blocked his efforts to move more assertively against Hitler. They charged the President with deceptive tactics and deliberate conspiracy to keep Pacific commanders in the dark. Their analyses contain much of historical value, but they are marred by personal bitterness, irrelevant criticism, and failure to prove their points.

Similarly outdated are some early defenders of Roosevelt who relied on a simplistic morality to justify American policies and rested their rebuttals on dissecting the revisionists' evidence and even their words and phrases. While charging detractors of F.D.R.'s administration with minimizing the aggressive designs of Berlin and Tokyo and ignoring Japan's treaty violations, they begged the more fundamental question of alternative policies Roosevelt might have followed, and assumed a threat to our global security and national interests without demonstrating it. Some supporters of the President found extenuation for his deceptions in the shortsighted opposition of isolationists, excusing while admitting Clare Booth Luce's memorable charge, "He lied the American people into war because he could not lead them into it."

Before turning to the writers represented in the following selections, something more may be said of those who dealt with the problem of Roosevelt's Asian policy in the immediate postwar period. Not all who questioned the wisdom of that policy may be dismissed. Former ambassador to Japan Joseph C. Grew, British historian Francis C. Jones, and the late William L. Neumann offered a revisionist view that contributes to clarifying our understanding of prewar policy. Their arguments anticipate some of those represented in these readings. Avoiding personal attacks and allegations of bad faith, these authors make an effort to see Japan's viewpoint. Mistaken though it may have been, as they admit, they imply that the United States would have had much to gain in recognizing Japan's problems. Japanese leaders were convinced that Western power and influence in Asia was a threat to their country's security and prosperity. Militaristic, racist, and chauvinistic, the Japanese government made the error of thinking that Britain and the United States would not fight a long and costly war to defend areas so remote.

In this revisionist view, the United States likewise erred in considering that it had a vital national interest in blocking Japanese expansion in Asia, and ignored the role a strong Japan could play in blocking Communist expansion in Asia, along with Japan's vital interest in doing so. Roosevelt's advisers ignored the importance of China to Japan. Nor did China, for its part, see advantages in close Sino-Japanese cooperation. China's resistance to Japanese offers of help against communism is a major point made in John Toland's later book, *Rising Sun,* which sees the Sino-Japanese war more as a product of shortsighted Chinese policy than of Japanese aggression. The Roosevelt administration, with strong pressure from Britain, overrated the importance of a free China and attempted to maintain the status quo in the Pacific without considering the impossibility of preserving an old power structure that had become obsolete with the disintegration of China's Nationalist government and the rising strength of Japan and the Soviet Union.

This revisionist school of thought holds that the United States mistakenly assumed it could coerce Japan, through economic pressure and threats of naval force, into yielding. Instead this policy drove Japan to further expansion in Southeast Asia, practically guaranteeing war with the United States. Our military leaders warned Roosevelt and Hull of their need for time to prepare, but the administration's concern for moral principles and national interests overreached our limited military capacity. Unaware of the pressure of time on Japanese leaders and their determination, Roosevelt—with some misgivings—maintained the firm stance urged on him by cabinet members like Morgenthau, Stimson, and Ickes. The more cautious Hull ultimately agreed. As war appeared more and more inevitable, the F.D.R. administration, according to the revisionists, failed to give the Pacific outposts adequate warnings. In retrospect the revisionists see the war's outcome as the ultimate irony—the United States attained neither strategic, political, nor economic goals. The country was left without trade or influence in China. And Asia gained neither stability nor security.

In the selections that follow, continued disagreement about America's policy toward Japan and the military and intelligence arrangements that accompanied that policy is both stated and implied. But recent writers have been more concerned to learn how war came, what influences were at work—to understand rather than to justify or condemn. Through these writers, the reader may come to understand the differences between Japan and the United States for oneself and arrive at one's own judgments.

In the first section readers will find how a few of the participants in policymaking on both sides viewed the measures they were advocating. The attitudes of many others will be found quoted in later sections.

The second section presents a number of general accounts of the confrontation between the powers in the western Pacific. Disagreeing among themselves about the actual basis for United States policy, they differ further on many points of interpretation. Tansill sees ominous mistakes in United States policy beginning long before Roosevelt came to office. Two writers, Feis and Schroeder, are completely opposed in their judgments about the necessity or wisdom of this country's actions. Burns, Graebner, and Iriye, benefiting from more recent perspectives, present somewhat more analytical view-points.

In forming conclusions about influences on Roosevelt and his Secretary of State, the reader may find accounts of attitudes in the State Department's Far Eastern Division and in the U.S. Navy establishment useful. Historians have found reasons to discount the influence on Roosevelt of other individuals, groups, or forces in America, as noted in the introductory note to the third section. But the reader should be well aware of the impact of the struggle in Europe and of British policy on the courses of action taken by the administration in dealing with Japan, even though some historians view the two areas in which we fought as only accidentally and incidentally connected and suggest that policies adopted toward aid to Hitler's victims should have been divorced from our problem with Japan.

Finally, the fourth group of readings addresses the problem of why the Pearl Harbor attack caught American forces by surprise. Ladislas Farago recounts the story of Japanese espionage and of the secret knowledge the United States obtained about Japanese plans. In Washington, MAGIC was the code name for important intelligence materials. For reasons of security such data was limited in distribution to a very few government and military leaders. Much of the information came from messages sent by the Japanese to their own diplomats in their top diplomatic code, which American cipher experts intercepted, broke, and designated PURPLE.

Samuel Eliot Morison defends the Roosevelt administration against those who judged it guilty of knowing about the attack on Pearl Harbor ahead of time and of failing to warn Admiral Kimmel and General Short, commanders in Hawaii. Admiral Kimmel, victim of the surprise attack, defends himself and charges Washington with failure to keep him informed. In the last selection, Roberta Wohlstetter sums up the problems encountered by military and intelligence groups in order to provide some understanding of why they were unable to warn Washington and Hawaii of the sneak attack.

Inherent in these last selections is the question of how our knowledge of Japan's concealed purposes, great though it was, nevertheless did not disclose their American targets. Did perceptions of the Japanese threat of expansion in Southeast Asia blind those, from the White House to the decks of ships in Pearl Harbor, to the danger to our own Pacific installations?

Victory in World War II brought the United States enhanced world power and, seemingly, world responsibility, readily embraced in the fifties and early sixties. Events from the Danube to the Yalu, from Peking, Moscow, and Berlin to Damascus, Tel Aviv, and Cairo, and especially the long agony of Vietnam have tempered this commitment. Today's readers may be considerably less optimistic about the capacity of the United States to intervene constructively in crises around the world.

The reader may tend, therefore, to be critical of the course America followed toward Japan in 1941. But hindsight, however valuable, should not prevent an understanding of how matters appeared to the adversaries at the time. Out of these accounts one may enhance one's awareness both of the responsibilities and the limitations of world power.

CHRONOLOGY

1931	Japan invades Manchuria
1931	Hoover's Secretary of State announces the *Stimson Doctrine*
1933	Japan leaves the League of Nations
1935	Italy attacks Ethiopia
1936	Spanish Civil War; Germany reoccupies the Rhineland
1937	"China Incident." Clash between China and Japan at Marco Polo Bridge escalates into undeclared war
1935–37	U.S. passes Neutrality Acts
1937	Roosevelt's *Quarantine Speech*
1938	Hitler takes Austria; British and French sign the *Munich Pact* "appeasing" Hitler
March 1939	Hitler takes Czechoslovakia; Mussolini invades Albania
July 1939	U.S. gives Japan notice of abrogation of reciprocal trade treaties
August 1939	Germany and Russia sign nonaggression pact
September 3, 1939	WAR: Hitler invades Poland; Britain and France declare war on Germany
November 1939	U.S. Congress repeals arms embargo, puts trade with belligerents on "cash and carry" basis
April–June 1940	*Blitzkrieg:* Fall of Denmark, Norway, The Netherlands, Belgium, France
September 1940	Destroyer-Bases Agreement
September 1940	Congress passes Selective Service Act, by one-vote margin
September 1940	Japan, Germany, and Italy sign Tripartite Pact
November 1940	Roosevelt reelected for third term
January–March 1941	Joint military staff talks, U.S. and Britain
March 1941	Lend-Lease Act
March 1941	Hull and Nomura begin talks in Washington
April 1941	Roosevelt orders U.S. Navy to patrol in western Atlantic
June 1941	Hitler attacks Russia
July 1941	U.S. occupies Iceland bases
July 1941	Japanese Imperial Conference determines to continue policy in Asia
July 24, 1941	Japan moves into Indochina
July 26, 1941	U.S. freezes Japanese assets

August 9–14, 1941	Atlantic Conference: Roosevelt and Churchill meet at Argentia
August 17, 1941	U.S. warning to Japan
August–September 1941	Prime Minister Konoye requests meeting with Roosevelt
September–October 1941	U.S. destroyers attacked in Atlantic
September 6, 1941	Konoye offers proposals to U.S.
October 2, 1941	U.S. note rejecting Konoye's proposals and deferring proposed meeting
October 17, 1941	Konoye Cabinet falls; Tojo becomes Prime Minister
November 7, 1941	U.S. rejects Japanese Imperial Conference's "Proposal A"
November 17, 1941	Kurusu arrives in Washington to join Nomura
November 20, 1941	U.S. rejects Japanese "Proposal B"
November 22–26, 1941	Hull weighs idea of a "modus vivendi," and rejects it
November 26, 1941	U.S. offers comprehensive proposal to Japan
November 27, 1941	U.S. Army and Navy send war warnings to Hawaii, Philippines, Guam, and other outposts
December 5–6, 1941	Japanese destroying codes and preparing to close embassy. Troop movements south from Indochina
December 6, 1941	Roosevelt sends personal plea to Japanese Emperor
December 6, 1941	U.S. begins interception of fourteen-part Japanese message rejecting November 26 offer
December 7, 1941	1:50 p.m.: Washington learns of Pearl Harbor attack

I FROM THE RECORD

Cordell Hull

HULL'S TESTIMONY BEFORE CONGRESS

To the Joint Committee investigating the Pearl Harbor attack after the war, Hull submitted a written statement from which the following selection is taken. Hull, from Tennessee, was Secretary of State from 1933 to 1944. He personally conducted the lengthy negotiations with Japan's Ambassador Nomura and finally with Special Envoy Kurusu as well. In the months leading to Pearl Harbor he met them frequently, often in the privacy of his own apartment in the evenings. More moderate than outright interventionists among his fellow cabinet members or even his chief adviser, Stanley Hornbeck, Hull nevertheless could not go along with those advising a more conciliatory policy, such as Joseph C. Grew, Ambassador to Japan, or Maxwell Hamilton, another of his advisers. In this he had the backing of his chief, President Roosevelt. Here he gives the official version of America's policy.

Conversations and Developments Prior to July 1941

On February 14, 1941, the President received the new Japanese Ambassador, Admiral Nomura, in a spirit of cordiality and said that they could talk candidly. He pointed out that relations between the United States and Japan were deteriorating and mentioned Japanese movements southward and Japanese entry into the Tripartite Agreement. The President suggested that the Ambassador might like to reexamine and frankly discuss with the Secretary of State important phases of American-Japanese relations.

On March 8, in my first extended conversation with the Japanese Ambassador, I emphasized that the American people had become fully aroused over the German and Japanese movements to take charge of the seas and of the other continents for their own arbitrary control and to profit at the expense of the welfare of all of the victims.

On March 14 the Japanese Ambassador saw the President and me. The President agreed with an intimation by the Ambassador that matters between our two countries could be worked out without a military clash and emphasized that the first step would be removal of suspicion regarding Japan's intentions. With the Japanese Foreign

From *Pearl Harbor Attack: Hearings before the Joint Committee on the Investigation of the Pearl Harbor Attack* (Washington, D.C.: U.S. Government Printing Office, 39 parts, 1946), II, 418–37.

Minister Matsuoka on his way to Berlin, talking loudly, and Japanese
naval and air forces moving gradually toward Thailand, there was
naturally serious concern and suspicion.

On April 16 I had a further conversation with the Japanese Ambassador. I pointed out that the one paramount preliminary question
about which our Government was concerned was a definite assurance in advance that the Japanese Government had the willingness
and power to abandon its present doctrine of conquest by force and
to adopt four principles which our Government regarded as the
foundation upon which relations between nations should rest, as
follows:

1. Respect for the territorial integrity and the sovereignty of each
    and all nations;
2. Support of the principle of noninterference in the internal af-
    fairs of other countries;
3. Support of the principle of equality, including equality of
    commercial opportunity.
4. Nondisturbance of the status quo in the Pacific except as the
    status quo may be altered by peaceful means.

I told the Japanese Ambassador that our Government was willing
to consider any proposal which the Japanese Government might
offer such as would be consistent with those principles.

On May 12 the Japanese Ambassador presented a proposal for a
general settlement. The essence of that proposal was that the United
States should request Chiang Kai-shek to negotiate peace with Japan, and, if Chiang should not accept the advice of the United States,
that the United States should discontinue its assistance to his government; that normal trade relations between the United States and
Japan should be resumed; and that the United States should help
Japan acquire access to facilities for the exploitation of natural
resources—such as oil, rubber, tin and nickel—in the southwest
Pacific area. There were also other provisions which Japan eventually
dropped, calling for joint guaranty of independence of the Philip-
pines, for the consideration of Japanese immigration to the United
States on a nondiscriminatory basis, and for a joint effort by the
United States and Japan to prevent the further extension of the
European war and for the speedy restoration of peace in Europe.

The proposal also contained an affirmation of Japan's adherence
to the Tripartite Pact and a specific reference to Japan's obligations

thereunder to come to the aid of any of the parties thereto if attacked by a power not at that time in the European war or in the Sino-Japanese conflict, other than the Soviet Union which was expressly excepted.

The peace conditions which Japan proposed to offer China were not defined in clear-cut terms. Patient exploring, however, disclosed that they included stipulations disguised in innocuous-sounding formulas whereby Japan would retain control of various strategic resources, facilities and enterprises in China and would acquire the right to station large bodies of Japanese troops, professedly for "joint defense against communism," for an indefinite period in extensive key areas of China proper and Inner Mongolia.

Notwithstanding the narrow and one-sided character of the Japanese proposals, we took them as a starting point to explore the possibility of working out a broad-gauge settlement, covering the entire Pacific area, along lines consistent with the principles for which this country stood.

On May 14, Mr. Matsuoka, the Japanese Minister of Foreign Affairs, in the course of a conversation with Ambassador Grew, said that both Prince Konoye and he were determined that Japan's southward advance should be carried out only by peaceful means, "unless," he added significantly, "circumstances render this impossible."

In reply to the Ambassador's inquiry as to what circumstances he had in mind, Mr. Matsuoka referred to the concentration of British troops in Malaya and other British measures. When the Ambassador pointed out that such measures were of a defensive character, the Minister's reply was that those measures were regarded as provocative by the Japanese public, which might bring pressure on the Government to act.

On May 27, 1941, President Roosevelt proclaimed the existence of an "unlimited national emergency" and in a radio address on the same day he declared that our whole program of aid for the democracies had been based on concern for our own security. He warned of the conditions which would exist should Hitler be victorious.

The President and I were sure that the proclamation would be noticed not only by Hitler but also by the Japanese warlords.

On May 28 I told the Japanese Ambassador that I had it in mind before passing from our informal conversations into any negotiations with Japan to talk out in strict confidence with the Chinese government the general subject matter involved in the proposals.

During the next few weeks there were a number of conversations for the purpose of clarifying various points and narrowing areas of difference. We repeatedly set forth our attitude on these points—the necessity of Japan's making clear its relation to the Axis in case the United States should be involved in self-defense in the war in Europe; application of the principle of noninterference in the internal affairs of another country and withdrawal of Japanese troops from Chinese territory; application of the principle of nondiscrimination in commercial relations in China and other areas of the Pacific and assurance of Japan's peaceful intent in the Pacific. I emphasized that what we were seeking was a comprehensive agreement which would speak for itself as an instrument of peace.

The Japanese pressed for a complete reply to their proposals of May 12. Accordingly, on June 21, the Ambassador was given our views in the form of a tentative redraft of their proposals. In that redraft there was suggested a formula which would make clear that Japan was not committed to take action against the United States should the latter be drawn by self-defense into the European war. It was proposed that a further effort be made to work out a satisfactory solution of the question of the stationing of Japanese troops in China and of the question of economic cooperation between China and Japan. There also was eliminated any suggestion that the United States would discontinue aid to the Chinese Government. Various other suggested changes were proposed in the interest of clarification or for the purpose of harmonizing the proposed settlement with our stated principles.

Japan's Warlords Disclose Their Intention of Further Aggression

On June 22, Germany attacked the Soviet Union, and this action started a chain of developments in Japan.

Following an Imperial conference at Tokyo on July 2, in which, according to an official announcement, "the fundamental national policy to be taken toward the present situation was decided," Japan proceeded with military preparation on a vast scale. One to two million reservists and conscripts were called up. Japanese merchant vessels operating in the Atlantic Ocean were suddenly recalled. Restrictions were imposed upon travel in Japan. Strict censorship of mails and communications was carried out.

During this period the Japanese press stressed the theme that Japan was being faced with pressure from many countries. It charged the United States with an intention to establish military bases in Kamchatka and with using the Philippine Islands as a "pistol aimed at Japan's heart." It warned that if the United States took further action in the direction of encircling Japan, Japanese-American relations would face a final crisis.

In July our Government began receiving reports that a Japanese military movement into southern Indochina was imminent. This Japanese movement into southern Indochina threatened the Philippine Islands, the Netherlands East Indies, and British Malaya. It also threatened vital trade routes. We immediately brought these reports to the attention of the Japanese representatives, pointed out the inconsistency between such a military movement and the discussions which were then proceeding, and requested information as to the facts.

On July 23, the Japanese Ambassador stated in explanation of the Japanese advance in Indochina that Japan needed to secure an uninterrupted source of supplies and to ensure against encirclement of Japan militarily. The Acting Secretary of State, Mr. Welles, replied that the agreement which was being discussed between the American and Japanese representatives would give Japan far greater economic security than she could gain by occupying Indochina. He pointed out that the United States policy was the opposite of an encirclement policy. He said that the United States could only regard the action of Japan as constituting notice that Japan was taking the last step before proceeding on a policy of expansion and conquest in the region of the South Seas. Under instructions from me, he told the Ambassador that in these circumstances I could not see any basis for pursuing further the conversations with the Japanese Ambassador.

Thereafter, no conversations were held on the subject of a general agreement with Japan until in August the Japanese Government took a new initiative.

On July 24 President Roosevelt made a proposal to the Japanese Government that Indochina be regarded as a "neutralized" country. That proposal envisaged Japan's being given the fullest and freest opportunity of assuring for itself a source of food supplies and other raw materials which—according to Japanese accounts—Japan was seeking to obtain. The Japanese Government did not accept the President's proposal.

It is pertinent to allude briefly to the estimate which we made of the situation at this juncture.

The hostilities between Japan and China had been in progress for four years. During those years the United States had continued to follow in its relations with Japan a policy of restraint and patience. It had done this notwithstanding constant violation by Japanese authorities or agents of American rights and legitimate interests in China, in neighboring areas, and even in Japan, and notwithstanding acts and statements by Japanese officials indicating a policy of wide-spread conquest by force and even threatening the United States.

The American Government had sought, while protesting against Japanese acts and while yielding no rights, to make clear a willing-ness to work out with Japan by peaceful processes a basis for continuance of amicable relations with Japan. It had been desired to give the Japanese every opportunity to turn of their own accord from their program of conquest toward peaceful policies.

The President and I, in our effort to bring about the conclusion of an agreement, had endeavored to present to the Japanese Govern-ment a feasible alternative to Japan's indicated program of conquest. We had made abundantly clear our willingness to cooperate with Japan in a program based upon peaceful principles. We had re-peatedly indicated that if such a program were adopted for the Pacific, and if thereafter any countries or areas within the Pacific were menaced, our Government would expect to cooperate with other governments in extending assistance to the region threatened.

While these discussions were going on in Washington, many re-sponsible Japanese officials were affirming in Tokyo and elsewhere Japan's determination to pursue a policy of cooperation with her Axis allies. Both Mr. Matsuoka and his successor as Minister of Foreign Affairs had declared that the Three Power Pact stood and that Japanese policy was based upon that pact. Large-scale preparation by Japan for extension of her military activities was in progress, especially since early July. Notwithstanding our efforts expressly to impress upon the Japanese Government our Government's concern and our objection to movement by Japan with use or threat of force into Indochina, the Japanese Government had again obtained by duress from the Vichy Government an authorization and Japanese armed forces had moved into southern Indochina, occupied bases there, and were consolidating themselves there for further southward movements.

The Japanese move into southern Indochina was an aggravated, overt act. It created a situation in which the risk of war became so great that the United States and other countries concerned were confronted no longer with the question of avoiding such risk but from then on with the problem of preventing a complete undermining of their security. It was essential that the United States make a definite and clear move in self-defense.

Accordingly, on July 26, 1941, President Roosevelt issued an executive order freezing Chinese and Japanese assets in the United States. That order brought under the control of the Government all financial and import and export trade transactions in which Chinese or Japanese interests were involved. The effect of this was to bring about very soon virtual cessation of trade between the United States and Japan.

On August 6 the Japanese Ambassador presented a proposal which he said was intended to be responsive to the President's proposal regarding neutralization of Indochina. In essence, the Japanese proposal was that:

1. The Japanese Government should undertake to refrain from stationing troops in regions of the southwest Pacific, to withdraw from French Indochina after "settlement of the China incident," to guarantee Philippine neutrality, and to cooperate in the production and procurement of natural resources in east Asia essential to the United States; and
2. The United States should undertake to "suspend its military measures in the southwestern Pacific areas" and to recommend similar action to the Governments of the Netherlands and Great Britain, to cooperate in the production and procurement of natural resources in the Southwestern Pacific essential to Japan, to take measures to restore normal commerce between the United States and Japan, to extend its good offices toward bringing about direct negotiations between Japan and the Chungking Government, and to recognize Japan's special position in Indochina even after withdrawal of Japanese troops.

The proposals advanced by the Japanese Government completely ignored the President's proposal, and on August 8 I so indicated to the Japanese Ambassador.

The movement of Japanese forces into Indochina continued unabated after the President's proposal was made known to the

Japanese Government. Also since then Japanese forces bombed Chungking more intensely then ever before, Japanese troops were massing on the Thailand frontier, Japan was making demands on Thailand, and Japanese troops were massing on the Siberian frontier of the Soviet Union.

At the same time, on August 8 and again on August 15, an official Japanese spokesman declared that encirclement of Japan by the ABCD powers—the United States, Great Britain, China, and the Netherlands—was an actual fact. The Japanese press, while affirming its approval of efforts by the Japanese Government to improve relations with the United States, stressed that the basis for any negotiations must be predicated upon there being under no circumstances any change in Japan's policies, namely, the "settlement of the China Incident, the firm establishment of the Co-Prosperity Sphere, and the Axis Alliance."

Japanese Proposal for Roosevelt-Konoye Meeting

In the conversation which I had with the Japanese Ambassador on August 8, the Ambassador inquired whether it might not be possible for the responsible heads of the two Governments to meet with a view to discussing means for reaching an adjustment of views. After reviewing briefly the steps which had led to a discontinuance of the informal conversations, I said that it remained to the Japanese Government to decide whether it could find means of shaping its policies along lines which would make possible an adjustment of views.

At the Atlantic Conference in August, Mr. Churchill had informed President Roosevelt that the British Government needed more time to prepare for resistance against a possible Japanese attack in the Far East. This was true also of our defense preparations. Furthermore, President Roosevelt and Mr. Churchill had agreed that the American and British Governments should take parallel action in informing Japan that, in the event the Japanese Government should take further steps of aggression against neighboring countries, each of them would be compelled to take all necessary measures to safeguard the legitimate rights and interests of its country and nationals and to insure its country's safety and security. The President and Mr. Churchill were also of the view that the American Government should be prepared to continue its conversations with the Japanese Government and by such means to offer Japan a reasonable and just alternative to the course upon which Japan was engaged.

Accordingly, President Roosevelt on August 17, the day of his return to Washington, informed the Japanese Ambassador that if the Japanese Government took any further steps in pursuance of a program of military domination by force or threat of force of neighboring countries our Government would be compelled to take any and all steps necessary toward safeguarding its legitimate rights and interests and toward insuring the security of the United States. At the same time President Roosevelt informed the Japanese Ambassador, in reply to the Ambassador's requests of previous weeks, that we were prepared to resume the conversations.

At this meeting on August 17 the President also informed the Japanese Ambassador that before proceeding with plans for a meeting of the heads of the American and Japanese Governments, as suggested by the Japanese Government, it would be helpful if the Japanese Government would furnish a clearer statement than had as yet been given of its present attitude and plans.

On August 28 the President was given a message from the Japanese Prime Minister, Prince Konoye, urging that the meeting of the heads of the two governments be arranged to discuss all important problems by Japan and the United States covering the entire Pacific area. Accompanying that message was a statement containing assurances, with several qualifications, of Japan's peaceful intent.

The President in his reply given on September 3 expressed a desire to collaborate with the Japanese Prime Minister to see whether there could be made effective in practice a program such as that referred to by the Japanese Government and whether there could be reached a meeting of minds on fundamentals which would afford prospect of success for such a meeting. It was suggested that to this end there take place immediately in advance of the proposed meeting preliminary discussions on fundamental and essential questions on which agreement was sought and on the manner in which the agreement would be applied. We felt that only in this way could a situation be brought about which would make such a meeting beneficial.

On September 6 the Japanese Ambassador presented a new draft of proposals. These proposals were much narrower than the assurances given in the statement communicated to the President on August 28. In the September 6 Japanese draft the Japanese gave only an evasive formula with regard to their obligations under the Tripartite Pact. There was a qualified undertaking that Japan would not "without any justifiable reason" resort to military action against any region south of Japan. No commitment was offered in regard to the nature of the terms which Japan would offer to China; nor any assurance of an intention by Japan to respect China's territorial integrity and sovereignty, to refrain from interference in China's internal affairs, not to station Japanese troops indefinitely in wide areas of China, and to conform to the principle of nondiscrimination in international commercial relations. The formula contained in that draft that "the economic activities of the United States in China will not be restricted *so long as pursued on an equitable basis*" [italic added] clearly implied a concept that the conditions under which American trade and commerce in China were henceforth to be conducted were to be a matter for decision by Japan.

On September 6 Prime Minister Konoye in a conversation with the American Ambassador at Tokyo indicated that the Japanese Government fully and definitely subscribed to the four principles which this Government had previously set forth as a basis for the reconstruction of relations with Japan. However, a month later the Japanese Minister for Foreign Affairs indicated to the American Ambassador that while these four points had been accepted "in principle," certain adjustments would be necessary in applying these principles to actual conditions.

A meeting between the President and Prince Konoye would have been a significant step. Decision whether it should be undertaken by our Government involved several important considerations.

We knew that Japanese leaders were unreliable and treacherous. We asked ourselves whether the military element in Japan would permit the civilian element, even if so disposed, to stop Japan's course of expansion by force and to revert to peaceful courses. Time and again the civilian leaders gave assurances; time and again the military took aggressive action in direct violation of those assurances. Japan's past and contemporary record was replete with instances of military aggression and expansion by force. Since 1931 and especially since 1937 the military in Japan exercised a controlling voice in Japan's national policy.

Japan's formal partnership with Nazi Germany in the Tripartite Alliance was a hard and inescapable fact. The Japanese had been consistently unwilling in the conversations to pledge their Government to renounce Japan's commitments in the alliance. They would not state that Japan would refrain from attacking this country if it became involved through self-defense in the European war. They held on to the threat against the United States implicit in the alliance.

Our Government could not ignore the fact that throughout the conversations the Japanese spokesmen had made a practice of offering general formulas and, when pressed for explanation of the meaning, had consistently narrowed and made more rigid their application. This suggested that when military leaders became aware of the generalized formulas they insisted upon introducing conditions which watered down the general assurances.

A meeting between the President and the Japanese Prime Minister would have had important psychological results.

It would have had a critically discouraging effect upon the Chinese.

If the proposed meeting should merely endorse general principles, the Japanese in the light of their past practice could have been expected to utilize such general principles in support of any interpretation which Japan might choose to place upon them.

If the proposed meeting did not produce an agreement, the Japanese military leaders would then have been in a position to declare that the United States was responsible for the failure of the meeting.

The Japanese had already refused to agree on any preliminary steps toward reversion to peaceful courses as for example adopting the President's proposal of July 24, regarding the neutralization of Indochina. Instead they steadily moved on with their program of establishing themselves more firmly in Indochina.

It was clear to us that unless the meeting produced concrete and clear-cut commitments toward peace, the Japanese would have distorted the significance of the meeting in such a way as to weaken greatly this country's moral position and to facilitate their aggressive course.

The acts of Japan under Konoye's Prime Ministership could not be overlooked.

He had headed the Japanese Government in 1937 when Japan attacked China and when huge Japanese armies poured into that country and occupied its principal cities and industrial regions.

He was Prime Minister when Japanese armed forces attacked the U.S.S. *Panay* on the Yangtze River on December 12, 1937.

He was Prime Minister when Japanese armed forces committed notorious outrages in Nanking in 1937.

He as Prime Minister had proclaimed in 1938 the basic principles upon which the Japanese Government, even throughout the 1941 conversations, stated that it would insist in any peace agreement with China. Those principles in application included stationing large bodies of Japanese troops in north China. They would have enabled Japan to retain a permanent stranglehold on China.

He had been Prime Minister when the Japanese Government concluded in 1940 with the Chinese quisling regime at Nanking a "treaty" embodying the stranglehold principles mentioned in the preceding paragraph.

Prince Konoye had been Japanese Prime Minister when Japan signed the Tripartite Pact with Germany and Italy in 1940.

As a result of our close-up conversations with the Japanese over a period of months, in which they showed no disposition to abandon their course of conquest, we were thoroughly satisfied that a meeting with Konoye could only result either in another Munich or in nothing at all, unless Japan was ready to give some clear evidence of a purpose to move in a peaceful direction. I was opposed to the first Munich and still more opposed to a second Munich.

Our Government ardently desired peace. It could not brush away the realities in the situation.

Although the President would, as he said, "have been happy to travel thousands of miles to meet the Premier of Japan," it was felt that in view of the factors mentioned the President could go to such a meeting only if there were first obtained tentative commitments offering some assurance that the meeting could accomplish good. Neither Prince Konoye nor any of Japan's spokesmen provided anything tangible.

At various times during September discussions were held with the Japanese. On September 27 the Japanese Ambassador presented a complete new redraft of the Japanese proposals. He urged an early reply.

On October 2, I gave the Japanese Ambassador a memorandum of an "oral statement" reviewing significant developments in the conversations and explaining our Government's attitude toward various points in the Japanese proposals which our Government did not consider consistent with the principles to which this country was committed. Disappointment was expressed over the narrow character of the outstanding Japanese proposals, and questions were raised in regard to Japan's intentions regarding the indefinite stationing of Japanese troops in wide areas of China and regarding Japan's relationship to the Axis Powers. While welcoming the Japanese suggestion of a meeting between the President and the Japanese Prime Minister, we proposed, in order to lay a firm foundation for such a meeting, that renewed consideration be given to fundamental principles so as to reach a meeting of the minds on essential questions. It was stated in conclusion that the subject of the meeting proposed by the Prime Minister and the objectives sought had engaged the close and active interest of the President and that it was the President's earnest hope that discussion of the fundamental questions might be so developed that such a meeting could be held.

During this period there was a further advance of Japanese armed forces in Indochina, Japanese military preparations at home were increased and speeded up, and there continued Japanese bombing of Chinese civilian populations, constant agitation in the Japanese press in support of extremist policies, and the unconciliatory and bellicose utterances of Japanese leaders.

For example, Capt. Hideo Hiraide, director of the naval intelligence section of Imperial Headquarters, was quoted on October 16 as having declared in a public speech:

> *America, feeling her insecurity . . . is carrying out naval expansion on a large scale. But at present America is unable to carry out naval operations in both the Atlantic and Pacific simultaneously.*
>
> *The imperial navy is prepared for the worst and has completed all necessary preparations. In fact, the imperial navy is itching for action, when needed.*
>
> *In spite of strenuous efforts by the Government, the situation is now approaching a final parting of the ways. The fate of our empire depends upon how we act at this moment. It is certain that at such a moment our Navy should set about on its primary mission.*

Tojo Cabinet and Continuation of Conversations

On October 16, 1941 the Konoye Cabinet fell. On the following day it was replaced by a new cabinet, headed by General Tojo.

The new cabinet informed our Government that it desired to continue the exploratory conversations looking to peace in the Pacific and to an agreement with the United States. But it showed no willingness to effect any fundamental modification of the Japanese position. Instead, Japanese bellicose utterances continued.

On October 17 the American press carried the following statement by Major General Kiyofuku Oamoto:

Despite the different views advanced on the Japanese-American question, our national policy for solution of the China affair and establishment of a common co-prosperity sphere in East Asia remains unaltered.

For fulfillment of this national policy, this country has sought to reach an agreement of views with the U.S. by means of diplomatic means. There is, however, a limit to our concessions, and the negotiations may end in a break with the worst possible situation following. The people must therefore be resolved to cope with such a situation.

Clearly, the Japanese warlords expected to clinch their policy of aggrandizement and have the United States make all the concessions.

On October 30 the Japanese Foreign Minister told the American Ambassador that the Japanese Government desired that the conversations be concluded successfully without delay and he said that "in order to make progress, the United States should face certain realities and facts," and he thereupon cited the stationing in China of Japanese armed forces.

The general world situation continued to be very critical, rendering it desirable that every reasonable effort be made to avoid or at least to defer as long as possible any rupture in the conversations. From here on for some weeks especially intensive study was given in the Department of State to the possibility of reaching some stop-gap arrangement with the Japanese so as to tide over the immediate critical situation and thus to prevent a breakdown in the conversations, and even perhaps to pave the way for a subsequent general agreement. The presentation to the Japanese of a proposal which would serve to keep alive the conversations would also give our Army and Navy time to prepare and to expose Japan's bad faith if it did not accept. We considered every kind of suggestion we could find which might help or keep alive the conversations and at the same time be consistent with the integrity of American principles.

In the last part of October and early November messages came to this Government from United States Army and Navy officers in China and from Generalissimo Chiang Kai-shek stating that he believed that a Japanese attack on Kunming was imminent. The Generalissimo requested that the United States send air units to China to defeat this threat. He made a similar request of the British Government. He also asked that the United States issue a warning to Japan.

At this time the Chinese had been resisting the Japanese invaders for four years. China sorely needed equipment. Its economic and financial situations were very bad. Morale was naturally low. In view of this, even though a Chinese request might contain points with which we could not comply, we dealt with any such request in a spirit of utmost consideration befitting the gravity of the situation confronting our hard-pressed Chinese friends.

I suggested that the War and Navy Departments study this Chinese appeal. In response, the Chief of Staff and the Chief of Naval Operations sent a memorandum of November 5 to the President giving an estimate concerning the Far Eastern situation. At the conclusion of this estimate the Chief of Staff and the Chief of Naval Operations recommended:

> That the dispatch of United States armed forces for intervention against Japan in China be disapproved.
> That material aid to China be accelerated consonant with the needs of Russia, Great Britain, and our own forces.
> That aid to the American Volunteer Group be continued and accelerated to the maximum practicable extent.
> That no ultimatum be delivered to Japan.

I was in thorough accord with the views of the Chief of Staff and the Chief of Naval Operations that United States armed forces should not be sent to China for use against Japan. I also believed so far as American foreign policy considerations were involved that material aid to China should be accelerated as much as feasible, and that aid to the American Volunteer Group should be accelerated. Finally, I concurred completely in the view that no ultimatum should be delivered to Japan. I had been striving for months to avoid a showdown with Japan, and to explore every possible avenue for averting or delaying war between the United States and Japan. That was the cornerstone of the effort which the President and I were putting forth with our utmost patience.

On November 14 the President replied to Generalissimo Chiang Kai-shek, in line with the estimate and recommendations contained in the memorandum of November 5 of the Chief of Staff and the Chief of Naval Operations. The Generalissimo was told that from our information it did not appear that a Japanese land campaign against Kunming was immediately imminent. It was indicated that American air units could not be sent and that the United States would not issue

a warning but there were outlined ways, mentioned in the memorandum of the Chief of Staff and the Chief of Naval Operations, in which
the United States would continue to assist China.

On November 7, I attended the regular Cabinet meeting. It was the
President's custom either to start off the discussion himself or to ask
some member of the Cabinet a question. At this meeting he turned to
me and asked whether I had anything in mind. I thereupon pointed
out for about 15 minutes the dangers in the international situation. I
went over fully developments in the conversations with Japan and
emphasized that in my opinion relations were extremely critical and
that we should be on the lookout for a military attack anywhere by
Japan at any time. When I finished, the President went around the
Cabinet. All concurred in my estimate of the dangers. It became the
consensus of the Cabinet that the critical situation might well be
emphasized in speeches in order that the country would, if possible,
be better prepared for such a development.

Accordingly, Secretary of the Navy Knox delivered an address on
November 11, 1941, in which he stated that we were not only confronted with the necessity of extreme measures of self-defense in the
Atlantic, but we were "likewise faced with grim possibilities on the
other side of the world—on the far side of the Pacific"; and the
Pacific no less than the Atlantic called for instant readiness for
defense.

On the same day Under Secretary of State Welles in an address
stated that beyond the Atlantic a sinister and pitiless conqueror had
reduced more than half of Europe to abject serfdom and that in the
Far East the same forces of conquest were menacing the safety of all
nations bordering on the Pacific. The waves of world conquest were
"breaking high both in the East and in the West," he said, and were
threatening, more and more with each passing day, "to engulf our
own shores." He warned that the United States was in far greater
peril than in 1917; that "at any moment war may be forced upon us."

Early in November the Japanese Government decided to send Mr.
Saburo Kurusu to Washington to assist the Japanese Ambassador in
the conversations.

On November 7 the Japanese Ambassador handed me a document
containing draft provisions relating to Japanese forces in China,
Japanese forces in Indochina, and the principle of nondiscrimination.
That proposal contained nothing fundamentally new or offering any

real recessions from the position consistently maintained by the Japanese Government.

In telegrams of November 3 and November 17 the American Ambassador in Japan cabled warnings of the possibility of sudden Japanese attacks which might make inevitable war with the United States.

In the first half of November there were several indeterminate conversations with the Japanese designed to clarify specific points. On November 15 I gave the Japanese Ambassador an outline for a possible joint declaration by the United States and Japan on economic policy. I pointed out that this represented but one part of the general settlement we had in mind. This draft declaration of economic policy envisaged that Japan could join with the United States in leading the way toward a general application of economic practices which would give Japan much of what her leaders professed to desire.

On November 12 the Japanese Foreign Office, both through Ambassador Grew and through their Ambassador here, urged that the conversations be brought to a settlement at the earliest possible time. In view of the pressing insistence of the Japanese for a definitive reply to their outstanding proposals, I was impelled to comment to the Japanese Ambassador on November 15 that the American Government did not feel that it should be receiving such representations, suggestive of ultimatums.

On November 15 Mr. Kurusu reached Washington. On November 17 he and the Japanese Ambassador called on me and later on the same day on the President.

In those conversations Mr. Kurusu said that the Japanese Prime Minister, General Tojo, seemed optimistic in regard to adjusting the question of applying the principle of nondiscrimination and the question of Japan's relation to the Tripartite Alliance, but he indicated that it would be difficult to withdraw Japanese troops from China. Mr. Kurusu offered no new suggestions on those two points. This was further evidence that Japan was bent on exercising a position of military, political, and economic control and dominance of China. The President made clear the desire of this country to avoid war between our two countries and to bring about a settlement on a fair and peaceful basis in the Pacific area.

On November 18 the Japanese Ambassador and Mr. Kurusu called on me. In that conversation the question of Japan's relation to the Tripartite Pact was discussed at length. I asked the Japanese Ambassador if he did not think that something could be worked out on this vital question. The Ambassador made no helpful comment in regard to the continued stationing of Japanese troops in China.

The Ambassador and Mr. Kurusu suggested the possibility of a temporary arrangement or a modus vivendi. The Ambassador brought up the possibility of going back to the status which existed before the date in July when, following the Japanese entry into southern French Indochina, the United States put freezing measures into effect.

said that if we should make some modifications in our embargo on the strength of such a step by Japan as the Ambassador had mentioned, we would not know whether the troops to be withdrawn from French Indochina would be diverted to some equally objectionable movement elsewhere. I said that it would be difficult for our Government to go a long way in removing the embargo unless we believed that Japan was definitely started on a peaceful course and had renounced purposes of conquest. I said that I would consult with the representatives of other countries on this suggestion. On the same day I informed the British Minister of my talk with the Japanese about the suggestion of a temporary limited arrangement.

On November 19 the Japanese Ambassador and Mr. Kurusu again called on me at their request. During that conversation the Ambassador made it clear that Japan could not abrogate the Tripartite Alliance and felt bound to carry out its obligations.

Japanese Ultimatum of November 20 and Our Reply

On November 20 the Japanese Ambassador and Mr. Kurusu presented to me a proposal which on its face was extreme. I knew, as did other high officers of the Government, from intercepted Japanese messages supplied to me by the War and Navy Departments, that this proposal was the final Japanese proposition—an ultimatum.

The proposal read as follows:

1. *Both the Governments of Japan and the United States undertake not to make any armed advancement into any of the regions in the Southeastern Asia and the Southern Pacific area excepting the part of French Indochina where the Japanese troops are stationed at present.*

2. *The Japanese Government undertakes to withdraw its troops now stationed in French Indochina upon either the restoration of peace between Japan and China or the establishment of an equitable peace in the Pacific Area.*

   In the meantime the Government of Japan declares that it is prepared to remove its troops now stationed in the southern part of French Indochina to the northern part of the said territory upon the conclusion of the present arrangement which shall later be embodied in the final agreement.

3. *The Government of Japan and the United States shall cooperate with a view to securing the acquisition of those goods and commodities which the two countries need in Netherlands East Indies.*

4. *The Governments of Japan and the United States mutually undertake to restore their commercial relations to those prevailing prior to the freezing of the assets.*

   The Government of the United States shall supply Japan a required quantity of oil.

5. *The Government of the United States undertakes to refrain from such measures and actions as will be prejudicial to the endeavors for the restoration of general peace between Japan and China.*

The plan thus offered called for the supplying by the United States to Japan of as much oil as Japan might require, for suspension of freezing measures, for discontinuance by the United States of aid to China, and for withdrawal of moral and material support from the recognized Chinese Government. It contained a provision that Japan would shift her armed forces from southern Indochina to northern Indochina, but placed no limit on the number of armed forces which Japan might send into Indochina and made no provision for withdrawal of those forces until after either the restoration of peace between Japan and China or the establishment of an "equitable" peace in the Pacific area. While there were stipulations against further extension of Japan's armed force into southeastern Asia and the southern Pacific (except Indochina), there were no provisions which would have prevented continued or fresh Japanese aggressive activities in any of the regions of Asia lying to the north of Indochina—for example, China and the Soviet Union. The proposal contained no provisions pledging Japan to abandon aggression and to revert to peaceful courses.

On November 21 Mr. Kurusu called alone upon me and gave me a draft of a formula relating to Japan's obligations under the Tripartite Pact. That formula did not offer anything new or helpful. I asked Mr.

Kurusu whether he had anything more to offer on the subject of a peaceful settlement as a whole. Mr. Kurusu replied that he did not.

On November 21 we received word from the Dutch that they had information that a Japanese force had arrived near Palao, the nearest point in the Japanese Mandated Islands to the heart of the Netherlands Indies. Our Consuls at Hanoi and Saigon had been reporting extensive new landings of Japanese troops and equipment in Indochina. We had information through intercepted Japanese messages that the Japanese Government had decided that the negotiations must be terminated by November 25, later extended to November 29. We knew from other intercepted Japanese messages that the Japanese did not intend to make any concessions, and from this fact taken together with Kurusu's statement to me of November 21 making clear that his Government had nothing further to offer, it was plain, as I have mentioned, that the Japanese proposal of November 20 was in fact their "absolutely final proposal."

The whole issue presented was whether Japan would yield in her avowed movement of conquest or whether we would yield the fundamental principles for which we stood in the Pacific and all over the world. By mid-summer of 1941 we were pretty well satisfied that the Japanese were determined to continue with their course of expansion by force. We had made it clear to them that we were standing fast by our principles. It was evident, however, that they were playing for the chance that we might be overawed into yielding by their threats of force. They were armed to the teeth and we knew they would attack whenever and wherever they pleased. If by chance we should have yielded our fundamental principles, Japan would probably not have attacked for the time being—at least not until she had consolidated the gains she would have made without fighting.

There was never any question of this country's forcing Japan to fight. The question was whether this country was ready to sacrifice its principles.

To have accepted the Japanese proposal of November 20 was clearly unthinkable. It would have made the United States an ally of Japan in Japan's program of conquest and aggression and of collaboration with Hitler. It would have meant yielding to the Japanese demand that the United States abandon its principles and policies. It would have meant abject surrender of our position under intimidation.

The situation was critical and virtually hopeless. On the one hand our Government desired to exhaust all possibilities of finding a means to a peaceful solution and to avert or delay an armed clash, especially as the heads of this country's armed forces continued to emphasize the need of time to prepare for resistance. On the other hand, Japan was calling for a showdown.

There the situation stood—the Japanese unyielding and intimidating in their demands and we standing firmly for our principles.

The chances of meeting the crisis by diplomacy had practically vanished. We had reached the point of clutching at straws.

Three possible choices presented themselves.

> Our Government might have made no reply. The Japanese warlords could then have told their people that the American Government not only would make no reply but would also not offer any alternative.
>
> Our Government might have rejected flatly the Japanese proposal. In that event the Japanese warlords would be afforded a pretext, although wholly false, for military attack.
>
> Our Government might endeavor to present a reasonable counter-proposal.

The last course was the one chosen.

In considering the content of a counter-proposal consideration was given to the inclusion therein of a possible modus vivendi. Such a project would have the advantages of showing our interest in peace to the last and of exposing the Japanese somewhat in case they should not accept. It would, if it had served to prolong the conversations, have gained time for the Army and Navy to prepare. The project of a modus vivendi was discussed and given intensive consideration from November 22 to November 26 within the Department of State, by the President, and by the highest authorities of the Army and Navy. A first draft was completed on November 22 and revised drafts on November 24 and 25. It was also discussed with the British, Australian, Dutch, and Chinese Governments.

The projected modus vivendi provided for mutual pledges by the United States and Japan that their national policies would be directed toward lasting peace; for mutual undertakings against advances by military force or threat of force in the Pacific area; for withdrawal by Japan of its armed forces from southern Indochina; for a modification by the United States of its freezing and export restrictions to permit resumption of certain categories of trade, within certain specified limits, between the United States and Japan; for the corresponding modification by Japan of its freezing and export restrictions; and for an approach by the United States to the Australian, British and Dutch Governments with a view to their taking similar measures. There was also an affirmation by the United States of its fundamental interest that any settlement between the Japanese and Chinese Governments be based upon the principles of peace, law, order, and justice. There was provision that the modus vivendi would remain in force for three months and would be subject to further extension.

It was proposed as a vital part of the modus vivendi at the same time to give to the Japanese for their consideration an outline of a peace settlement which might serve as a basis for working out a comprehensive settlement for the Pacific area along broad and just lines. On November 11 there had been prepared in the Division of Far Eastern Affairs for possible consideration a draft of a proposal along broad lines. This draft like others was drawn up with a view to keeping the conversations going (and thus gaining time) and to leading, if accepted, to an eventual comprehensive settlement of a nature compatible with American principles. This draft proposal contained statements of general principles, including the four principles which I had presented to the Japanese on April 16, and a statement of principles in regard to economic policy. Under this draft the United States would suggest to the Chinese and Japanese Governments that they enter into peace negotiations, and the Japanese Government would offer the Chinese Government an armistice during the period of the peace negotiations. The armistice idea was dropped because it would have operated unfairly in Japan's favor.

A further proposal to which I gave attention was a revision in tentative form made by the Department on November 19 of a draft of a proposed comprehensive settlement received from the Treasury Department on the previous day. This tentative proposal was discussed with the War and Navy Departments. In subsequent revisions points to which objections were raised by them were dropped. A third proposal which I had under consideration was that of the modus vivendi.

What I considered presenting to the Japanese from about November 22 to November 26 consisted of our modus vivendi draft and an outline of a peace statement which might serve as a basis for working out a comprehensive settlement for the Pacific area along broad and just lines. This second and more comprehensive part followed some of the lines set forth in the November 11 draft and in the November 19 draft.

While the modus vivendi proposal was still under consideration, I emphasized the critical nature of this country's relations with Japan at the meeting of the War Council on November 25. The War Council, which consisted of the President, the Secretaries of State, War and Navy, the Chief of Staff and the Chief of Naval Operations, was a sort of a clearing house for all the information and views which we were currently discussing with our respective contacts and in our respective circles. The highlights in the developments at a particular juncture were invariably reviewed at those meetings. At that meeting I also gave the estimate which I then had that the Japanese military were already poised for attack. The Japanese leaders were determined and desperate. They were likely to break out anywhere, at any time, at any place, and I emphasized the probable element of surprise in their plans. I felt that virtually the last stage had been reached and that the safeguarding of our national security was in the hands of the Army and the Navy.

In a message of November 24 to Mr. Churchill, telegraphed through the Department, President Roosevelt added to an explanation of our proposed modus vivendi the words, "I am not very hopeful and we must all be prepared for real trouble, possibly soon."

On the evening of November 25 and on November 26 I went over again the considerations relating to our proposed plan, especially the modus vivendi aspect.

As I have indicated, all the successive drafts, of November 22, of November 24 and of November 25 contained two things: (1) the possible modus vivendi; and (2) a statement of principles, with a suggested example of how those principles could be applied—that which has since been commonly described as the 10-point proposal.

I and other high officers of our Government knew that the Japanese military were poised for attack. We knew that the Japanese were demanding—and had set a time limit, first of November 25 and extended later to November 29, for—acceptance by our Government of their extreme, last-word proposal of November 20.

It was therefore my judgment, as it was that of the President and other high officers, that the chance of the Japanese accepting our proposal was remote.

So far as the modus vivendi aspect would have appeared to the Japanese, it contained only a little chickenfeed in the shape of some cotton, oil and a few other commodities in very limited quantities as compared with the unlimited quantities the Japanese were demanding.

It was manifest that there would be widespread opposition from American opinion to the modus vivendi aspect of the proposal especially to the supplying to Japan of even limited quantities of oil. The Chinese Government violently opposed the idea. The other interested governments were sympathetic to the Chinese view and fundamentally were unfavorable or lukewarm. Their cooperation was a part of the plan. It developed that the conclusion with Japan of such an arrangement would have been a major blow to Chinese morale. In view of these considerations it became clear that the slight prospects of Japan's agreeing to the modus vivendi did not warrant assuming the risks involved in proceeding with it, especially the serious risk of collapse of Chinese morale and resistance and even of disintegration of China. It therefore became perfectly evident that the modus vivendi aspect would not be feasible.

The Japanese were spreading propaganda to the effect that they were being encircled. On the one hand we were faced by this charge and on the other by one that we were preparing to pursue a policy of appeasing Japan. In view of the resulting confusion, it seemed important to restate the fundamentals. We could offer Japan once more what we offered all countries, a suggested program of collaboration along peaceful and mutually beneficial and progressive lines. It had always been open to Japan to accept that kind of a program and to move in that direction. It still was possible for Japan to do so. That was a matter for Japan's decision. Our hope that Japan would so decide had been virtually extinguished. Yet it was felt desirable to put forth this further basic effort, in the form of one sample of a broad but simple settlement to be worked out in our future conversations, on the principle that no effort should be spared to test and exhaust every method of peaceful settlement.

In the light of the foregoing considerations, on November 26 I recommended to the President—and he approved—my calling in the Japanese representatives and handing them the broad basic proposals while withholding the modus vivendi plan. This was done in the late afternoon of that day.

The document handed the Japanese representatives on November 26 was divided into two parts:

The first part of the document handed the Japanese was marked "Oral." In it was reviewed briefly the objective sought in the exploratory conversations, namely, that of reaching if possible a settlement of questions relating to the entire Pacific area on the basis of the principles of peace, law and order and fair dealing among nations. It was stated that it was believed that some progress had been made in reference to general principles. Note was taken of a recent statement by the Japanese Ambassador that the Japanese Government desired to continue the conversations directed toward a comprehensive and peaceful settlement.

In connection with the Japanese proposals of November 20 for a modus vivendi, it was stated that the American Government most earnestly desired to afford every opportunity for the continuance of discussions with the Japanese Government directed toward working out a broad-gauge program of peace throughout the Pacific area. Our Government stated that in its opinion some features of the Japanese proposals of November 20 conflicted with the fundamental principles which formed a part of the general settlement under consideration and to which each government had declared that it was committed.

Our Government suggested that further effort be made to resolve the divergences of views in regard to the practical application of the fundamental principles already mentioned. Our Government stated that with this object in view it offered "for the consideration of the Japanese Government a plan of a broad but simple settlement covering the entire Pacific area as one practical exemplification of a program which this Government envisages as something to be worked out during our further conversations."

The second part of the document embodied the plan itself which was in two sections.

In section I there was outlined a mutual declaration of policy containing affirmations that the national policies of the two countries were directed toward peace throughout the Pacific area, that the two countries had no territorial designs or aggressive intentions in that area, and that they would give support to certain fundamental principles of peace upon which their relations with each other and all other nations would be based. These principles were stated as follows:

1. The principle of inviolability of territorial integrity and sovereignty of each and all nations.
2. The principle of noninterference in the internal affairs of other countries.

3. The principle of equality, including equality of commercial opportunity and treatment.
4. The principle of reliance upon international cooperation and conciliation for the prevention and pacific settlement of controversies and for improvement of international conditions by peaceful methods and processes.

This statement of policy and of principle closely followed the line of what had been presented to the Japanese on several previous occasions beginning in April.

In section I there was also a provision for mutual pledges to support and apply in their economic relations with each other and with other nations and peoples liberal economic principles. These principles were enumerated. They were based upon the general principle of equality of commercial opportunity and treatment.

This suggested provision for mutual pledges with respect to economic relations closely followed the line of what had previously been presented to the Japanese.

In section II there were outlined proposed steps to be taken by the two governments. One unilateral commitment was suggested, an undertaking by Japan that she would withdraw all military, naval, air and police forces from China and from Indochina. Mutual commitments were suggested along the following lines:

a. To endeavor to conclude a multilateral nonaggression pact among the governments principally concerned in the Pacific area;
b. To endeavor to conclude among the principally interested governments an agreement to respect the territorial integrity of Indochina and not to seek or accept preferential economic treatment therein;
c. Not to support any government in China other than the National Government of the Republic of China with capital temporarily at Chungking;
d. To relinquish extraterritorial and related rights in China and to endeavor to obtain the agreement of other governments now possessing such rights to give up those rights;
e. To negotiate a trade agreement based upon reciprocal most-favored-nation treatment;
f. To remove freezing restrictions imposed by each country on the funds of the other;
g. To agree upon a plan for the stabilization of the dollar-yen rate

with Japan and the United States each furnishing half of the fund;

h.   To agree that no agreement which either had concluded with any third power or powers shall be interpreted by it in a way to conflict with the fundamental purpose of this agreement; and

i.   To use their influence to cause other governments to adhere to the basic political and economic principles provided for in this suggested agreement.

The document handed the Japanese on November 26 was essentially a restatement of principles which have long been basic in this country's foreign policy. The practical application of those principles to the situation in the Far East, as embodied in the ten points contained in the document, was along lines which had been under discussion with the Japanese representatives in the course of the informal exploratory conversations during the months preceding delivery of the document in question. Our Government's proposal embodied mutually profitable policies of the kind we were prepared to offer to any friendly country and was coupled with the suggestion that the proposal be made the basis for further conversations.

A vital part of our program of standing firm for our principles was to offer other countries worthwhile plans which would be highly profitable to them as well as to ourselves. We stood firmly for these principles in the face of the Japanese demand that we abandon them. For this course there are no apologies.

Our Government's proposal was offered for the consideration of the Japanese Government as one practical example of a program to be worked out. It did not rule out other practical examples which either Government was free to offer.

We well knew that, in view of Japan's refusal throughout the conversations to abandon her policy of conquest and domination, there was scant likelihood of her acceptance of this plan. But it is the task of statesmanship to leave no possibility for peace unexplored, no matter how slight. It was in this spirit that the November 26 document was given to the Japanese Government.

When handing the document of November 26 to the Japanese representatives, I said that the proposed agreement would render possible practical measures of financial cooperation which, however, had not been referred to in the outline for fear that they might give rise to misunderstanding. I added also that I had earlier informed the

Ambassador of my ambition of settling the immigration question but that the situation had so far prevented me from realizing that ambition.

It is not surprising that Japanese propaganda, especially after Japan had begun to suffer serious defeats, has tried to distort and give a false meaning to our memorandum of November 26 by referring to it as an "ultimatum." This was in line with a well-known Japanese characteristic of utilizing completely false and flimsy pretexts to delude their people and gain their support for militaristic depredations and aggrandizement.

After November 26 the Japanese representatives at their request saw the President and me on several occasions. Nothing new developed on the subject of a peaceful agreement. . . .

Joseph C. Grew

TWO LETTERS TO THE PRESIDENT

Joseph C. Grew, Ambassador to Japan, 1932–1941, envisioned his place in history as one who would restore peace to Asia. A seasoned diplomat, he had attained his greatest success in negotiations that ended our hostilities with Turkey in 1923. His wife, who had lived in Japan and knew the language, was a descendent of Commodore Matthew C. Perry, who had opened Japan to the West in the 1850s. In Tokyo she was a distinct social and political asset to Grew.

Until midsummer of 1940 Grew had been optimistic about avoiding war. In "Red Light" messages to the State Department he had warned against coercive measures and urged conciliation. When he became convinced that failure of his country to heed his advice was encouraging aggression and pushing Japan into the arms of the Axis, he changed his stance and sent the "Green Light" dispatch to Hull on September 12, 1940 calling for a firm stand and a threat of force. In the following letter of December 14, 1940 to Roosevelt—an old friend—Grew repeated his belief that firmness at that point would entail less risk of war. His new position was based on the hope that such a policy would discredit the militarists in Japan, permitting more moderate elements to regain their voice. He recognized that America was resolved to stand firm. He wanted to swim with the tide, and to make sure that Japan realized that Roosevelt would not back down.

In his later letter of September 22, 1941 Grew was again urging conciliation and a meeting with Konoye, the Japanese Prime Minister. Grew was convinced that Konoye would be able to control the militarists and that he was sincere in seeking accommodation with the United States. Having thus returned to his "Red Light" position, Grew was disturbed at implications that the State Department was now charging him with vacillation. Hornbeck appeared to think he was advocating appeasement. The Ambassador insisted it was "constructive conciliation."

Were Roosevelt and Hull wrong in disregarding Grew, in believing that Konoye could not make any considerable concessions? Was Hull right in reminding Grew that Washington had a far broader field of view than the embassy in Tokyo? Had Grew himself been wrong when he earlier advocated getting tough with Japan as a way to avoid war?

Tokyo, December 14, 1940

DEAR FRANK: * * * About Japan and all her works. It seems to me to be increasingly clear that we are bound to have a showdown some

December 14, 1940 letter from *Pearl Harbor Attack: Hearings before the Joint Committee on the Investigation of the Pearl Harbor Attack* (Washington, D.C.: U.S. Government Printing Office, 1946), II, pp. 630–31; September 21, 1941 letter from *Foreign Relations of the United States: Diplomatic Papers, 1941* (Washington, D.C., Department of State, 1956), IV, pp. 468–69.

day, and the principal question at issue is whether it is to our advantage to have that showdown sooner or to have it later.

The chief factors in the problem would seem, from this angle, to be:

1. Whether and when Britain is likely to win the European war.
2. Whether our getting into war with Japan would so handicap our help to Britain in Europe as to make the difference to Britain between victory and defeat;
3. To what extent our own policy in the Far East must be timed with our preparedness program and with respect to the relative strength of the American and the Japanese Navies now and later.

Those are questions which, with our limited information here, I am not qualified even approximately to answer.

From the Tokyo angle we see the picture roughly as follows:

After eight years of effort to build up something permanently constructive to American-Japanese relations, I find that diplomacy has been defeated by trends and forces utterly beyond its control, and that our work has been swept away as if by a typhoon, with little or nothing remaining to show for it. Japan has become openly and unashamedly one of the predatory nations and part of a system which aims to wreck about everything that the United States stand for. Only insuperable obstacles will now prevent the Japanese from digging in permanently in China and from pushing the southward advance, with economic control as a preliminary to political domination In the areas marked down. Economic obstacles, such as may arise from American embargoes, will seriously handicap Japan in the long run, but meanwhile they tend to push the Japanese onward in a forlorn hope of making themselves economically self-sufficient.

History has shown that the pendulum in Japan is always swinging between extremist and moderate policies, but as things stand today we believe that the pendulum is more likely to swing still further toward extremes than to reverse its direction. Konoye, and especially Matsuoka, will fall in due course, but under present circumstances no Japanese leader or group of leaders could reverse the expansionist program and hope to survive.

Our own policy of unhurried but of inexorable determination in meeting every Japanese step with some step of our own has been eminently wise, and that policy has sunk deep into Japanese consciousness. But while important elements among the Japanese people deplore the course which their leaders are taking, those elements are nevertheless inarticulate and powerless and are likely to remain so. Meanwhile the Germans here are working overtime to push Japan into war with us. I have told Matsuoka point-blank that his country is heading for disaster. He has at least seen that his efforts to intimidate us have fallen flat and have had an effect precisely the reverse of that intended.

It therefore appears that sooner or later, unless we are prepared, with General Hugh Johnson, to withdraw bag and baggage from the entire sphere of "Greater East Asia including the South Seas" (which God forbid), we are bound eventually to come to a head-on clash with Japan.

A progressively firm policy on our part will entail inevitable risks—especially risks of sudden uncalculated strokes, such as the sinking of the Panay, which might inflame the American people—but in my opinion those risks are less in degree than the far greater future dangers which we would face if we were to follow a policy of laissez faire.

In other words, the risks of not taking positive measures to maintain our future security are likely to be much greater than the risks of taking positive measures as the southward advance proceeds. So far as I am aware, the great majority of the American people are in a mood for vigorous action. The principal point at issue, as I see it, is not whether we must call a halt to the Japanese program, but when.

It is important constantly to bear in mind the fact that if we take measures "short of war" with no real intention to carry those measures to their final conclusion if necessary, such lack of intention will be all too obvious to the Japanese, who will proceed undeterred, and even with greater incentive, on their way. Only if they become certain that we mean to fight if called upon to do so will our preliminary measures stand some chance of proving effective and of removing the necessity for war—the old story of Sir Edward Grey in 1914.

If by such action we can bring about the eventual discrediting of Japan's present leaders, a regeneration of thought may ultimately take shape in this country, permitting the resumption of normal relations with us and leading to a readjustment of the whole Pacific problem. . . .

Tokyo, September 22, 1941.

Dear Frank: I have not bothered you with personal letters for some time for the good reason that letters are now subject to long delays owing to the infrequent sailings of ships carrying our diplomatic pouches, and because developments in American-Japanese relations are moving so comparatively rapidly that my comments would generally be too much out of date to be helpful when they reached you. But I have tried and am constantly trying in my telegrams to the Secretary of State to paint an accurate picture of the moving scene from day to day. I hope that you see them regularly.

As you know from my telegrams, I am in close touch with Prince Konoye who in the face of bitter antagonism from extremist and pro-Axis elements in the country is courageously working for an improvement in Japan's relations with the United States. He bears the heavy responsibility for having allowed our relations to come to such a pass and he no doubt now sees the handwriting on the wall and realizes that Japan has nothing to hope for from the Tripartite Pact and must shift her orientation of policy if she is to avoid disaster; but whatever the incentive that has led to his present efforts, I am convinced that he now means business and will go as far as is possible, without incurring open rebellion in Japan, to reach a reasonable understanding with us. In spite of all the evidence of Japan's bad faith in times past in failing to live up to her commitments, I believe that there is a better chance of the present Government implementing whatever commitments it may now undertake than has been the case in recent years. It seems to me highly unlikely that this chance will come again or that any Japanese statesman other than Prince Konoye could succeed in controlling the military extremists in carrying through a policy which they, in their ignorance of international affairs and economic laws, resent and oppose. The alternative to reaching a settlement now would be the greatly increased probability of war—*Facilis descensus Averno est*—and while we would undoubtedly win in the end, I question whether it is in our own interest to see an impoverished Japan reduced to the position of a third-rate Power. I therefore must earnestly hope that we can come to terms, even if we must take on trust, at least to some degree, the continued good faith and ability of the present Government fully to implement those terms.

I venture to enclose a copy of a letter which I recently wrote to a Japanese friend who had expressed the hope that the United States would ultimately come to sympathize and to cooperate with Japan in pursuing her "legitimate interests and aspiration." The letter was sent by my friend, on his own initiative, to Prince Konoye.

My admiration of the masterly way in which you have led and are leading our country in the present turmoil in world affairs steadily increases.

Faithfully yours,   Joseph C. Grew

Japan's Basic National Policy Decisions

AGENDA FOR IMPERIAL CONFERENCE OF SEPTEMBER 6, 1941

In an Imperial Conference of July 2, 1941, Japan reached a decision to carry out a program to establish the Greater East Asia Co-Prosperity Sphere involving settlement of the China "incident," advance into Southeast Asia, and settlement of the "Soviet Question." The text of this policy is provided in the selection from Feis reprinted later in these readings. It resolved to carry out the national program "no matter what obstacles may be encountered," and in the event diplomatic negotiations did not clear the way it planned preparations for war with England and the United States.

In the agenda for the September 6 conference, below, a deadline of early October was set for the diplomats. Before the conference the Emperor expressed fear that preparations for war were taking priority over diplomatic efforts. During the conference Emperor Hirohito, in an unprecedented move, spoke out, reading a short verse by the Emperor Meiji, his grandfather, indicating his distress. His ministers assured him that stress was being put on negotiations and that war was contemplated only as a last resort.

But military preparations went forward; diplomatic efforts were not successful. When Konoye's cabinet fell, on October 18, the new Prime Minister, General Tojo, was informed that the Emperor, still worried over the possibility of war, wanted the new government to start with a clean slate, disregarding decisions made in the July and September conferences. Yet an Imperial Conference of November 5 decided for war if final proposals, A or B, were not acceptable to the United States. Proposal A assured America of access to China's trade but assumed a continuing Japanese army presence at least in North China, and in Indochina until war with China ended. It reaffirmed Japan's alliance with Germany and Italy. Proposal B was meant as a temporary measure if A failed, to avert war with the United States. It called for no further military moves by either side. The United States was to restore trade with Japan, including a supply of oil. And the United States was, in effect, to end its help to China. Neither proposal was acceptable to the United States (see Feis, below).

Hull's note of November 26 brushed aside Japan's proposals and merely restated the position of the United States. At an Imperial Conference on December 1, 1941 the Japanese leaders rejected what they considered Hull's "ultimatum" and decided to go to war.

From *Pearl Harbor Attack: Hearings before the Joint Committee on the Investigation of the Pearl Harbor Attack* (Washington, D.C.: U.S. Government Printing Office, 1946), XX, pp. 4022–23.

Plans for the Prosecution of the Policy
of the Imperial Government
(Agenda for a Council in the Imperial Presence)

In view of the increasingly critical situation, especially the aggressive plans being carried out by America, England, Holland and other countries, the situation in Soviet Russia and the Empire's latent potentialities, the Japanese Government will proceed as follows in carrying out its plans for the southern territories as laid in "An Outline of the Policy of the Imperial Government in View of Present Developments."

1. Determined not to be deterred by the possibility of being involved in a war with America (and England and Holland) in order to secure our national existence, we will proceed with war preparations so that they be completed approximately toward the end of October.
2. At the same time, we will endeavor by every possible diplomatic means to have our demands agreed to by America and England. Japan's minimum demands in these negotiations with America (and England), together with the Empire's maximum concessions are embodied in the attached document.
3. If by the early part of October there is no reasonable hope of having our demands agreed to in the diplomatic negotiations mentioned above, we will immediately make up our minds to get ready for war against America (and England and Holland).

   Policies with reference to countries other than those in the southern territories will be carried out in harmony with the plans already laid. Special effort will be made to prevent America and Soviet Russia from forming a united front against Japan.

Annex Document: A List of Japan's Minimum Demands
and Her Maximum Concessions in Her Negotiations
with America and England.

I. *Japan's Minimum Demands in Her Negotiations with America (and England).*

1. America and England shall not intervene in or obstruct a settlement by Japan of the China Incident.

(a) They will not interfere with Japan's plan to settle the China

Incident in harmony with the Sino-Japanese Basic Agreement and the Japan-China-Manchoukuo Tripartite Declaration.

(b) America and England will close the Burma Route and offer the Chiang Regime neither military, political nor economic assistance.

Note: The above do not run counter to Japan's previous declarations in the "N" plan for the settlement of the China Incident. In particular, the plan embodied in the new Sino-Japanese Agreement for the stationing of Japanese troops in the specified areas will be rigidly adhered to. However, the withdrawal of troops other than those mentioned above may be guaranteed in principle upon the settlement of the China Incident.[1]

Commercial operations in China on the part of America and England may also be guaranteed, insofar as they are purely commercial.

2. America and England will take no action in the Far East which offers a threat to the defense of the Empire.

(a) America and England will not establish military bases in Thai, the Netherlands East Indies, China or Far Eastern Soviet Russia.

(b) Their Far Eastern military forces will not be increased over their present strength.

Note: Any demands for the liquidation of Japan's special relations with French Indochina based on the Japanese-French Agreement will not be considered.[2]

3. America and England will cooperate with Japan in her attempt to obtain needed raw materials.

(a) America and England will restore trade relations with Japan and furnish her with the raw materials she needs from the British and American territories in the Southwest Pacific.

(b) America and England will assist Japan to establish close economic relations with Thai and the Netherlands East Indies.

II. *Maximum Concessions by Japan.*

It is first understood that our minimum demands as listed under I above will be agreed to.

---

[1] The China Incident is Japan's euphemism for the war between China and Japan. The Sino-Japanese Basic Agreement and the Japan-China-Manchoukuo Tripartite Declaration refer to arrangements between Japan, the puppet Chinese government at Nanking, and Japan's puppet state, Manchoukuo, in Manchuria. The *Tripartite Declaration* should not be confused with Japan's *Tripartite Pact* with Germany and Italy.—Ed.

[2] The Japanese-French Agreement was extorted from the German-dominated Vichy government of France in September 1940, permitting Japanese troops to occupy bases in Indochina.—Ed.

1. Japan will not use French Indochina as a base for operations against any neighboring countries with the exception of China.

Note: In case any questions are asked concerning Japan's attitude towards Soviet Russia, the answer is to be that as long as Soviet Russia faithfully carries out the Neutrality Pact and does not violate the spirit of the agreement by, for instance, threatening Japan or Manchuria, Japan will not take any military action.

2. Japan is prepared to withdraw her troops from French Indochina as soon as a just peace is established in the Far East.

3. Japan is prepared to guarantee the neutrality of the Philippine Islands.

Joseph W. Ballantine
MEMORANDA ON NEGOTIATIONS

Ballantine was assistant chief of the State Department's Division of Far Eastern Affairs. He attended many of Hull's meetings with Ambassador Nomura and Kurusu. Here he sets forth arguments against the Japanese modus vivendi (Proposal B) and reports on the reaction of the Japanese diplomats to Hull's rejection of Tokyo's final offer. Does this report suggest any unwillingness of the United States to carry on further discussions? Does Hull seem to be issuing an ultimatum?

Memorandum by Mr. Joseph W. Ballantine
to the Secretary of State

[Washington,] November 22, 1941.

Mr. Secretary: With reference to the Japanese proposal of November 20 for a modus vivendi and our memorandum containing

Memorandum, November 22, 1941, from *Foreign Relations of the United States, Diplomatic Papers, 1941* (Washington, D.C.: Department of State, 1956), IV, pp. 633–34. Memorandum, November 26, 1941, from *Papers Relating to the Foreign Relations of the United States, Japan, 1931–1941* (2 volumes; Washington, D.C., 1943), II, pp. 764–66.

suggestions for possible comment that might be made orally to the Japanese in regard to their proposal, there are given below additional suggestions for possible comment:

With reference to item three in regard to cooperation in obtaining from the Netherlands East Indies materials which our two countries need, it is not clear why the Japanese Government desires to limit this proposal to the Netherlands East Indies. It would appear to us that, if the Japanese Government could see its way clear to adopting our proposal in regard to commercial policy, the field for cooperation by the two countries would not be limited to any one area but would extend to the entire world. It would seem to us that the Japanese proposal takes no account of our broad offer which was renewed in very specific terms in the paper which was given to the Japanese Ambassador on November 15. It would seem to us that such a proposal would be open to possible criticism. That is to say that, whereas Japan was insisting on preferential treatment for itself in certain areas, in other areas it was asking for cooperation of the United States in obtaining for Japan the very kind of economic opportunities which Japan was trying to deny to third countries elsewhere. This Government has consistently advocated broadening the basis of world trade not from any selfish point of view but from the point of view of providing stable peace and elimination of chronic political instability and recurrent economic collapse. Such a program would provide means of raising living standards all over the world, thus promoting the well-being of all peoples.

With reference to the provision that the Government of the United States should supply Japan a required quantity of oil, it may be observed that until very recently the United States was supplying Japan with an ever-increasing amount of petroleum products, even to the extent where there was widespread public criticism in the United States of permitting this to continue. The period since 1937 was marked, on the one hand, by a tremendous increase in imports into Japan from the United States of petroleum products and, on the other hand, according to reports reaching us, by a progressive curtailment in the amounts of oil released in that country for normal peacetime consumption. There is no desire in this country to deny to Japan petroleum products needed for its normal economy, but the increased consumption of American petroleum products in Japan for a military purpose brings to the fore a question which we have called to the attention of the Japanese Ambassador, namely, that the Japanese association with the Axis powers is doing the United States tremendous injury.

With regard to the fifth point in the Japanese proposal, you might wish to emphasize again what you said to the Japanese Ambassador on November 20, namely, that, when the Japanese complain about our helping China, the public in this country wonders what is underneath the Anti-Comintern Pact; that Japanese statesmen ought to understand that we are helping China for the same reason that we are helping Britain; that we are afraid of the military elements throughout the world led by Hitler; and that the methods adopted by the Japanese military leaders in China are not unlike Hitler's methods. You might then ask what the Ambassador thinks would be the public reaction in this country if we were to announce that we had decided to discontinue aid to Great Britain. You might say that in the minds of American people the purposes underlying our aid to China are the same as the purposes underlying our aid to Great Britain and that the American people believe that there is a partnership between Hitler and Japan aimed at dividing the world between them.

J[oseph] W. B[allantine]

Memorandum of a Conversation

[Washington,] November 26, 1941.

The Japanese Ambassador [Nomura] and Mr. Kurusu called by appointment at the Department. The Secretary handed each of the Japanese copies of an outline of a proposed basis of an agreement between the United States and Japan and an explanatory oral statement.

After the Japanese had read the documents, Mr. Kurusu asked whether this was our reply to their proposal for a modus vivendi. The Secretary replied that we had to treat the proposal as we did, as there was so much turmoil and confusion among the public both in the United States and in Japan. He reminded the Japanese that in the United States we have a political situation to deal with just as does the Japanese Government, and he referred to the fire-eating statements which have been recently coming out of Tokyo, which he said had been causing a natural reaction among the public in this country. He said that our proposed agreement would render possible practical measures of financial cooperation, which, however, were not referred to in the outline for fear that this might give rise to misunderstanding. He also referred to the fact that he had earlier in the conversations acquainted the Ambassador of the ambition that had been his of settling the immigration question but that the situation had so far prevented him from realizing that ambition.

Mr. Kurusu offered various depreciatory comments in regard to the proposed agreement. He noted that in our statement of principles there was a reiteration of the Stimson doctrine. He objected to the proposal for multilateral nonaggression pacts and referred to Japan's bitter experience of international organizations, citing the case of the award against Japan by the Hague tribunal in the Perpetual Leases matter. He went on to say that the Washington Conference Treaties had given a wrong idea to China, that China had taken advantage of them to flaunt Japan's rights. He said he did not see how his Government could consider paragraphs (3) and (4) of the proposed agreement and that if the United States should expect that Japan was to take off its hat to Chiang Kai-shek and propose to recognize him Japan could not agree. He said that if this was the idea of the American Government he did not see how any agreement was possible.

The Secretary asked whether this matter could not be worked out.

Mr. Kurusu said that when they reported our answer to their Government it would be likely to throw up its hands. He noted that this was a tentative proposal without commitment, and suggested that it might be better if they did not refer it to their Government before discussing its contents further informally here.

The Secretary suggested that they might wish to study the documents carefully before discussing them further. He repeated that we were trying to do our best to keep the public from becoming uneasy as a result of their being harangued. He explained that in the light of all that has been said in the press, our proposal was as far as we would go at this time in reference to the Japanese proposal; that there was so much confusion among the public that it was necessary to bring about some clarification; that we have reached a stage when the public has lost its perspective and that it was therefore necessary to draw up a document which would present a complete picture of our position by making provision for each essential point involved.

The Secretary then referred to the oil question. He said that public feeling was so acute on that question that he might almost be lynched if he permitted oil to go freely to Japan. He pointed out that if Japan should fill Indochina with troops our people would not know what lies ahead in the way of a menace to the countries to the south and west. He reminded the Japanese that they did not know what tremendous injury they were doing to us by keeping immobilized so many forces in countries neighboring Indochina. He explained that we are primarily out for our permanent futures, and the question of Japanese troops in Indochina affects our direct interests.

Mr. Kurusu reverted to the difficulty of Japan's renouncing its support of Wang Ching-wei. The Secretary pointed out that Chiang Kai-shek had made an outstanding contribution in bringing out national spirit in China and expressed the view that the Nanking regime had not asserted itself in a way that would impress the world. Mr. Kurusu agreed with what the Secretary had said about Chiang, but observed that the question of the standing of the Nanking regime was a matter of opinion. His arguments on this as well as on various other points were specious, and unconvincing.

The Ambassador took the occasion to observe that sometimes statesmen of firm conviction fail to get sympathizers among the public; that only wise men could see far ahead and sometimes suffered martyrdom; but that life's span was short and one could only do his duty. The Ambassador then asked whether there was no other possibility and whether they could not see the President.

The Secretary replied that he had no doubt that the President would be glad to see them at any time.

Mr. Kurusu said that he felt that our response to their proposal could be interpreted as tantamount to meaning the end, and asked whether we were not interested in a modus vivendi.

The Secretary replied that we had explored that. Mr. Kurusu asked whether it was because the other powers would not agree; but the Secretary replied simply that he had done his best in the way of exploration.

The Ambassador when rising to go raised the question of publicity. The Secretary replied that he had it in mind to give the press something of the situation tomorrow, and asked what the Ambassador thought. The Ambassador said that they did not wish to question the Secretary's right to give out what he desired in regard to the American proposal. The Ambassador said he would like to have Mr. Wakasugi call on Mr. Ballantine on Thursday to discuss further details.

[Joseph W.] Ballantine

II HISTORIANS VIEW AMERICAN AND JAPANESE POLICY

Charles Callan Tansill

BACK DOOR TO WAR

Charles Callan Tansill (1890–1964), author of Back Door to War *(1952) from which the following selection is taken, was a bitter critic of President Roosevelt and strong opponent of our entry into World War II. A long-time diplomatic historian who taught at Fordham and Georgetown universities, he was also the author of a respected revisionist work critical of our entry into World War I,* America Goes to War *(1938).*

Despite personal bias Tansill presents an analysis of American foreign policy in the decade before Pearl Harbor that draws attention to aspects that other revisionists critical of the Roosevelt administration had missed. The reader will want to judge whether the interpretations Tansill draws from his evidence are valid.

He holds that Japan's actions resulted from an acute fear of Communist penetration in China, Japan's near neighbor and natural trading partner. The United States, he charges, failed to recognize the Russian threat to Asia and remained unsympathetic to the problem it posed for Japan. Instead America maintained its traditional stance in support of China, viewing Japan as the real threat. Tansill makes Henry L. Stimson responsible for perpetuating "a myth" that United States interests were linked with China. Does he find Stimson, formerly Hoover's Secretary of State, the most important figure in reinforcing this viewpoint when he became Roosevelt's Secretary of War?

Since Tansill wrote at the height of the red scare of the 1950s, does he imply, perhaps, that the United States should have been as concerned as Japan was at growing Russian influence in Asia? Does he believe that Roosevelt's administration was guilty of discounting the Communist threat?

Tansill appears to regard our mistaken effort to help China as the main reason for antagonism toward Japan, rather than seeing Japan more broadly as a threat to global security as some other authors represented in these readings do. Does this mean that Tansill would have had the United States accept Japanese domination of China and the entire Southeast Asian region as a counterweight to Russia?

CONTINUED FRICTION WITH JAPAN POINTS TOWARDS INEVITABLE WAR

Congress Enacts an Exclusion Law Which Angers Japan

As American statesmen looked from the troubled scenes in China to the quiet landscapes in Japan, it was not with relief but with suspicion that they viewed the placid picture of Old Nippon. The orderly

From Charles Callan Tansill, *Back Door to War: The Roosevelt Foreign Policy, 1933–1941.* Copyright © 1952. Reprinted by permission of the Henry Regnery Company. Excerpted from pp. 80–479.

ways of empire grated upon the sensibilities of many Americans who preferred the uneasy atmosphere of democracy to the regulated rhythm of the Mikado's Government. Since 1913, Japan had been under almost constant attack by the Department of State. The Wilson Administration had led a sustained assault against Japan along several fronts, and the inauguration of a Republican Administration in 1921 had led to the calling of the Washington Conference for the express purpose of checking Japanese plans for expansion. The climate of opinion in the United States was definitely hostile to Japan, and it was inevitable that clouds of misunderstanding between the two countries should gather along the diplomatic horizon. The first threat of a storm came in connection with the immigration question.

After the close of the World War [WWI] there was an increasing fear in the United States that the war-impoverished countries of Europe would send a huge wave of immigration to American shores. On May 19, 1921, in order to prevent such a contingency, Congress enacted a law that limited the number of aliens of any particular nationality that would be granted admission to the United States in any one year to 3 percent of the "number of foreign-born persons of such nationality resident in the United States" in the year 1910. Some months later a new act was framed which reduced the annual admission of any nationality to 2 percent of the foreign-born population of that nationality resident in the United States in 1890.[1] A high dike had been erected against the expected wave of immigration.

It was soon apparent that this new legislation would not be used merely to supplement the gentlemen's agreement with Japan which since 1907 had controlled the immigration of laborers from that country. In 1921 a movement began in the Far West to exclude by legislation any further immigration of Japanese laborers.

Background of the Manchurian Incident

Japan is Worried over the Spread of Communism in China. The outcome of the conflict between China and Soviet Russia in 1929 had important implications for Japan. First of all, it was clear that Russia had violated the provisions of the Sino-Russian agreement of 1924 which prohibited the spread of communistic propaganda in China.

[1] A. Whitney Griswold, *The Far Eastern Policy of the United States* (New York, 1938), pp. 369–70.

The vast amount of data seized by Chinese police in the Harbin Consulate left no doubt on this point. Russian denials carried no conviction to Japanese minds, and the fact that Chang Hsueh-liang had to fight alone against Soviet armed forces indicated that Chiang Kai-shek was either too weak to guard the frontiers of Manchuria effectively or was not deeply disturbed by the Russian chastisement of the war lord of the Three Eastern Provinces. The Japanese bastions of defense in North China were in evident danger.

This fact seemed apparent to Japanese statesmen when they looked at the ominous failure of Chiang Kai-shek to cope with Communist armies. In December 1930, Chiang mobilized troops, from Hunan, Hopeh, and Kiangsi provinces and sent them against the Communists. The Reds soon annihilated the Eighteenth Corps under General Chang Huei-tsan and caused the rapid retreat of the Fiftieth Corps. In February 1931, General Ho Ying-chin was given three army corps to attack the Reds but by May his forces were compelled to withdraw. In July, Chiang Kai-shek himself led a large army to the Nanchang front, but accomplished nothing decisive.[2] The Red menace was daily becoming more formidable and Japanese fears rapidly increased. The only way to insure Japanese security was through adequate measures of defense in Manchuria. These might violate some shadowy rights of sovereignty that China had over Manchuria, but these rights had not been successfully asserted since 1912 and would soon be extinguished by Russia if Japan took no action. For Japan, expansion in Manchuria was a national imperative. . . .

To Japan it appeared obvious that Manchuria was essential to her as a bastion of defense and as the keystone of her economic structure. Her statesmen hoped that the Department of State would recognize that North China was just as important to Japan as the Caribbean area was to the United States. The American Government had sent military forces to Haiti and to the Dominican Republic for the purpose of establishing administrations that would be responsive to American desires.[3] This armed intervention had been so recent and so effective that it led the American chargé in Peking to send a

[2] *Communism in China, Document A, Appendix No. 3* (Tokyo, 1932), pp. 3–5. This document was published by the Japanese Government as a part of the case of Japan. For a sympathetic account of the struggle of Chiang Kai-shek with the Chinese Communists see T'ang Leang-Li, *Suppressing Communist Banditry in China* (Shanghai, 1934), Chap. 5.

[3] Hallett Abend, *New York Times,* November 4, 1931.

dispatch to Secretary Kellogg which ended on a significant note:
"We cannot oppose Japanese plans in Manchuria ethically in view of
measures we have taken in our correspondingly vital zone—the
Caribbean. . . ."[4]

Japan was well aware of the danger that this Red tide might roll
over most of China. In the documents presented to the Lytton Commission in 1932, emphasis was placed upon this Communist menace
and upon the apparent inability of the Chinese Nationalist Government to control it.[5] It seemed to Tokyo that Japanese interests in
North China were about to be crushed between the millstones of
Chinese nationalism and Russian bolshevism. An appeal to the
League of Nations would accomplish little. Chinese nationalism had
found a sympathetic audience in the Western powers. Most of them
were inclined to accept the fictions and pretensions put forward by
the Nanking Government. The Japanese position in North China was
in grave danger of being infiltrated by Reds or successfully attacked
by fervent Chinese Nationalists whose patriotism had turned into a
"flame of hatred."[6] . . .

The dilemma that faced Japan is clearly and cogently stated by
George Sokolsky who was used as an intermediary between China
and Japan in 1931:

> It needs to be recalled here that in 1931 the last efforts were made to
> reconcile these countries [China and Japan]. Actually, I was an instru-
> ment in that attempted reconciliation, going to Japan from China to hold
> meetings with Baron Shidehara, Minister of Foreign Affairs, and others. I
> can say that the Japanese attitude was conciliatory; the Chinese, on the
> whole, antagonistic. . . . Two forces were at work to keep China and
> Japan quarreling: Soviet Russia and the League of Nations. Soviet Russia
> had been engaged since 1924 in an active program of stirring hate
> among the Chinese people against all foreigners except the Russians, but
> particularly against the British and the Japanese. . . .[7]

Secretary Stimson Prepares a Path to War

One of the reasons why Japan was "conciliatory" towards China in
1931 was because of the shaky structure of Japanese finance. A war

[4] Ferdinand L. Mayer to Secretary Kellogg, Peking, November 22, 1927. 894.51 So 8/4
MS, Department of State.
[5] *Communism in China, Document A, Appendix No. 3* (Tokyo, 1932).
[6] *Lytton Report* (Washington, 1932), p. 19.
[7] George Sokolsky, "These Days," *Washington Times-Herald,* March 14, 1951.

with China might lead to very serious consequences. On September 18, 1931, the American press published a summary of a report made by Dr. Harold G. Moulton, of the Brookings Institution, on economic conditions in the Japanese Empire. This survey had been undertaken upon the invitation of the Japanese Minister of Finance. In conclusion the summary stated that "military retrenchment, continuation of peaceful relations with the United States, and sharp restriction of the present rates of population are all essential if serious economic and financial difficulties in Japan are to be averted. . . . A balanced budget and tax reduction can be accomplished only if military outlays are curtailed."[8]

It was only with the greatest reluctance, therefore, that Japanese statesmen consented to support a program of expansion in Manchuria. After it was apparent that the Japanese Kwantung Army had seized certain cities in North China, Hugh Byas, writing from Tokyo, reported that the sudden movement of troops had not been "foreseen by the Japanese Government and had not been preventable."[9] Byas, as well as many other veteran observers in the Far East, had great confidence in the pacific disposition of Baron Shidehara, the Japanese Minister of Foreign Relations. Secretary Stimson shared this view and at first he was anxious to refrain from exerting too much pressure upon the Japanese Government because he feared such a policy would play into the hands of the militarists. . . .

The bombing of Chinchow by Japanese planes on October 8 [1931] provoked Stimson to take more vigorous action to preserve peace. He now began to consider the employment of sanctions against Japan in order to compel her to "respect the great peace treaties."[10] On October 10 he secured the President's [Hoover's] approval of a suggestion to have an American representative participate in all the sessions of the League Council which dealt with the enforcement of the Kellogg-Briand Pact. . . .

After this thrust against Japan, Stimson once more turned to the League and explained the basis of American action. Pressure from President Hoover had softened the tone of his notes. When Stimson in Cabinet meetings began to talk about coercing Japan by all "means short of actual use of armed force," the President informed

---

[8] Ware, op. cit., p. 206.
[9] *New York Times*, September 19, 1931.
[10] Henry L. Stimson, *The Far Eastern Crisis: Recollections and Observations* (New York, 1936), pp. 51–57.

him that "this was simply the road to war itself and he would have none of it."[11] . . .

. . . Elihu Root, thoroughly alarmed by the active measures Secretary Stimson was taking to stop Japanese expansion in Manchuria, wrote the Secretary a long letter of protest. Root had been Secretary of State from 1905 to 1909 and had negotiated the Root-Takahira Agreement that had given Japan a green light in Manchuria. He now warned Stimson about "getting entangled in League measures which we have no right to engage in against Japan." He also alluded to Japan's special interests in Manchuria through a long period of years, and spoke of the need for Japan to protect herself in a political sense against "the dagger aimed at her heart."

Root was a realist who did not want war with Japan. Stimson was a pacifist who loved peace so much he was always ready to fight for it. He wholeheartedly subscribed to the slogan—perpetual war for perpetual peace. In his answer to Root he expressed the belief that his intervention in the Manchurian muddle was necessary to save the whole structure of the peace treaties. He was the Atlas on whose stooping shoulders world peace was precariously balanced. A "new advance by Japan" would "undoubtedly create much adverse and even hostile sentiment in this country and much pressure upon us for some kind of action." As a man of action he was not inclined to draw back into any shell of neutrality. . . .[12]

SECRETARY STIMSON PRODUCES A PATTERN OF WAR

As one means of coping with the Japanese advance in North China, Stimson sent Joseph C. Grew to Tokyo as the American Ambassador. When Grew arrived in Japan in June 1932, the press was friendly and the Emperor was as agreeable as Mr. Grew's deafness permitted him to be. But the shadows of the Manchurian adventure fell across the threshold of the American Embassy and Grew soon realized that they would probably deepen and lengthen despite all his efforts to banish them with the bright light of some new Japanese-American understanding.

The main barrier across the road to friendly relations was the

---

[11] Ray L. Wilbur and Arthur M. Hyde, *The Hoover Policies* (New York, 1937), p. 603.
[12] Secretary Stimson to Elihu Root, December 14, 1931, Strictly Personal and Confidential, Box 129, Root Papers, Library of Congress.

Stimson doctrine itself.[13] The Japanese Government was determined to recognize Manchukuo in defiance of adverse opinion in the United States and in Europe. Secure control over North China appeared to Japanese statesmen, regardless of party affiliations, as a national necessity. As a source of essential raw materials and as a market for manufactured goods, Manchuria had special importance for Japan. Presidents Theodore Roosevelt and Woodrow Wilson had been willing to regard certain portions of North China as a Japanese sphere of influence, and the language of the Root-Takahira and the Lansing-Ishii agreements was so vaguely fertile that Japanese aspirations had enjoyed a rapid growth. Theodore Roosevelt, after boldly plucking the Panama pear, could not turn a deaf ear to Japanese pleas for a bite of Manchurian melon. And Woodrow Wilson, deep in his preparations for a crusade against wicked Germany, could not look too closely into Japanese motives in Manchuria. Encouraged by these friendly gestures of American Presidents, Japanese armies moved into many parts of North China. When Stimson suddenly flashed a red light of warning against any further advance, the Japanese Government made no real effort to obey the signal. Their Manchurian machine had gained too much momentum to be stopped by an American traffic cop who merely blew a tin whistle of non-recognition. . . .

In some circles in Japan the hope was expressed that a change in the Administration in Washington would bring a change in Far Eastern policy. But Stimson still had some six months to serve as Secretary of State, and there was the ominous possibility that during the period he would so firmly fix the pattern of policy that a new Secretary would be unable to alter it. Of one thing everyone in Japan could be certain—Stimson would not recede from the stand he had taken, no matter what the result. America might not be pushed to the point of actual conflict with Japan, but the road to war would be wide open and an invitation to hostilities would be ready for the anxious consideration of the President-elect.

In order to make sure that this invitation would be no empty affair, Stimson had consented to have Major General Frank R. McCoy serve

[13] The Stimson doctrine was the declaration by Hoover's Secretary of State, Henry L. Stimson, in a note sent to China and Japan on January 7, 1932 that the United States would not recognize treaties or agreements brought about by the use of force contrary to the Kellogg-Briand peace pact.—Ed.

as a member of the Lytton Commission of Enquiry. If this commission denounced Japanese aggression in North China in acidulous terms, General McCoy would bear a portion of the responsibility for such an indictment.

On October 1, 1932, the report of the Lytton Commission was published in Geneva. It made some interesting admissions. The rapid growth of the Communist Party was briefly described and the inability of Chiang Kai-shek to suppress it was clearly indicated.[14] But nothing was said about Soviet infiltration of Sinkiang and the absorption of Outer Mongolia. Japan was to be the culprit in China, not Russia. In order to prove this point the report expressed in very positive terms the belief that Japan made use of the Mukden Incident of September 18 to carry out a far-reaching plan of expansion in North China. It was admitted that Japan had "special interests" in Manchuria but these interests did not justify the erection of a semi-independent state like Manchukuo which would be under Japanese control. The report therefore recommended that Manchuria should enjoy "a large measure of autonomy" consistent "with the sovereignty and administrative integrity of China."[15]

The report mentioned the fact that the Japanese had erected the new state of Manchukuo on March 9, 1932, and had installed Henry Pu-yi, the boy Emperor of China, as the regent. It did not indicate who was to dethrone the regent or who was to assume the grave responsibility of pushing the large Japanese Army out of Manchukuo and thus permit Manchuria to resume its former status. Indirectly, this assertion of continued Chinese sovereignty over the Three Provinces was an endorsement of the Stimson nonrecognition principle. The commission conveniently closed its eyes to the fact of Japanese control over Manchukuo and assumed that the farce of nonrecognition would bring Japan to heel. It was a little shocked when Japan formally recognized Manchukuo on September 15, and Secretary Stimson felt outraged at this defiance of his doctrine. . . .

. . . Stimson found time to visit Hyde Park on January 9 [1933] where he found President-elect Roosevelt in a very receptive mood. He had no trouble in convincing Roosevelt that the Stimson doctrine should be one of the pillars of the foreign policy of the new Administration. Three days later he informed Ambassador Debuchi that

---

[14] *Lytton Report* (Washington, 1932), pp. 20–23.
[15] Ibid., p. 130.

the President-elect would adhere to the Stimson policy.[16] On January 16 this news was sent to our diplomatic representatives abroad, and on the following day Roosevelt, at a press conference at Hyde Park, insisted that America must stand behind the principle of the "sanctity of treaties."[17] Party lines in America had disappeared when it came to imposing discipline upon Japan. . . .

Even if Secretary Stimson had been sincere in his desire to make some gesture of conciliation towards Japan, it was apparent that time was against him. In a few weeks the Roosevelt Administration would take office and it would be most unusual for an outgoing Secretary of State to take a major diplomatic step which might not be in complete agreement with the policy already outlined by his successor in office after March 4, 1933. At any rate Stimson did nothing to conciliate Japanese statesmen who were now determined to take some radical action at Geneva. The Roosevelt statement at Hyde Park on January 17 in favor of the "sanctity of treaties" failed to make much of an impression upon them. They knew that the British and French empires had been built by the blood, sweat, and tears of millions of persons in conquered countries. Why all this sudden show of international virtue? As Matsuoka sagely remarked: "The Western Powers taught the Japanese the game of poker but after acquiring most of the chips they pronounced the game immoral and took up contract bridge."[18] It was obvious to most Japanese statesmen that the conscience of the Western powers barked only at strangers.

Matsuoka Marches Out of the League

At Geneva, Matsuoka was not inclined to listen to lectures in the League Assembly on public morals, and Ambassador Grew on February 23, 1933, informed Secretary Stimson that the Japanese Cabinet was in entire agreement with the viewpoint of their chief delegate. They regarded their position in Manchuria as an essential link in the "life line" of the Japanese Empire. They were determined to fight rather than yield to League pressure.[19] In the face of this

[16] Conversation between Secretary Stimson and Ambassador Debuchi, January 12, 1933. *Japan and the United States, 1931–1941*, I, 108–109.
[17] *New York Times*, January 18, 1933. Stimson had already assured the British Foreign Secretary, Sir John Simon, that the President-elect was committed to the Stimson doctrine. Sir John replied, January 14, that the British Government would adhere to the same doctrine. *Foreign Relations, 1933*, III, 89.
[18] Frederick Moore, *With Japan's Leaders* (1942), pp. 38–39.
[19] *Japan and the United States: 1931–1941*, I, 110–12. On February 7, 1933, with his

resolute Japanese attitude, the League went ahead and on February 24 it formally approved by an overwhelming vote the report of the Committee of Nineteen which had implemented the Lytton Report.[20]

This critical action on the part of the Assembly of the League of Nations provoked an immediate response from Matsuoka. After gravely stating that his government had "reached the limit of its endeavors to cooperate with the League," he marched stiffly from the hall of the Assembly. . . .

Hugh Wilson, representing the United States, was also in the Assembly as Matsuoka walked out. . . . He . . . realized that a crisis had been reached in world politics, and this crisis he knew had been precipitated by Stimson's nonrecognition policy. In his memoirs, Wilson tells the story of that fateful march of Matsuoka:

> The final session of the Assembly remains indelibly printed on my mind. . . . Matsuoka's speech on that day in the Assembly was delivered with a passionate conviction far removed from his usual businesslike manner. He pointed out the danger of pillorying a great nation. He warned that the Assembly was driving Japan from its friendship with the West toward an inevitable development of a self-sustaining, uniquely Eastern position. . . . For the first time the gravest doubts arose as to the wisdom of the course which the Assembly and my country were pursuing. I began to have a conception of the rancor and resentment that public condemnation could bring upon a proud and powerful people, and I began to question, and still do question whether such treatment is wise. . . . Condemnation creates a community of the damned who are forced outside the pale, who have nothing to lose by the violation of all laws of order and international good faith. . . . Not only did such doubts regarding arraignment arise in me, but for the first time I began to question the nonrecognition policy. More and more as I thought it over I became conscious that we had entered a dead-end street.[21]

It was apparent to seasoned diplomats that the manner in which Stimson endeavored to apply the nonrecognition formula was so provocative that war and not peace would be the result of his efforts. . . .

. . . On his way home from the debacle at Geneva, Matsuoka passed through the United States and hoped to have a conference

---

tongue in his cheek, Stimson instructed Hugh Wilson, United States Minister at Geneva, to make it clear that he was not in any way attempting "to guide or to influence or prejudice the League in its deliberations." *Foreign Relations, 1933*, III, 153.

[20] Russell M. Cooper, *American Consultation in World Affairs*, pp. 268–69.

[21] Hugh R. Wilson, *Diplomat Between Wars* (New York, 1941), pp. 279–81.

with President Roosevelt. When this news came to the Department of State, Mr. Hornbeck immediately wrote a memorandum indicating that it "would be undesirable to have the new President grant Mr. Matsuoka an interview." If he (Matsuoka) were "to speak with the President it would be only natural for the public to assume that Matsuoka had endeavored to convince the President of the justice of the Japanese case."[22] For some reason that is not clear, Mr. Hornbeck believed that the American public should not be placed under the strain of having to follow the arguments of Matsuoka. There was a chance that they might be too cogent and thus defeat the repressive policy of the Department of State. As a result of Mr. Hornbeck's advice, Matsuoka did not have an opportunity to present in private the case of Japan relative to Manchukuo. . . .

The Japanese press also expressed an ardent desire that the Roosevelt Administration would take an understanding view of the Manchurian situation and thereby lay the basis for "a restoration of friendly relations between the two nations." Matsuoka himself was quite optimistic with reference to Japanese-American relations. He thought that all talk of war between the two countries was "ridiculous." If Japan went to war in the near future, it would be with Soviet Russia, and Matsuoka expressed the view that in that event "he would not be surprised to see the United States on Japan's side."

There was no doubt that Japan had no wish for a war with the United States. Matsuoka was correct in his belief that the logical opponent for Japan in her next war would be Russia, but logic was not the basis for the foreign policy of the Roosevelt Administration. The wish that was closest to Stalin's heart was to involve Japan and the United States in a war that would remove the Japanese barrier that prevented the Red tide from overflowing the wide plains of China. The way that wish was gratified is the story of the succeeding chapters on Japanese-American relations. . . .

Japan Promotes Autonomy Movement in North China

It had been very clear to Theodore Roosevelt during his administration as President that Japan regarded Manchuria as a bulwark of

---

[22] Memorandum by Mr. Hornbeck, Division of Far Eastern Affairs, February 28, 1933. 811.4611 Japan/24, MS, Department of State. On March 31, 1933, Matsuoka had a brief interview with Secretary Hull. He was "very affable" and "urged that Japan be given time in which to make herself better understood." With reference to this conversation, Mr. Hull remarks: "I was courteous but virtually silent while he was offering these parting remarks." *Foreign Relations, 1933*, p. 264.

defense and as the keystone in the economic structure of the empire. Japan could not retire from her position in that province and any attempt to force her withdrawal would lead to open warfare. President Franklin D. Roosevelt and Secretary Hull by adopting the Stimson formula of nonrecognition had opened a Pandora's box of troubles in the Far East. When they applied the formula to Japan and remained silent concerning Russia's absorption of Outer Mongolia, they emptied every evil in the box and led them to stalk along the Manchurian frontier stirring up discontent. . . .

Soviet Russia Promotes a War between China and Japan

It is apparent from the diplomatic correspondence that came to the Department of State from Nanking and Tokyo that in the summer of 1937 many Chinese officials were spoiling for a fight between Japan and China. In June 1937, Mr. Andrews, second secretary of the American Embassy in Tokyo, had a conversation with Dr. Mar who held a similar position in the Chinese Embassy. After Ambassador Grew read a report of this conversation he noted that Dr. Mar's attitude was "one of truculence and undue optimism, thus reflecting the enhanced sense of security that has been developed in a section of Chinese officialdom as a consequence of the development of the past year." China, and not Japan, was ready for the outbreak of hostilities.

In China the Japanese Ambassador kept speaking in a conciliatory vein which stressed the idea that "the time would come when there would be 'understandings' between China and Japan." As a result of these pacific words Mr. Gauss, the American Consul-General at Shanghai, reported that in informed quarters it was believed that "the Japanese are unlikely to display a strong attitude or to take any aggressive measures in North China while the question of an Anglo-Japanese understanding is being explored."

It is evident that many foreign observers in June–July 1937 regarded an outbreak of war between China and Japan as quite improbable. The Konoye Ministry seemed intent upon carrying out the pacific policy of the preceding administrations. It was with distinct surprise, therefore, that the governments of the major powers heard that armed hostilities had taken place near Peking. On the night of July 7, in the vicinity of the famous Marco Polo bridge, some

Japanese troops became involved in a sharp fight with some units of the Chinese Twenty-ninth Army.[23] A new drama that would end on a curtain line announcing Russian domination of the Far East had opened with an ominous fanfare. The whole world became an interested audience with few of the spectators realizing that the progress of the play was pointed towards a Russian conclusion. Chinese, Japanese, and Americans would move across the Far Eastern stage in intricate patterns that finally proclaimed a definite Muscovite motif. The Moscow theater never staged a more effective puppet show. . . .

Japanese military authorities did not at first appear to realize the strength of this tie between the Communists and the Nationalists, and they hoped for an early settlement of the clash on the night of July 7. Some of them were inclined to believe that "the firing by Chinese troops which started the incident was not premeditated."[24] This conciliatory attitude led to the agreement of July 11 which was formally signed by General Chang on the nineteenth. Its terms were mild. There would be an apology and some punishment for the Chinese captain responsible for the outbreak of hostilities. There would also be assurances for the future which provided for the voluntary retirement of Chinese officials in North China who impeded Sino-Japanese cooperation and the expulsion of the communistic elements from the Peking district.[25]

On July 12 the Japanese Ambassador (Saito) had a long conversation with Secretary Hull during the course of which he explained the policy of the Foreign Office. At the conclusion of Saito's remarks, Hull expressed his approval of Japanese efforts "to work out a friendly settlement" of the incident.[26] On the following day Ambassador Grew informed the Department of State that he believed that "if some way of avoiding general hostilities without losing face could be found, the Japanese Government might possibly still be pleased to find this way."[27]

It seemed to Mr. Hornbeck that the Japanese Foreign Office was

[23] This China Incident, as the Japanese called it, led to the long war between China and Japan, 1937–1945. But have more recent events in China borne out Tansill's conclusion that Russia would end up dominating Asia?—Ed.

[24] Walter H. Mallory, "Japan Attacks, China Resists," *Foreign Affairs*, XVI (October 1937), 129–33.

[25] Memorandum by the ambassador in Japan (Grew), Tokyo, July 22, 1937. *United States and Japan, 1931–1941*, I, 333–34.

[26] Memorandum by Secretary Hull, July 12, 1937. Ibid., pp. 316–18.

[27] Ambassador Grew to Secretary Hull, Tokyo, July 13, 1937. Ibid., pp. 319–20.

taking the position that conversations should not be held by representatives of the Chinese and Japanese governments "but between Japanese officials in North China and the local Chinese officials on the theory that North China is a political entity separate from the authority and control of the Chinese (Nanking) Government." It was his opinion that the American Government should "make no approach to either the Chinese or the Japanese authorities and make no public comment."[28]

Secretary Hull followed this advice. On the evening of July 13 he summoned Ambassador Saito to his apartment in the Carlton Hotel and frankly informed him that the American Government was "paramountly concerned in the preservation of peace." Because of this fact it would confine its utterances "to phrases entirely within range of its impartial, friendly attitude towards all alike." Its action would "stop entirely short of any question or phase of mediation."[29]

This "hands off" attitude would continue to be observed by the Department of State if no general war followed the clash at Peking. In the event of long-continued hostilities tremendous pressure would be exerted upon Secretary Hull to undertake some form of mediation. But in the early days of July 1937 there still seemed some hope for peace. It was true, however, that the action of the Chinese Nationalist Government in disavowing the agreement of July 11 was causing deep concern in the minds of many observers. When this disavowal was followed by the dispatch of "a large body of troops" to the Peking area, it was obvious that a crisis had arrived.[30] . . .

The British Foreign Office favored a "combined Anglo-American démarche" in Tokyo and Nanking rather than an invocation of the Nine-Power Treaty, and Foreign Secretary Eden suggested this to Ambassador Bingham. From Tokyo, Ambassador Grew expressed a strong dissent from this view. He could see "no reason why we should take action."[31] He also indicated that in Japan the unanimity of opinion relative to the situation in North China was "striking." It was not "a case of unwilling deference by the Government to military

---

[28] Memorandum by Mr. Hornbeck, July 13, 1937. 793.94/8737, 8922, MS, Department of State.
[29] Memorandum by Secretary Hull, July 13, 1937. *United States and Japan, 1931–1941*, I, 320–22.
[30] Ambassador Grew to Secretary Hull, Tokyo, July 13, 1937. 793.94/8741, MS, Department of State.
[31] Ambassador Grew to Secretary Hull, Tokyo, July 13, 1937. 793.94/8742, MS, Department of State.

initiative. The Cabinet enjoys high prestige, is wholly in command and lends full support to steps recently taken by the Japanese Army in North China. . . . At no time during the period of my assignment at this post have I observed indications of so strong and unanimous a determination on the part of the Japanese Government to resist even at the cost of extensive hostilities any movement which might tend to weaken the position of Japan in North China." Mr. Grew also remarked that there was not sufficient evidence to justify the hypothesis that "either the Japanese Government or the Army deliberately engineered the incident in order to force a 'show down.' "[32] . . .

On July 16, Ambassador Grew reported from Tokyo that "the steady development of plans of the Chinese Government to mobilize its forces and to concentrate them in North China was the principal cause for the decision taken yesterday by the Japanese Government to send reinforcements from Japan to North China."

* * *

The Communist menace in China gave Secretary Hull little concern. He was now thoroughly aroused over reports of indiscriminate bombings in China by the Japanese. In a long instruction to Ambassador Grew he spoke his mind very plainly. It appeared to him that Japanese unresponsiveness to American protests against bombings showed that the Japanese Government did not set a high value upon American efforts "to cultivate good will, confidence, and stability in general." If the Japanese Government would just follow the high principles enunciated by the American Government on July 16 the situation in the Far East would probably improve. While the American Government had endeavored to follow an "absolutely impartial course" during the current crisis in China, the actions of the Japanese armed forces had shocked American opinion. It would be expedient for the Japanese Government to keep in mind that their course in China was looked upon in America with the same degree of disapproval that it had evoked in Britain. American public opinion "has been outraged by the methods and strategy employed by the combatants, particularly by the Japanese military, and has become

---

[32] Ambassador Grew to Secretary Hull, Tokyo, July 13, 1937. 793.94/8745, MS, Department of State.

gradually more critical of Japan." It was high time the Japanese Government gave heed to the principles so often expressed by the Department of State.[33]

It is evident that the statement of American principles by Secretary Hull on July 16 was a verbal bombshell directed against Japan. All talk of an "absolutely impartial course" towards China and Japan during the July crisis was mere diplomatic eyewash which no realistic statesmen took seriously. Hull was definitely antagonistic towards Japan, and his statement of July 16 was a prelude to the quarantine speech of President Roosevelt on October 5. . . .

The quarantine speech of October 5 had many macabre overtones designed to frighten the American people. It indicated that large portions of the world were experiencing a "reign of terror," and that the "landmarks and traditions which have marked the progress of civilization toward a condition of law, order and justice" were being "wiped away." "Innocent peoples and nations" were being "cruelly sacrificed to a greed for power and supremacy" which was "devoid of all sense of justice and humane consideration." If this sad condition of affairs existed in other parts of the world it was vain for anyone to "imagine that America will escape, that it may expect mercy, that this Western Hemisphere will not be attacked, and that it will continue tranquilly and peacefully to carry on the ethics and the arts of civilization."

Newspapers of a one-world persuasion sprang to the President's support. The *New York Times* and the *World-Telegram* promptly attacked the "unrealities of isolation,"[34] while the *New York Daily News* suggested a long-range Anglo-American naval blockade of Japan if that nation were to overrun China and threaten the interests of the Western powers."[35]

Some papers advocated an economic boycott as a means to bring Japan to reason. The *Washington Post* urged that America "immediately cease to buy Japanese goods,"[36] and this opinion was strongly seconded by the *Washington Evening Star*[37] and the Rochester *Democrat and Chronicle*.[38] The *Atlanta Constitution* expressed the

---

[33] Secretary Hull to Ambassador Grew, September 2, 1937. *United States and Japan, 1931–1941*, I, 361–64.
[34] October 6, 8, 1937.
[35] October 3, 7, 1937.
[36] October 8, 1937.
[37] October 6, 7, 1937.
[38] October 6, 1937.

emphatic opinion that "war-diseased nations must be quarantined,"[39] and the *Birmingham News*[40] and the Raleigh *News and Observer*[41] joined the chorus. In the Middle West the *Chicago Daily News*,[42] the *St. Louis Globe-Democrat*,[43] and the *Cincinnati Enquirer*[44] expressed agreement with the "general principles" of the President's address. On the Pacific Coast the *San Francisco Chronicle*,[45] the *Los Angeles Timoo*,[46] and the *Portland Morning Oregonian*[47] adopted a favorable attitude.

But there was a large legion of newspapers that rejected any thought of economic sanctions against Japan. Such action would lead to war. The *New York Herald Tribune* believed that the President's speech had been based upon the "identical sands of confusion, emotion and wishful thinking which so tragically engulfed Mr. Wilson's great vision."[48] The New York *Sun* warned the President that American public opinion would not approve any policy of "pulling chestnuts out of the fire for any association of foreign nations."[49] The *Boston Herald* boldly declared that "Americans must not embark on another costly attempt to reform the world,"[50] while even the staunchly Democratic *Boston Post* cried out in protest: "He [the President] must know that the American people are in no mood for a crusade."[51]

The *Chicago Tribune* was openly hostile to any threat of a boycott against Japan. Economic sanctions would lead America down the road to war.[52] The *Detroit Free Press* voiced the opinion that there was no "adequate reason for remarks that were evangelistic rather than statesmanlike, and were manifestly designed to stir emotions rather than provoke careful thought."[53] The *Milwaukee Journal* remarked that a boycott is a "first cousin to outright war,"[54] and the

[39] October 7, 1937.
[40] October 6, 11, 1937
[41] October 6, 8, 1937
[42] October 6, 8, 1937.
[43] October 15, 1937.
[44] October 7, 8, 1937.
[45] October 6, 1937.
[46] October 6, 7, 1937.
[47] October 6, 1937.
[48] October 6, 8, 1937.
[49] October 6, 7, 1937.
[50] October 6, 7, 1937.
[51] October 11, 1937.
[52] October 6, 1937.
[53] October 7, 1937.
[54] October 10, 1937

Spokane *Spokesman-Review* stated ominously that the President's Chicago address "approximated a declaration of war."[55]

The columnists were divided in their opinions of the Chicago address. Boake Carter was fearful that the President suffered from the "disease of moral fervor for reform."[56] Paul Mallon regarded the address as a clever move to divert attention from the unfortunate appointment of Hugo Black to the Supreme Court,[57] while General Hugh S. Johnson was worried that America, as in 1917, would play the role of "sucker."[58]

On the other hand, David Lawrence hailed the address as the "speech the whole world has been waiting for several months to hear,"[59] Dorothy Thompson was delighted that she could now envisage the end of American "neutrality,"[60] and Walter Lippmann praised the President for a much-needed clarion call to the democracies to resist aggressor nations.[61]

The Catholic press had few words of praise for the President's Chicago challenge. *America* flatly stated that the "people of the United States positively are opposed to foreign imbroglios";[62] the *Ave Maria* was filled with misgivings,[63] while Father Gillis, in the *Catholic World,* was sharply critical of any pressure in favor of American intervention in the Far East.[64]

It is interesting to note that the *Christian Century,* which reflected the Protestant viewpoint, was distinctly suspicious of the Chicago speech. In a forecast of the future it warned that if America went to war on behalf of China the result would be a victory for Russia.[65]

This Russian angle of the situation in the Far East was clearly perceived by many observers. On October 12 the Division of Far Eastern Affairs prepared a memorandum for the use of Secretary

[55] October 6, 7, 1937.
[56] *Boston Daily Globe,* October 8, 1937.
[57] *Boston Herald,* October 8, 1937.
[58] *New York World-Telegram,* October 6, 1937.
[59] *Chicago Daily News,* October 7, 1937.
[60] *New York Herald Tribune,* October 10, 1937.
[61] *New York Herald Tribune,* October 16, 1937.
[62] October 16, 1937.
[63] October 23, 1937, pp. 534–35.
[64] December 1937, pp. 257–65. On October 9, 1937, Senator David I. Walsh wrote a note to Secretary Hull in which he inclosed a telegram from the Maryknoll Fathers in Japan. They deeply regretted the "recent change official attitude towards Sino-Japanese trouble," and urgently requested his influence "towards restoring previous attitude impartial tolerance as most practical policy." 793.94/10546, MS, Department of State.
[65] October 20, 1937, pp. 1287–88.

Hull. With reference to possible economic sanctions, the memorandum asks the question whether the United States should take the lead in such a movement. In answer to this question it remarks: "It is believed that the assuming of such a position by any country would bring that country face to face with a very real hazard. . . . It seems to me [Mr. Hamilton, chief of the Division] that public opinion in the United States is definitely opposed to the United States assuming a position of leadership in the imposing of restrictive measures directed at Japan. Moreover it should be borne in mind that if restrictive measures should take the form of economic 'sanctions,' the United States would be called upon to carry the heaviest burden.[66] . . . If some program could be worked out which would give Japan a reasonable prospect of economic security and which would remove Japan's fear of communism and attack from the Soviet Union, there would be removed some basic elements in the situation responsible for Japan's present imperialistic program."[67]

[66] In a letter to Mr. Hornbeck, Mr. Taneo Taketa, a representative of the South Manchuria Railway, points out the close economic ties between the United States and Japan. The South Manchuria Railway alone had purchased "far more than $100,000,000 worth of equipment from the United States." Other firms had purchased large amounts. 793.94/10708, MS, Department of State.
[67] Memorandum prepared by the Division of Far Eastern Affairs, October 12, 1937. 793.94/10706, MS, Department of State.

Herbert Feis

THE ROAD TO PEARL HARBOR

Herbert Feis argues in this selection that Roosevelt and Hull could follow no other course than to oppose Japanese aggression while offering every possible incentive to Japan to forego its Axis connection. For Feis it was a reasonable and righteous defense of the treaty structure in the Pacific, and Hull's proposals of November 26 were realistic and fair. How does this analysis compare with Tansill's? Does Feis agree completely with Hull's view as set forth in the first selection? Why did the policy fail to avert war? How does Feis explain Hull's rejection of a meeting with Konoye, and Japan's proposed modus vivendi?

Feis was a government adviser and served on the policy planning staff of the State Department. He has held a Guggenheim Fellowship. A Pulitzer Prize winner, he has written of the continuing diplomacy and strategy of the United States in Churchill, Roosevelt, and Stalin *(1957);* Japan Subdued *(1961);* The China Tangle *(1953); and* The Potsdam Conference *(1960).*

After Our Elections:
Steps towards a Concerted Program

November 1940; the Roosevelt administration was safely confirmed in power. It could properly construe the election result as approval of its opposition to the Axis and its support of Britain short of war. But, because of the terms in which he had expounded these policies during the campaign, the President was obliged still to move warily and on the slant. The words spoken during the election contest lived on to complicate and confine decision for the times ahead.

Americans had been told that they need not take part in the battles then being fought in Europe and Asia and that the government would not cause them to do so.[1] They had been urged to

Selections from Herbert Feis, *The Road to Pearl Harbor* (copyright 1950 by Princeton University Press, Princeton Paperback, 1971), pp. 133–328. Reprinted by permission of Princeton University Press.

[1] The most unguarded of these statements, amounting to a promise, was made by the President in a speech in Boston on October 30 when he said:

"And while I am talking to you mothers and fathers, I give you one more assurance.

"I have said this before, but I shall say it again and again and again:

"Your boys are not going to be sent into any foreign wars.

"They are going into training to form a force so strong that, by its very existence, it will keep the threat of war far away from our shores.

"The purpose of our defense is defense."

It can, of course, be well argued that the question of what is or is not a "foreign war" is not to be learned from a map alone. But the manner in which it was used during the campaign seemed to give it a simple meaning of wars fought in and by provide weapons and resources to fend off the danger of having to go to war. British resistance, the expressed thought ran, was giving us time to become so strong that no country, or group of countries, would dare attack us. While if the Axis won, the United States would become exposed to its fury and forced to fight near or within our own land. This was a correct judgment of the meaning to us of the wars in Europe and Asia. It was a well-founded basis for the program sponsored by the government and for the acceptance of the connected risks. But it left the President open to a charge of blunder or bad faith if the United States found itself at war.

The government avoided all actions which could not be construed as defensive. It continued—and it was no easy thing to do—to refuse to enter into any accord which carried an obligation to go to war. But it shaped our policies in conference with other governments and fitted its action to theirs. We were about to form a common front against Japan without admitting it or promising to maintain it by force.

Before leaving the subject, a comment may be added about the information given the American people during the months after the election—the winter of 1940–41. Some things that were done were wholly told, some vaguely told, and a few, such as naval talks and movements, were hardly told at all. The President's utterances of this period did not provide all the explanatory knowledge that could have been wanted to follow and judge American policy in action. For they were not systematic statements of the situation facing the United States and the choice before it. They were emotional appeals to the American people to hurry along their military preparations and to stand firm and hard against the Axis. They were written as such, not by essayists but by political advisers and dramatists. They were pinpointed explosives.[2] They were exertions of leadership in behalf of measures that were secretly in the making, or rather in the taking.

*　*　*

---

foreign countries. The term was, unless I am mistaken, taken over from the opponents of intervention. A cousinly term was effectively used by Charles A. Beard in the title of a virulent article that he published in *Harper's Magazine* for September 1939, "Giddy Minds and Foreign Quarrels."

Willkie spoke in the same strain as Roosevelt; in fact he set the pace in providing assurance that the United States need not and should not enter the war. The isolationists were far more extreme, denouncing any and all acts of intervention.

[2] To adopt a description used by Robert E. Sherwood—*Roosevelt and Hopkins* (New York, 1948), p. 184—who writes that Willkie's radio speeches "sounded" harsh, hurried and diffuse—short-range blasts of birdshot rather than pinpointed high explosive shells."

While keeping the American fleet at American bases, while refusing to say what it would or would not do if Japan sailed into the
Southwest Pacific, the American government—within a month after
the elections—put together a program of subtly adjusted measures to
hinder Japan.

First came the decisions in regard to aid for China in response to
Chiang Kai-shek's appeals. On November 30 the President announced that we would put another $100 million at his disposal. Fifty
modern pursuit planes at once were promised him, with as many
more as possible. Steps were taken to issue passports to American
citizens who wished to go to China to serve as aviators or aviation
instructors. A plan for providing China with long-range bombers so
that it could hit back at Tokyo was excitedly discussed with the
British and Chinese. To the chagrin of all, it was found impractical.[3]
These measures were the outcome of a tense effort to make sure that
the Chiang Kai-shek regime would be able and willing to keep in the
fight.

Ships and planes were sent out to the Philippines. Six submarines
went, with more to follow. Plans were made to assemble the whole
Asiatic fleet at Manila and to increase its size. Hull urged that the
Navy send as well a whole squadron of cruisers to southernmost
Philippine ports. The President was briefly for this, but changed his
mind. He also wanted to publish the news of our naval movements,
but he took Hull's advice to let them become known by reports that
were certain to seep out, as the ships were seen. A public announcement, he thought, might cause trouble of two kinds: objection
within the United States which would lessen the effect upon Japan;
and excitement within Japan. Japan was not to be threatened publicly, but to be left guessing.

"I believed in letting them guess as to when and in what set of

---

[3] This seems to have been inspired by a remark of the President that it would be a
good thing if the Chinese could bomb Japan. Morgenthau took it up, and talked it over
with Lothian and T. V. Soong who enthusiastically cabled Chiang Kai-shek. Hull said he
was for it, but it might occur to skeptical spirits who knew him that he saw no need to
catch that arrow in his hand since it would soon fall to earth. Chiang Kai-shek
answered that he would carry out the plan, provided the United States supplied not
only the bombers but escort planes and the necessary ground organization. We, of
course, had none of these to spare; the bombers would have had to be taken from the
allotments destined for Britain, Hawaii, and the Philippines. The idea was dropped at a
meeting on December 23, when General Marshall demonstrated how impractical it was.
Morgenthau diary, entries for December 3, 7, 8, 10, 18, 20, 22, and 23, 1940.

circumstances we would fight. While Japan continued to guess, we continued to get ready for anything she might do."[4]

The Japanese were not the only ones compelled to guess. The British were just as uncertain. A month later Harry Hopkins from London was reporting to the President that "Eden asked me repeatedly what our country would do if Japan attacked Singapore or the Dutch East Indies, saying it was essential to their policy to know."[5]

The thought may be carried further. Not only did the British not know what we would do, but neither did Roosevelt or Hull know. Would the President ask Congress to declare war on Japan? Or would he merely take some lesser measures—such as turning submarines over to the British, or using American naval forces to maintain a patrol and convoy system in the Pacific? Or, because that might waste naval forces, would he not even do that?

He was spared the need of deciding. Most fortunately so. For grave uses for the fleet in the Atlantic loomed up more clearly than before, and a great need to face Hitler with unengaged forces. On December 8, Churchill, by letter, put before the President (through Hull) a lucid and compelling summary of the situation faced by Britain and of the aid it would need to carry on. Among its parts were these: "The danger of Great Britain being destroyed by a swift, overwhelming blow has for the time being very greatly receded. In its place there is a long, gradually maturing danger, less sudden and less spectacular, but equally deadly. This mortal danger is the steady and increasing diminution of sea tonnage. . . . The decision for 1941 lies upon the seas. Unless we can establish our ability to feed this island, to import the munitions of all kinds which we need, unless we can move our armies to the various theatres where Hitler and his confederate Mussolini must be met, and maintain them there . . . we may fall by the way, and the time needed by the United States to complete her defensive preparations may not be forthcoming. It is, therefore, in shipping and in the power to transport across the oceans, particularly the Atlantic Ocean, that in 1941 the crunch of the whole war will be found."[6]

In drafting this, Churchill had before him Stark's memo of

---

[4] Hull, *The Memoirs of Cordell Hull* (New York, 1948), I, p. 915.
[5] Sherwood, *Roosevelt and Hopkins* (New York, 1948), p. 259.
[6] Winston S. Churchill, *Their Finest Hour* (Boston, 1949), p. 560.

November 12. A copy had been sent on to him by the British naval representative in Washington, along with Stark's remark that it would be useful if the Prime Minister endorsed the basic suggestions therein contained. The advice was taken to heart. The Prime Minister's analysis left no doubt that the United States would have to do more than it had done.

While the President was still in the Caribbean, the problem drew together Hull, Knox, Stimson, Stark, and Marshall. They hunted for the response that would be sufficient yet possible. All agreed with the comment that Stimson wrote in his diary while these talks were on: "It is very apparent that nothing will save Great Britain from the starvation of her supplies, which Stark estimates will necessarily take place in six months, except assistance from us by convoy in the Atlantic. . . ."[7] When Stimson so proposed in the cabinet (on December 19), "The President said he hadn't quite reached that yet."[8]

But, short of that, the resolve emerged from these December conferences to extend American naval protection over the Atlantic as far and as fast as might be necessary, and in the face of any risks of fighting at sea. This was enough (though not the sole) reason for refusing to promise to join the defense of Singapore and the Indies; enough reason why the President could not know or tell what he might do if Japan attacked them. A season was ahead in which the forces of the Allies were to be most wanly stretched. . . .

In the disturbed realm of diplomacy which the United States and Japan had entered, the language used is in part symbolic, in part spoken. Battleships and economic controls are the symbol of power in reserve, symbols used to give edge to verbal warnings, a way of saying "Do you see what I mean?" without saying it. But at the same time the American government was giving secret spoken warnings to Japan.

Dooman, the experienced Counselor of the American Embassy in Tokyo, had been on leave in the United States. He was known by the Japanese to be a firm and straightforward friend. So it was thought that his report of the state of American opinion might be accepted as advice rather than as a threat. On February 14 (Tokyo time) he put before Ohashi, the Vice-Minister for Foreign Affairs, the "philosophy" of the American position. The Vice-Minister was told that the Ameri-

---

[7] Stimson diary, entry for December 16, 1940.
[8] Ibid., entry for December 19, 1940.

can people were determined to support Britain even at the risk of war; that if Japan or any other country menaced that effort it "would have to expect to come into conflict with the United States"; that if Japan were to occupy Dutch or British areas in the Pacific it would create havoc with the British situation in the war; and that the United States had abstained from an oil embargo in order not to impel Japan to create a situation that could only lead to the most serious outcome.

On the same date, February 14 (Washington time), the President had his first talk with the new Japanese Ambassador, Admiral Nomura. He made no such blunt affirmations. By being affable and eager, the President sought to show that he wished peace, not war. He spoke as though the danger of war lay in a chance error or incident rather than because of any basic clash of interest. The purpose was to encourage the Japanese government to talk with us. If, as was thought, and correctly thought, in Washington, there was still a division of opinion in the Japanese government, an engagement to talk with us would help the proponents of peace. The light touch was chosen for heavy work, for critical work.[9]

In summary, then, American policy during this winter period of alarm (January–February) was a compound of warning gestures, slowly spreading coercion, earnest advice, and an invitation to talk.

The reports that came back from Tokyo were taken to mean that this policy was, at least for the time being, effective. Grew reported on the 18th of February that the Japanese officials were much disturbed by the reactions abroad; and that Matsuoka was being compelled again to defend himself against criticisms of the Tripartite Pact. The Japanese Foreign Office denied in a calm note on the 20th to the British that there was any basis for their alarm; nor for the warlike preparations which the British and the Americans were taking to meet unreal contingencies in the South Seas.

On February 20, or thereabouts, it became confirmed that Matsuoka was about to leave for Moscow, Berlin, and Rome. "For the purpose," Churchill informed the President, "of covering the failure of action against us."[10] This was not an adequate explanation. But

---

[9] Hull's memorandum of this talk is printed in *Foreign Relations: Japan,* II, 387–89.
[10] In this message of February 20, reprinted in *Pearl Harbor Attack,* Part 19, p. 3454, Churchill attributed the postponement of the attack to fear of the United States. He was doing his best to keep the fear alive, as when on the 24th he remarked to the Japanese Ambassador in London that it would be a pity if Japan, already at war with China, should find itself at war with Great Britain and the United States. But he took occasion

about the direction of Matsuoka's mind at any given moment any guess seemed to be as good as another—so like a twisted rope was he. As when told by Grew that everything that Dooman had said to Ohashi had his (Grew's) entire concurrence and approval, he answered that he entirely agreed with what Dooman had said.[11] To Craigie at about the same time he said that Japan's motto was "No conquest, no oppression, no exploitation."

Matsuoka's words were not trusted. But the allowance of time was a great relief. And beyond that a great chance—both to strive further to avert war with Japan, and to get ready for the fight if war came. Projects for each purpose were in secret course. Two ladders were being built for history; no one knew which would be used. . . .

In weighing all that came after, these four points should be borne in mind, for they marked out the ground on which the American government stood. In some phases of the talks with Japan, it was deemed discreet to leave them in the background. But they were never forgotten. In order they were:

1. Respect for the territorial integrity and the sovereignty of each and all nations.
2. Support of the principle of noninterference in the internal affairs of other countries.
3. Support of the principle of equality, including equality of commercial opportunity.
4. Nondisturbance of the status quo in the Pacific except as the status quo may be altered by peaceful means.

The Japanese government did not want to argue principles; abstract principles, which took no account of place, time, or degree. It wanted an end to American aid to China, a lifting of the embargoes, economic independence, a commanding place in the Far East. Thus, the Japanese records verify, it studied this list of commandments glumly. They made a cavern in which Japan could become lost and delayed. But the Japanese government was to find that there was no way round them. Or, as the matter was regarded by the heads of that government (and so stated in their later defense), American insistence that Japan subscribe to these four principles was

---

also to assure the Japanese government that the measures taken by Britain were only for defense, that no attack would be made upon Japan or Japanese forces.
[11] *Foreign Relations: Japan,* II, 143.

"symptomatic of a doctrinairism which was to exercise a baleful influence throughout."[12] . . .

On July 2 there came together in the presence of the Emperor the chief figures of the civil and military governments of Japan. These included the Prime Minister, Prince Konoye; the Foreign Minister, Matsuoka; the Minister for War, General Tojo; the Minister for the Navy, Admiral Oikawa; the Chief of the Army General Staff, General Sugiyama; the Chief of the Naval General Staff, Admiral Nagano; the President of the Privy Council, Hara; and the Minister for Home Affairs, Hiranuma. The plans ratified at this Imperial Conference set into determined motion the acts and responses that six months later resulted in war between Japan and the United States. The tail of the serpent wound round to its mouth.

From the text of the resolution adopted at this conference the course of events that followed can now be clearly traced. It is not very long and the reader, I think, will want to have most of it.[13]

An Outline of the Policy of the Imperial Government in View of Present Developments (Decision reached at the Conference held in the Imperial Presence on July 2)

I. Policy

1. The Imperial Government is determined to follow a policy which will result in the establishment of the Greater East Asia Co-Prosperity Sphere and world peace, no matter what international developments take place.

2. The Imperial Government will continue its effort to effect a settlement of the China Incident and seek to establish a solid basis for the security and preservation of the nation. This will involve an advance into the southern regions and, depending on future developments, a settlement of the Soviet Question as well.

3. The Imperial Government will carry out the above program no matter what obstacles may be encountered.

---

[2] *Far East Mil. Trib.*, Defense Document No. 3100.

[3] I have selected the translation of this "Outline of the Policy of the Imperial Government in View of Present Developments" contained in the "Konoye Memoirs" (as printed in *Pearl Harbor Attack*, Part 20, pp. 4018–19), in preference to that contained in the text presented to the *International Military Tribunal* (Exh. No. 588). Between these two translations there are points of difference, both in the order of exposition and in the tone, though no basic difference in meaning. The translation presented to the *International Military Tribunal* reads as though the Japanese government were virtually determined on war with the United States, while the one herein used seems to regard that event as a possibility against which Japan was to prepare but still seek to avoid.

II. Summary

1. *Steps will be taken to bring pressure on the Chiang Regime from the southern approaches in order to bring about its surrender. Whenever demanded by future developments the rights of a belligerent will be resorted to against Chungking and hostile concessions taken over.*

2. *In order to guarantee national security and preservation, the Imperial Government will continue all necessary diplomatic negotiations with reference to the southern regions and also carry out various other plans as may be necessary. In case the diplomatic negotiations break down, preparations for a war with England and America will also be carried forward. First of all, the plans which have been laid with reference to French Indochina and Thai will be prosecuted, with a view to consolidating our position in the southern territories.*

In carrying out the plans outlined in the foregoing article, we will not be deterred by the possibility of being involved in a war with England and America.

3. *Our attitude with reference to the German-Soviet War will be based on the spirit of the Tripartite Pact. However, we will not enter the conflict for some time but will steadily proceed with military preparations against the Soviet and decide our final attitude independently. At the same time, we will continue carefully correlated activities in the diplomatic field.*

. . . In case the German-Soviet War should develop to our advantage, we will make use of our military strength, settle the Soviet question and guarantee the safety of our northern borders. . . .

4. *In carrying out the preceding article all plans, especially the use of armed forces, will be carried out in such a way as to place no serious obstacles in the path of our basic military preparations for a war with England and America.*

5. *In case all diplomatic means fail to prevent the entrance of America into the European War, we will proceed in harmony with our obligations under the Tripartite Pact. However, with reference to the time and method of employing our armed forces we will take independent action.*

6. *We will immediately turn our attention to placing the nation on a war basis and will take special measures to strengthen the defenses of the nation.*

7. *Concrete plans covering this program will be drawn up separately.*

The main lines of this policy were set and most stubbornly held by the forces who spoke through General Tojo. They did not get their whole way, but a ruinous share of it. They thought that if Japan acquired a self-sufficient base of operation in the south it could wear down China, and stand, if need be, a long war against Britain and the United States. The Army and Navy were to get ready for such a war. But the hope remained that it would not have to be fought. It was expected that if Germany defeated Russia, the United States and

Britain would give way; that they would allow Japan to establish the New Order in East Asia at the expense of others.

To Matsuoka this course of action was a rebuff and a mistake. But he buoyed himself up with the belief that his views would prevail later. Thus he busied himself with excuses, assuring Ribbentrop that Japan was preparing for all eventualities and when the time came would turn against Russia; in the meantime the advancing vigil in the Pacific was no less a contribution to the common cause.[14] To Konoye and the Imperial Household the resolution of July 2 was at least a temporary respite from the disputes with which they were surrounded. All gambled on the chance that the German armies would bring both the Soviet Union and the British down before winter came. Then there would be only one strong possible enemy left—the United States. This was the strategy that failed. But it might have won.

Japan's actions during the next few months followed this plan:

The economic resources of the country were organized for war.

The entry into Indochina was begun. Before July ended the demands were served upon Petain, and the Japanese Navy and Army moved into Indochina.

The Army hastened its operational plans against Malaya, Java, and other points in the Netherlands East Indies, Borneo, the Bismarck Archipelago, and the Philippines.[15]

The Navy developed corresponding plans—among them one highly secret tactic. It began to practice the Pearl Harbor attack, conceived first in January. The fleets went into Kagoshima Bay and there the planes practiced coming in low over the mountains, dive bombing, and the use of torpedoes, specially designed for shallow waters.[16]

The Japanese government gave the government of the Soviet Union on July 2 formal assurances that it would observe the neutrality pact.[17] The size of the Kwantung Army was increased (from some 300,000 men to about twice that number). But troops were withdrawn

[14] Ibid., Exh. Nos. 636, 796, 1113.

[15] Testimony of General Tanaka (Shinichi), Chief of the Operations Section, General Staff of the Army. The studies were ordered by General Sugiyama, Chief of the General Staff, with the approval of Tojo and General Muto, Chief of the (so-called) Military Affairs Bureau of the War Minister.

[16] Interrogation of Admiral Nagano, ibid., Exh. No. 1127 (a).

[17] When first asked about this by the Soviet Ambassador, Smetanin, on June 25, Matsuoka evaded and left the matter doubtful. Extract from Smetanin's diary, entry for June 25, 1941, ibid., Exh. No. 793.

from the borders of Manchukuo and concentrated at interior points. Orders were given to avoid border troubles with Russian forces and compose any incidents as quickly as possible.[18] At the same time a new plan of operations against Siberia was prepared; in contrast to former ones it contemplated simultaneous attacks on several fronts.

All these items of preparation looked towards war. And yet most of the Konoye Cabinet still eagerly wished to avoid war with the United States. If persuasion and the use of the least offensive forms could keep the United States quiet, they would not be economized.[19] . . .

By July 20 "Magic," as well as other sources, supplied the answers as to whether the reformed Konoye Cabinet would renounce its attachment to Germany or its plan to occupy Indochina. It did not intend to do either. A message which Toyoda had broadcast on July 19 (Tokyo time) to various Japanese diplomatic missions was intercepted. This stated "that although the Cabinet has changed there will be no departure from the principle that the Tripartite Pact forms the keystone of Japanese national policy." Another intercepted message of July 20 (Tokyo time) revealed that Toyoda told Kato (the Japanese Ambassador in Vichy) that the Japanese Army was ready and would advance into Indochina on the 24th, whether or not the French government consented. . . .

We Freeze Japan's Funds

On the next day, the 24th, the radio reported that Japanese warships had appeared off Camranh Bay, and that twelve troop transports were on their way south from Hainan. . . .

At eight o'clock in the evening the President's office at Poughkeepsie passed out to the press a release which stated that, in view of the unlimited national emergency, the President was issuing an Executive Order freezing Japanese assets in the United States. "This measure," the press release continued, "in effect, brings all financial and import and export trade transactions in which Japanese interests are involved under the control of the government. . . ."[20]

---

[18] Testimony of General Tanaka.
[19] Testimony of General Tominago (Kijoji), Section Chief, War Ministry, ibid., Exh. No. 705; of General Yanagita (Genzo), Chief, Army Special Service Agency, Harbin, ibid., Exh. No. 723; of General Otsubo (Kazuma), Chief of Staff, Third Front of Kwantung Army, ibid., Exh. No. 837.
[20] Press release issued at Poughkeepsie, N.Y., by the White House at 8 P. M., July 25, 1941.

The step had been taken which was to force Japan to choose between making terms with us or making war against us. No longer would the United States be providing the resources which left her better able to fight if she should so decide. . . .

. . . If Japan was to fight, the longer it waited the greater the risk that the battle might be lost for lack of oil or other essential raw materials. So the oil gauge influenced the time of decision.

Not only the time of decision, but the war plans. The wish to obtain economic reserves for a long war was an important factor in determining the spheres to be occupied. It was decided by Imperial Military Headquarters that to be sure of enough oil, rubber, rice, bauxite, iron ore, it was necessary to get swift control of Java, Sumatra, Borneo, and Malaya. In order to effect the occupation and protect the transport lines to Japan, it was necessary to expel the United States from the Philippines, Guam, and Wake, and Britain from Singapore. Thus it can be said that the points of attack and occupation were settled by placing these vital raw material needs alongside of the estimate of Japan's military means. And having settled these, the question of the weather entered in to hurry the final action.[21]

The Army and Navy feared even to see two, three, or four *months* elapse. For on their strategic calendar October and November were the best months for landing operations. December was possible but difficult, January or later, impossible.[22] If the plan were to include an attack on Pearl Harbor by the Great Circle Route, navigational and weather conditions would, it was judged, become unfavorable after January.[23] Furthermore the sooner the southern operations were

[21] This brief comment on the way in which the wish to obtain economic reserves affected the plans with which Japan began the war is drawn from several studies made available to me by the Military Intelligence Division of the Supreme Headquarters of the Allied Command in Tokyo; especially the information furnished by Colonel Hattori (Takushiro), former Chief of the Operations Section of the General Staff of the Japanese Army. It corresponds also to the explanations of Admiral Toyoda (Soemu), former Commanding Officer, Kure Naval District.

[22] Tojo deposition, *Far East Mil. Trib.*, Exh. No. 3655. As stated by Admiral Shimada, Minister of the Navy, in his disposition, Exh. No. 3565: "With the advent of December, northeasterly monsoons would blow with force in the Formosan Straits, the Philippines, and Malayan areas rendering military operations difficult."

[23] This forecast of weather conditions was borne out by the event—in early December. "The start (for the attack on Pearl Harbor) was from Saeki, the training harbor, about November 17, 1941; then north and across the Pacific, just south of the Aleutians, then south to Pearl Harbor. We had studied this route for a long time. Upon returning we suffered from heavy seas and strong winds." Interrogation of Captain Watanabe, on Admiral Yamamoto's staff.

under way, the less the chance that the Soviet Union could attack from the north; if they could be completed before the end of winter, that danger need not be feared.[24]

Thus, leaving Konoye to go on with his talks with the United States, the Army and Navy threw themselves at once into the plans for action. The Operations Section of the Army began to get ready to capture Malaya, Java, Borneo, the Bismarck Archipelago, the Indies, and the Philippines; it was to be fully ready by the end of October. The Navy finished its war games. These included the surprise attack on Pearl Harbor and the American fleet there. At the end of the games the two general staffs conferred on the result and found it satisfactory.[25]

By the end of September these steps towards war—if diplomacy should fail—were well under way. Still Konoye and Toyoda found themselves reading the unchanging reports of American resistance. The President was still in the White House—planning to go no further than Warm Springs. Hull and his draftsmen were still dissecting every document which came from Tokyo with the scalpel of mistrust. In his apartment in the Wardman Park Hotel there seemed to be no sense of hurry. No calender hung there with October ringed in red.

Time had become the meter of strategy for both governments. But one did not mind its passing, while the other was crazed by the tick of the clock. . . .

The world may long wonder what would have happened had the President agreed then to meet with Konoye. Grew and Dooman, at the time and later, had a sense that the refusal was a sad error. To them it seemed that the American government had missed a real chance to lead Japan back to peaceful ways. Konoye, they thought, was sincere in his acceptance of those principles of international conduct for which the American government stood, and with the support of the Emperor would be able to carry through his promises. In words which Grew confided to his diary:

> *It is my belief that the Emperor, the Government of Prince Konoye and the militant leaders of Japan (the leaders then in control) had come to accept the status of the conflict in China, in conjunction with our freezing*

[24] As stated by General Tojo in his defense deposition, and by Colonel Hattori in his study for the Supreme Command of the Allied Powers.
[25] See evidence of records of Admiral Nagano and Admiral Yamamoto, Commander in Chief of the Combined Fleet, ibid., Exh. Nos. 1126 and 1127. For interesting details, see Captain Ellis M. Zacharias, *Secret Missions* (New York [1946]), pp. 243, *et seq.*

*measures and Japan's economic condition as evidence of failure or com-
parative incapacity to succeed.*

Our attitude, he thought (and others since have thought the same), showed a lack both of insight and suppleness, if not of desire. The mistake sprang, in this view, from failure to appreciate why Konoye could not be as clear and conclusive as the American government wished; and to admit that Japan could correct its course only in a gradual and orderly way. Wise American statesmanship, thus, would have bartered adjustment for adjustment, agreeing to relax our economic restraints little by little as Japan, little by little, went our way. Instead, the judgment ends, it was dull and inflexible. By insisting that Japan promise in black and white, then and there, to conform to every American requirement, it made Konoye's task impossible.

It will be always possible to think that Grew was correct; that the authorities in Washington were too close to their texts and too soaked in their disbelief to perceive what he saw. That the American government was as stern as a righteous schoolmaster cannot be denied. Nor that it was unwilling either to ease Japanese failure, or to provide any quick or easy way to improve their hard lot. But the records since come to hand do not support the belief that a real chance of maintaining peace in the Pacific—on or close to the terms for which we had stood since 1931—was missed. They do not confirm the opinion that Konoye was prepared, without reserve or trickery, to observe the rules set down by Hull.[26] Nor that he would have been able to do so, even though a respite was granted and he was allowed to grade the retreat gently.

If Konoye was ready and able—as Grew thought—to give Roosevelt trustworthy and satisfactory promises of a new sort, he does not tell of them in his "Memoirs." Nor has any other record available to me disclosed them. He was a prisoner, willing or unwilling, of the terms precisely prescribed in conferences over which he presided. The latest of these were the minimum demands specified

---

[26] For example, the decisions in regard to China. How reconcile two of Hull's principles (those stipulating nonintervention in domestic affairs and respect for the integrity and independence of China) with the terms specified on September 6 and reaffirmed by a Liaison Conference of September 13, as "Magic" revealed? China was to be required to assent to the stationing of Japanese Army units "for a necessary period" in prescribed areas in Inner Mongolia and North China, and for the stationing of Japanese warships and military units in Hainan, Amoy, and other localities. There was to be a Sino-Japanese economic coalition.

by the Imperial Conference of September 6, just reviewed. It is unlikely that he could have got around them or that he would have in
some desperate act discarded them. The whole of his political career
speaks to the contrary.

In proof of his ability to carry out his assurances, Konoye stressed
first, that his ideas were approved by the Army and Navy; and second, that senior officials (Vice-Chiefs of Staff) of both branches
would accompany him on his mission. If and when he said "Yes,"
they would say "Yes"; and thus the United States could count upon
unified execution of any accord. But it seems to me far more likely
that the Army and Navy had other thoughts in mind on assigning
high officials to go along with him. They would be there to see that
Konoye did not yield to the wish for peace or the will of the President. The truer version of the bond is expressed in the title of one of
the subsections of Konoye's "Memoirs": "The Independence of the
Supreme Command and State Affairs from Each Other: The Anguish
of Cabinets from Generation to Generation."

Konoye could have honestly agreed that Japan would stop its
southern advance and reduce its forces in China to the minimum
needed to assure compliance with its wishes. That is really all. To the
seekers of the New Order in East Asia this seemed much; to the
American government it seemed too little. The error, the fault, in
American policy—if there was one—was not in the refusal to trust
what Konoye could honestly offer. It was in insisting that Japan
entirely clear out of Indochina and China (and perhaps out of Manchukuo) and give up all exclusive privileges in these countries.

In any case, the President and Hull were convinced that Konoye's
purposes were murky and his freedom of decision small. Therefore
they concluded that to meet with him before Japan proved its intentions would be a great mistake.[27] It could bring confusion into both
American policies and our relations with the other opponents of the
Axis. So Grew's earnest appeal for a daring try did not influence the
responses to Japan that Hull's drafting squad was putting together.

---

[27] Ott's judgment of the prospect was at the time the same as that reached by the
American government. He thought that even though certain circles about Konoye
genuinely sought a *détente* with the United States, the effort was certain to fail in the
end. He reported that the purpose of Konoye's mission was being pictured to the Navy
and activist circles as a last step to convince the Japanese people that a peaceful
settlement was not possible. Acceptance of the American terms would, Ott predicted,
swiftly result in grave inner convulsions. (See Most Urgent telegram, Ott to Ribbentrop,
September 4, 1941. *Far East Mil. Trib.* Exh. No. 801A.)

They took nothing that came from Tokyo for granted; wanted everything shown. The Army and Navy were both saying that they could use well all the time they could get. Both Stimson and Knox approved "stringing out negotiations." But neither wanted Roosevelt to meet Konoye or to soften American terms just to gain time.[28]

Hull was guided by these thoughts in the prepared answer which he gave Nomura on October 2, the answer on which the plans of Japan hung. The Japanese proposals (of September 6), this said in effect, did not provide a basis for a settlement, and were on essential points ambiguous.[29] The meeting between the President and Konoye was put off till there was a real meeting of minds about the application of the four principles—which were the essential foundations of proper relations.

Upon reading this, the opinion nurtured by Konoye and Toyoda, that Japanese and American terms could be reconciled, dropped. This, the note of October 2, rather than the one of November 26 on which controversy has centered, ended the era of talk. For the crisis that followed in Japan brought into power a group determined to fight us rather than move further our way. Thereafter war came first, diplomacy second. . . .

The American government, while talking with Japan, could not forget that it was allied with Germany and Italy. American planes and warships were now providing watch and ward over wide areas of the Middle and Western Atlantic and around Iceland.[30] Encounters were becoming frequent. On September 11 the President, having discussed his words with Hull, Stimson, and Knox, broadcast: "The aggression is not ours. Ours is solely defense. But let this warning be clear. From now on, if German or Italian vessels of war enter the waters, the protection of which is necessary for American defense, they do so at their own peril. The orders which I have given as Commander-in-Chief of the United States Army and Navy are to carry out that policy—at once."[31]

---

[28] Stimson diary, entry for October 6, 1941.

[29] The text is to be found in *Foreign Relations: Japan*, II, 656, *et seq.*

[30] On August 25 Atlantic fleet forces were ordered to destroy surface raiders which attacked shipping along sea lanes between North America and Iceland, or which approached these lanes sufficiently closely to threaten such shipping. On September 3 the Western Atlantic area of operations covered by the United States Atlantic fleet was extended eastward. These were changes, Nos. 2 and 4, to W.P.L. 51. *Pearl Harbor Attack*, Part 5, p. 2295.

[31] While this speech was in preparation, the President had the impulse to be more explicit in his statements but Hull warned against any reference to shooting.

On September 26 the Navy issued orders to protect all ships engaged in commerce in our defensive waters—by patrolling, covering, escorting, reporting, or destroying German and Italian naval, land, and air forces encountered.[32] As the President wrote to Mackenzie King, Prime Minister of Canada, ". . . we have begun to have practically sole charge of the safety of things to twenty-six degrees longitude, and to a further extension in the waters well to the eastward of Iceland."[33]

Further, it was foreseen that before long American merchant ships, manned by American crews, would soon be making the whole voyage to Britain. By the end of September, agreement had been reached between the President and Congressional leaders that the Neutrality Act should be so amended as to permit American merchant ships to enter combat areas and the ports of belligerents. The President's message so recommending was sent to Congress October 8.

Would this bring war with Germany? Hull did not think so; Hitler would not, he thought, declare a war as a result of any action of ours unless he thought it to his own advantage.[34] But should this turn out to be wrong, how would Japan construe its obligations under Article III of the Tripartite Pact? It was not possible to deduce a reliable answer from either the Japanese talk or texts. The American government sought to have Japan, in some form or other, cancel the obligation. The Konoye Cabinet lived in an agony of division over the issue. Unwilling to separate from Germany, but equally unwilling to lose a chance for a settlement with the United States, it fell into bigamous vows. . . .

On November 5, the same day that the Japanese government decided to go to war if its final proposals (A or B) were rejected, Stark and Marshall (with Chiang Kai-shek's appeal before them) summed up their judgment of the line to be held. Their memorandum to the President advised that:

---

[32] This was Western Hemisphere Defense Plan, No. 5 (W.P.L. 52), effective October 11, 1941.

[33] Letter, Roosevelt to King, September 27, 1941. Churchill understood these orders to mean that American ships would attack any Axis ships found in the prohibited zone and assume responsibility for all fast British convoys other than troop convoys between America and Iceland. See his message to General Smuts of September 14, 1941. Churchill, *The Grand Alliance*, p. 517.

[34] The event proved Hull to be correct. On September 17 the German Navy asked Hitler to change its orders to permit, among other things, attacks on escorting forces in any operational area at any time. Hitler decided against such action for the time being, until the outcome of the fighting in Russia was decided, which he expected soon. *Fuehrer Conferences*, 1941, II, 33.

(a) The basic military policies and strategy agreed to in the United States–British Staff conversations remain sound. The primary objective of the two nations is the defeat of Germany. If Japan be defeated and Germany remain undefeated, decision will still have not been reached. In any case, an unlimited offensive war should not be undertaken against Japan, since such a war would greatly weaken the combined effort in the Atlantic against Germany, the most dangerous enemy.

(b) War between the United States and Japan should be avoided while building up defensive forces in the Far East, until such time as Japan attacks or directly threatens territories whose security to the United States is of very great importance. Military action against Japan should be undertaken only in one or more of the following contingencies: (1) A direct act of war by Japanese armed forces against the territory or mandated territory of the United States, the British Commonwealth, or the Netherlands East Indies; (2) The movement of Japanese armed forces into Thailand to the West of 100° East, or South of 10° North; or into Portuguese Timor, New Caledonia, or the Loyalty Islands.[35]

(d) Considering world strategy, a Japanese advance against Kunming, into Thailand except as previously indicated, or an attack on Russia would not justify intervention by the United States against Japan.

(e) All possible aid short of actual war against Japan should be extended to the Chinese Central Government.

Specifically, they recommend:

That the dispatch of United States armed forces for intervention against Japan in China be disapproved.

That material aid to China be accelerated consonant with the needs of Russia, Great Britain, and our own forces.

That aid to the American Volunteer Group be continued and accelerated to the maximum practicable extent.

That no ultimatum be delivered to Japan.[36]

The President followed this traced line. On the 6th he told Stimson that he might propose a truce in which there would be no movement of armed forces for six months, during which China and Japan might come to terms. Stimson wanted time also but objected to this means of getting it. The movement of forces to the Philippines, he thought, should not be halted. And the Chinese, in his opinion, should not be left alone with the Japanese; they would, he correctly forecast, balk at any such arrangement.[37] The President placed the idea of a truce aside, but not far.

On this next day, November 7, the President asked the Cabinet for

[35] The thought was that any movement of this kind would be a plan to go into the Gulf of Siam, on the way to attack the Malay-Kra Peninsula.
[36] *Pearl Harbor Attack*, Part 14, pp. 1061–62.
[37] Stimson diary, entry for November 6, 1941.

advice. All agreed with a statement made by Hull that the situation was extremely serious and that Japan might attack at any time. The position being maintained in the talks with Japan was approved; the current program for the extension of military forces in the Southwest Pacific area was endorsed; the cohesion between our own activities in that area and those of Britain, Australia, and the Indies was noted with satisfaction. Thus it was decided to "carry on," and to leave Japan to decide whether to turn about or attack. The President took a poll, asking whether the people would back the government up if it struck at Japan in case it attacked English or Dutch territories in the Pacific. All the Cabinet was of the opinion that it would. It was agreed that speeches should be made to acquaint the country with the situation.[38]

In the evening after this Cabinet meeting Nomura paid his first call on Hull since the advent of the Tojo Cabinet. Earnestly he presented Proposal A and asked a quick answer. Hull, after a rapid glance at the contents (which he already knew) indicated his attitude by observing what a wonderful chance Japan had to launch forth on a real new order which would gain it moral leadership in the Far East.

Nomura asked to talk to the President, and was received on the 10th. He had an invisible naval escort not of his own choosing. Not many hours before he entered the White House, his former colleague, Vice-Admiral Nagumo, on board the aircraft carrier *Akagi,* issued Striking Force Operations Order, No. 1. All ships in this force were directed to complete battle preparations by November 20, and to assemble in Hitokappu Bay, Etorofu Island, Kuriles. This was the force that was to attack Pearl Harbor.

Nomura did not know either the schedule or geography written in this order, one of many placing the Japanese Navy in location for war. But he knew that he was in a race with such orders, and that only some miracle of conversion could stop them. The smoke was over the funnels. Thus he pleaded for acceptance of what he came to offer on the ground that Japan was doing all it could in the light of reason and of history. But his two American listeners were unmoved. Their books, open and secret, contained the record of Japan's desertion of the ways of peace and order. . . .

Nomura placed Proposal B before Hull on November 20. The En-

---

[38] Ibid., entry for November 7, and the written statement by Hull, *Pearl Harbor Attack,* Part 2, p. 429.

glish text, as cabled some days before, had been intercepted and read. Hull knew that it was regarded in Tokyo as the last bargain; the hinge on the breech of the cannon.

There were five numbered points on the white piece of paper which Nomura gave to Hull. They have been printed in many other places, but I think the reader will want them before him as he follows the narrative:

> 1. Both the Government of Japan and the United States undertake not to make any armed advancement into any of the regions in the South-eastern Asia and the Southern Pacific area excepting the part of French Indochina where the Japanese troops are stationed at present.
> 2. The Japanese Government undertakes to withdraw its troops now stationed in French Indochina upon either the restoration of peace between Japan and China or the establishment of an equitable peace in the Pacific area.
>
> In the meantime the Government of Japan declares that it is prepared to remove its troops now stationed in the southern part of French Indochina to the northern part of the said territory upon the conclusion of the present arrangement which shall later be embodied in the final agreement.
> 3. The Government of Japan and the United States shall cooperate with a view to securing the acquisition of those goods and commodities which the two countries need in Netherlands East Indies.
> 4. The Government of Japan and the United States mutually undertake to restore their commercial relations to those prevailing prior to the freezing of the assets.
>
> The Government of the United States shall supply Japan a required quantity of oil.
> 5. The Government of the United States undertakes to refrain from such measures and actions as will be prejudiced to the endeavors for the restoration of general peace between Japan and China.[39]

Whoever insisted on the last paragraph—Tojo and the Army certainly did—insisted on war.

Hull glanced over the text to make sure it was the same as that which was known. It was. Then, on two points in particular, he spoke out. Linking Japan's treatment of China to Hitler's actions, he defended our aid to China. Kurusu remarked that perhaps this point (No. 5) in the Japanese terms might be construed to mean that the United States would end its help only at the time when talks between

[39] *Foreign Relations: Japan*, II, 755–56.

Japan and China would have started. Hull also dwelt on the fact that
his truce would leave Japan a full member of the Axis pact, and
hence still a potential enemy of the United States and Great Britain.
To this Kurusu had no answer.[40]

Hull found no dissent, either within the State Department or at the
White House, to his opinion that the proposal was "clearly unaccept-
able." His reasons for finding it so are summed up again in his
"Memoirs":

> *The commitments we should have to make were virtually a surrender. We
> on our part should have to supply Japan as much oil as she might
> require, suspend our freezing measures, and resume full commercial rela-
> tions with Tokyo. We should have to discontinue aid to China and with-
> draw our moral and material support from the recognized Chinese Gov-
> ernment of Chiang Kai-shek. We should have to help Japan obtain prod-
> ucts of the Netherlands East Indies. We should have to cease augment-
> ing our military forces in the western Pacific.*
>
> *Japan, on her part, would still be free to continue her military opera-
> tions in China, to attack the Soviet Union, and to keep her troops in
> northern Indochina until peace was effected with China. . . . Japan thus
> clung to her vantage point in Indochina which threatened countries to
> the south and vital trade routes.*
>
> *The President and I could only conclude that agreeing to these pro-
> posals would mean condonement by the United States of Japan's past
> aggressions, assent to future courses of conquest by Japan, abandon-
> ment of the most essential principles of our foreign policy, betrayal of
> China and Russia, and acceptance of the role of silent partner aiding and
> abetting Japan in her effort to create a Japanese hegemony over the
> western Pacific and eastern Asia.*[41]

* * *

War might be in the secret messages; it might be in the nerves;
but the wish to avoid it was still alive. Hull began to compound a
counter-offer to Proposal B which might defer the climax without
giving Japan an advantage, or destroying the faith of our allies. The
drafting squad ransacked the files for old memoranda, and drew
upon a refreshingly new one from the Treasury. . . .

The very making of the offer seemed likely to have troublesome, if
not ruinous, effects. It would be self-defeating to give a true and full
explanation to the American people. A confused domestic debate
was apt to follow and be in full flow when the war crisis came. More

[40] Ibid., II, 753–55.
[41] Hull, op. cit., II, 1069–70.

worrisome still was the prospect that, despite whatever was said, the other nations fighting the Axis would feel let down. There was no time to convince Chiang Kai-shek that China would not suffer and would not be deserted.[42] The other members of the coalition were showing themselves lukewarm—not opposing the truce, but not welcoming it. Was it, as Hull averred, only a maneuver, or was it a wavering in the ranks?

Sometime during the night of the 25th, Churchill's answer to the President arrived.[43] It left the American government free to do what it thought best, but seemed to fall in with the view that a truce with Japan was unfair to China. Doubt seemed to overrule enthusiasm. The text is given so that the reader may judge for himself:[44]

Most Secret for the President from the Former Naval Person. Your message about Japan received tonight. Also full accounts from Lord Halifax of discussions and your counter project to Japan on which Foreign Secretary has sent some comments. Of course, it is for you to handle this business and we certainly do not want an additional war. There is only one point that disquiets us. What about Chiang Kai-shek? Is he not having a very thin diet? Our anxiety is about China. If they collapse our joint dangers would enormously increase. We are sure that the regard of the United States for the Chinese cause will govern your action. We feel that the Japanese are most unsure of themselves.[45]

Hull, in the course of the night, added up the sum of pros and cons. The reason for going ahead with the counterproposal had come to

[42] The intercepted message, No. 821, from Togo to Nomura on the 24th read in part: ". . . our demand for a cessation of aid to Chiang . . . is a most essential condition." Loc. cit.

[43] There is a conflict of report as to when this cable or its substance was known to the President and Hull. According to the time stamps on the face of the original, it was sent from London at 6 a.m. on November 26, received by the code room of the State Department at 12:55 a.m., November 26, which is before the time of dispatch, allowance being made for five hours' time difference. It also carries the notation that it was sent over to the White House at 9:05 a.m., on the 26th.

But two of the participants in the afternoon and evening meetings with Hull on the 25th have the remembered impression that either the cable or the substance of it was known to them then; they recall even Hull's comments that Churchill's message did not seem to agree entirely with Eden's. Despite the absence of any record, it is possible that the substance of this message was transmitted earlier in the day through the British Embassy in Washington or some other channel. Hull's reference to this point in his book (op. cit., II, 1081) can be read either way, but suggests that Hull knew its contents on the night of the 25th.

[44] In the minute that Churchill sent to Eden on November 23 he indicated favor towards the counterproposal being prepared by the State Department, provided the United States and Britain remained free to continue their aid to China. But on this point he found the draft which Hull submitted inadequate. Churchill, *The Grand Alliance*, pp. 595–96.

[45] *Pearl Harbor Attack*, Part 14, p. 1300.

seem unreal. What we had to offer, it was all but certain, would not buy even time. The objections seemed many and hard to meet. He decided to discard it and let events take their course. The verdict was reached after tormenting uncertainty. But once reached, a calm sense followed that he had done all that a man could do. . . .

The long Ten-Point Memorandum on principles, which was our response to Proposal B, was received in Tokyo on the morning of the 27th. Along with it Nomura and Kurusu sent a convoy of troubled comment. They thought the answer hard and dumbfounding. But they found nothing in it compelling Japan to resort to war. They were afraid, as "Magic" let Washington know, that the United States and Britain might try to forestall Japan by occupying the Indies, thus bringing on war. Even this late, Nomura advised his government to keep on with the effort to reach a peaceful accord. He recalled a remark the President had made in an earlier talk—that there would be "no last words."[46] But, he added, if his counsel was not taken, it would be best not to keep up a false front of friendliness, and to strike from behind it. Kurusu, also, tried to be calming. He attributed our statement in part to knowledge of the Japanese military movements and concentrations in the south.[47]

Another Liaison Conference was called as soon as the American paper was read (November 27). This summarily dismissed our statement of principles as a humiliating ultimatum. It was resolved to proceed with the program adopted on November 5; that is, to go to war as soon as the striking forces were in position. Stratagem had failed. Force would be used. Japan would do or die.

As was natural, the men who made this decision pleaded later that it was compelled by the terms placed upon peace by the United States. Thus, the former Foreign Minister, Togo, one of the more conciliatory members of the government, argued that "Japan was now asked not only to abandon all the gains of her years of sacrifice, but to surrender her international position as a power in the Far East.["] That surrender, as he saw it, would have amounted to national suicide. ["]The only way to face this challenge and defend ourselves was war."[48]

---

[46] Intercepted Telegrams, Nos. 1180, 1189, and 1190, Nomura to Togo, November 26, 1941, set forth the Ambassador's views at length.

[47] Telegram, No. 1206, Nomura to Togo, November 27, and memorandum of telephone conversation between Kurusu and Yamamoto on November 27.

[48] Togo deposition, *Far East Mil. Trib.*, Exh. No. 3646.

This was not a valid attitude. The idea that compliance with the American terms would have meant "extinction" for Japan, or so deeply hurt it that it could not guard its just interests, is an absurdity. Japan was not asked to give up any land or resources except those which it held by force of arms. Its independence was not in peril. Its Army, Navy, and Air Force would have remained in being. Its chances to trade with the rest of the world would have been restored. Its struggle against the extension of communism could have combined with that of China and the West. Extinction threatened the plan for expansion in Asia, but not Japan or the Japanese.

James MacGregor Burns

SHOWDOWN IN THE PACIFIC

The following selection is from the Pulitzer Prize-winning volume with which James MacGregor Burns concludes his two-volume biography of Franklin D. Roosevelt. Burns focuses here on a somewhat shorter period than the selection from Feis, viewing the last months before Pearl Harbor from a broader and more recent perspective. On the one side he demonstrates Roosevelt's failure to make clear to our allies, our potential foes, and to the American public just what United States policy was and how far it would go. On the other side, from postwar Japanese sources, he illuminates the struggle within Japan between moderates and militarists. Note particularly the question of what Emperor Hirohito could or would do as it bears on the proposal for a Roosevelt-Konoye meeting. The Burns account reflects the President's indecision and his lapses into lethargy, perhaps, as Burns suggests, partly attributable to Roosevelt's poor health. But was the United States also in a strategic plight, unable to abandon ideals in order to appease Japan yet unready to risk war to enforce its position?

News of Argentia broke up Washington's summer doldrums, at least for a time.[1] Democratic leaders in Congress hailed the Atlantic Charter as a magnificent statement of war aims—indeed, as a signpost to "real and lasting peace." Hiram Johnson and Robert Taft accused Roosevelt of making a secret alliance and planning an invasion of Europe. The *New York Times,* billing the pledge to destroy Nazi tyranny in an eight-column headline, proclaimed that this was the end of isolationism, while the New York *Journal-American* accused the President of retracing, one by one, all the steps toward war taken by Wilson. Colonel McCormick's Chicago *Tribune,* irked by the Roosevelt-Churchill togetherness, reminded its readers that the President was "the true descendant of that James Roosevelt, his great-grandfather, who was a Tory of New York during the Revolution and took the oath of allegiance to the British King." Both friend and foe saw the meeting as a prelude to more aggressive action.

[1] Argentia, in Placentia Bay, Newfoundland, was the place of the historic meeting between Roosevelt and Winston Churchill in August 1941, when the two leaders drew up the "Atlantic Charter," a declaration of their common principles for attaining a peaceful world.—Ed.

But not Roosevelt, evidently. Having taken a dramatic step forward, he executed his usual backward hop. Aside from a lackluster message to Congress incorporating the declaration, he took little action to follow it up. At the first press conference after the meeting on the *Potomac,* reporters found him cautious. What about actual implementation of the broad declarations, he was asked. "Interchange of views, that's all. Nothing else." Were we any closer to entering the war? "I should say, no." Could he be quoted directly? "No, you can quote indirectly."

But the meeting at sea did seem popular with the people, according to the pollsters. Seventy-five percent of those polled had heard about the eight-point credo, and of those about half indicated full or partial approval, while only a quarter of them were cool or hostile. Many were indifferent or uninformed, however, and this number grew as time passed. Five months later most people remembered the two men meeting, but few remembered anything about the Charter itself.

Nor did the conference seem measurably to change popular attitudes toward Roosevelt's aid-to-Britain program. Those attitudes seemed almost fixed during most of 1941. Asked in May, "So far as you, personally, are concerned, do you think President Roosevelt has gone too far in his policies of helping Britain?" about a quarter answered "too far," about a quarter "not far enough," and half "about right." This pattern persisted with remarkable stability into the fall; evidently the President was shifting step by step with the movement of opinion. On the face of it he was acting as a faithful representative of the people; a majority endorsed his policies and he fell evenly between the critics of both wings. As he took increasingly interventionist action "short of war," he was holding the great bulk of public support.

The troubling question remained whether, in view of the critical situation abroad, he should be more in advance of opinion than representative of it, more of a catalytic or even a divisive agent than a consensual one, more of a creator and exploiter of public feeling than a reflector and articulator of it.

This was the question Stimson kept raising. When the President phoned him early in the summer to tell him that he had some good news—that a forthcoming Gallup Poll was going to be much more favorable than the Gallup people had expected—Stimson reminded him again that all these polls omitted one factor which the President seemed to neglect—"the power of his own leadership." Roosevelt had not denied this but had complained that he simply did not feel peppy enough.

It was leadership and decision, after all, that American strategists needed, not merely symbol and pageantry. Early in July the President had asked Stimson to join with Knox and Hopkins in exploring over-all production needs in order to "defeat our potential enemies." For ten weeks the defense Secretaries had struggled with the question, and then given up. Everything depended on what assumptions they were working under, Stimson wrote to his chief—whether the United States promptly engaged in an avowed all-out military effort against Germany, or merely continued its present policy of helping nations fighting the Axis with munitions, transport, and naval help. The Army, Navy, and Air strategists were united in preferring active participation in the war against Germany, Stimson went on, but work could not be concluded until the President's views were known.

The military uncertainty was reflected right down the army line. A *Nation* reporter spent ten days in August tramping up and down Times Square talking with over three hundred Regular soldiers, draftees, National Guardsmen. They were a breezy, cocky lot, confident that any one of them could lick the Germans or an infinite number of Japanese. But, except for the Regulars, they hated the Army, Roosevelt, General Marshall, and Negroes in about equal degree. Few had any idea why they were in the Army or what the Army was for. Some were American Firsters—but they had little suspicion that the Commander in Chief was trying to drag the United States into war. They simply seemed confused. They neither attacked nor defended Roosevelt's foreign policy; they just did not seem to care.

But there was some logic to their position. They understood the President's policy of aid to Britain short of war, but if the nation was not preparing to fight Germany, "Why this Army?"

The Winds and Waves of Strife

The President had promised Churchill at Argentia that he would use hard language in his message to Tokyo; the Prime Minister had feared that the State Department would try to water it down, and he was right. Hull and his aides felt that the warning might arouse the extremist wing in Japan, and by the time they finished massaging the message it was one more general warning. The President went along with the change. He decided that he could deliver the warning more

effectively at a direct confrontation with Nomura. On Sunday afternoon, August 17, 1941, the Japanese Ambassador arrived at the
White House.

The old Admiral was hard of hearing, had a glass eye, spoke
English uncertainly, and was so fuzzy at times that Hull wondered if
he understood his own government's position, let alone Washington's. But he was affable and had an encouraging way of
nodding responsively, with an occasional mirthless chuckle, to
Roosevelt's and Hull's main points. The President, in fine fettle after
his two weeks at sea, made some pleasant remarks and then spoke
gravely, contrasting his country's peaceful and principled record in
the Far East, as he saw it, with Japan's conquests through force. Did
the Admiral have any proposal in mind? Nomura did. Pulling a paper
from his pocket, he said that his government was earnestly desirous
of peaceful relations—and Premier Konoye proposed a meeting with
the President midway in the Pacific.

The President seemed unperturbed at losing the initiative just as
he was about to issue his warning. He read the watered-down statement anyway. Even this weak message Roosevelt presented almost
defensively. Indeed—or so Nomura reported to Tokyo—the President
finally handed him the oral remarks as a matter of information. The
lion's roar of Argentia had become a lamb's bleat. Even so, Roosevelt
reported to Churchill that his statement to Nomura was "no less
vigorous" than the one they had planned.

Konoye's offer to meet Roosevelt was a weak card played from a
shaky hand. Dropping Matsuoka had not eased the Premier's situation at home. Washington's reaction to the Indochina occupation had
been sharper than Tokyo expected; the freeze seemed a direct threat
to national survival. The Emperor, Konoye knew, was uneasy about
the drift toward conflict with America. The Army under Tojo still took
its old expansionist line, but now, to the Premier's alarm, the oil-
conscious Navy was swinging to a more militant stance. The jingo
press was attacking Washington for sending oil to Russia via Vladivostok and "Japanese" waters; officials lived under heavy police
guard against assassination; extremists in the middle ranks of the
Navy and Army were a constant threat. A dramatic meeting with
Roosevelt might break the deepening spiral, Konoye calculated,
arouse the moderates among the people, enlist the Emperor's backing, and present the militarists with a fait accompli. He won Tojo's

grudging acquiescence to a parley on condition that if the meeting failed—as the War Minister expected it would—the Premier would return home not to resign but ready to lead the war against the United States.

Playing for the highest stakes, Konoye was so eager for a summit conference that he had Foreign Minister Toyoda sit down with Ambassador Grew and plead, on a long, stifling evening, for Grew's support for the idea. He prepared a special ship for the voyage to the conference and planned to take a brace of admirals and generals, all of them moderates, to "share responsibility" with him. In order to bypass Hull, Nomura would deliver Konoye's invitation to the President personally; a conciliatory note was prepared for Hull in a style calculated not to excite him.

The notes that Nomura handed Roosevelt on the morning of August 28 were full of benevolence and vague promises. Konoye renewed his invitation to meet—and to do so soon in the light of the present situation, which was "developing swiftly and may produce unforeseen contingencies." Roosevelt remarked that he liked the tone and spirit of Konoye's message. The note from the Japanese government indicated its willingness to withdraw from Indochina as soon as the China incident was settled, not to attack Russia, and indeed not to attack anyone, north or south. Roosevelt interrupted the reading of the note to offer some small rebuttals, and he could not resist the temptation, with what seemed to Nomura a cynical smile, to ask whether there would be an invasion of Thailand while he might be meeting with Konoye, just as Indochina had been invaded during Hull's conversations with Nomura.

Still, Roosevelt was sorely tempted to parley. A rendezvous in the Pacific would be a dramatic counterpart to his trip to Argentia; the Japanese seemed to be in a conciliatory mood; and he always had confidence in his ability to persuade people face to face. He even proposed Juneau as a place to confer, on the ground that it would require him to be away two weeks rather than three. But now the President ran into serious difficulties among his advisers.

Hull and the old Far Eastern hands in his Department opposed a conference unless the major questions were settled—and settled to Washington's liking—in advance. The Secretary seemed to take a mixed approach to Japan: he never tired of stating his principles and flailing Japan for not living up to them; he opposed conciliation because he had no faith in Konoye's ability to check the military; but he also opposed drastic action. He had both a devil theory of Japanese politics and an aversion to a showdown—an ambivalence that precluded any consistent policy except endless pieties, conversations, and delays. And Hull could hardly have welcomed another ocean conference where the President, off in the heady sea breezes with advisers like Welles and Hopkins, might take steps—like the warning to Japan drawn up at Argentia—that could upset Hull's patient diplomacy.

In Tokyo, Grew took the opposite stand. Though long a hard-liner toward Japan, he had seized on a Pacific rendezvous as the last-best hope of averting a showdown. He urged Hull not to reject the Japanese proposal "without very prayerful consideration." Konoye would not request such a meeting, he argued, unless he was willing to make concessions; he was determined to overcome the extremists, even at peril to his own life. At the most, Grew contended, Japan would make concessions on Indochina and China; at the very least a meeting would slow the growing momentum toward a head-on collision. He ended with a grim warning: if the meeting did not take place, new men would come to power and launch a do-or-die effort to take over all of Greater East Asia—which would mean war with the United States.

When faced with conflicting advice Roosevelt rarely made immediate clear-cut choices; in this case he took the expedient course of continuing to talk hopefully of a meeting while following Hull's advice to demand agreement on fundamental principles before consenting to a rendezvous. Calling Nomura to the White House on September 3, the President carefully dealt with the Japanese proposal of the week before. He appreciated Konoye's difficulties at home, he told the Ambassador, but he had difficulties, too. While Hull sat by, Roosevelt read the Secretary's four fundamental principles: respect for other nations' territorial integrity and sovereignty; noninterference in other nations' internal affairs; equality of commercial opportunity; nondisturbance of the status quo in the Pacific except through peaceful means. He was pleased, said the President, that Japan had endorsed these principles explicitly in its note of August 28. But, since there was opposition to such principles in certain quarters in Japan, what concrete concessions would Tokyo make in advance of the summit conference?

While Roosevelt played for time, other less visible decision-makers in Japan were facing their own urgencies during August. Washington's freezing order of late July along with increasing indications that Russia would hold on were forcing Army and Navy planners in Tokyo to abandon thoughts of attacking the Soviets from the rear, at least during 1941, and to look south. The only way to overcome American, British, and Dutch power, it was decided, was through a series of lightning attacks. Such a plan would be heavily dependent on weather—on tides, phases of the moon, monsoons—and on moving fast, before oil gave out. On September 3 the military chiefs and the Cabinet met in a liaison conference. "We are getting weaker," Navy Chief of Staff Osami Nagano stated bluntly at the outset. "The enemy is getting stronger." A timetable must be set. Military preparations must get under way even while diplomacy continued. While Cabinet members sat by, Navy and Army chiefs soberly discussed plans. Finally it was agreed: "If, by the early part of October, there is still no prospect of being able to attain our demands, we shall immediately decide to open hostilities against the United States, Great Britain, and the Netherlands."

So a timetable had been set. In all the tortuous windings toward war, this was the single most crucial step. Why did Konoye agree? Partly because he had high hopes for his conference with Roosevelt—he would let the military play their game if they would let him play his. And partly because of the Emperor, who presumably could keep the military in line. On September 5 Konoye's Cabinet unanimously approved the action of the liaison conference. The Premier then hurried to the palace to inform the Emperor.

Hirohito was in an almost imperious mood. He listened to Konoye with apparently rising concern, then questioned him sharply. Were war preparations gaining precedence over diplomacy? Konoye said no, but suggested that the Emperor ask the military chiefs. Nagano and the Chief of the Army General Staff, Hajime Sugiyama, were summoned to the throne room. The Emperor questioned Sugiyama on military aspects of the plan. How long would a war with the United States last? For the initial phase about three months, the General said. The Emperor broke in: Sugiyama as War Minister in 1937 had said that the China incident would be over in a month; it was still going on. This was different, Sugiyama said; China was a vast hinterland, while the southern area was composed of islands.

This only aroused the Emperor further. "If you call the Chinese hinterland vast would you not describe the Pacific as even more immense?" Sugiyama looked down at his boots and was silent.

Next morning Hirohito called in his Lord Keeper of the Privy Seal, Koichi Kido. In a few minutes an imperial conference was to start; the Emperor had decided that he would speak out, he told Kido, and inform the military that he would not sanction war as long as the possibility of a settlement remained. Kido said smoothly that he had already asked Yoshimichi Hara, the President of the Privy Council, to ask the questions for the Emperor; it would be more appropriate for His Majesty to make any comments at the end.

Soon the Cabinet and the Chiefs of Staff were seated across from the Emperor on hard chairs in the east wing of the palace. One after another his ministers went through their carefully prepared recitations. The Empire would go to war by the end of October, declared Konoye, unless diplomacy had achieved its "minimum demands." These were: America and Britain should not hinder settlement of the China incident; they would cease helping the Chungking regime; they would not strengthen their military position in the Far East; they would cooperate with Japan economically. Japan's "maximum concessions" were: not to advance militarily from Indochina; to withdraw its forces from Indochina after peace was established; to guarantee the neutrality of the Philippines.

Nagano spoke next. Vital supplies—especially oil—were dwindling. Time was vital. He sketched the necessary strategy if war broke out. If the enemy aimed for a quick war and early decisions and dispatched their fleet, "this would be the very thing we hope for." With aircraft "and other elements" he could beat them in the Pacific. More likely, though, "America will attempt to prolong the war, utilizing her impregnable position, her superior industrial power, and her abundant resources." In a long war Japan's only chance, after the first quick strikes, was to seize the enemy's major military areas, establish an impregnable position, and develop military resources. Sugiyama then spoke up. He expressed the Army's complete agreement with Nagano. Japan must not mark time and be trapped by Anglo-American intrigue and delays. Intensive troop movements were required. If negotiations failed, a decision for war must be made within ten days of the failure at the latest. Others spoke, but there was no break in the united front.

The Emperor became flushed as Hara went through set questions and received set replies. A hush fell on the room. His Majesty was not satisfied with the assurances about diplomacy first. He drew a slip from his pocket and in his high voice read a poem composed by his grandfather the Emperor Meiji:

> *All the seas, in every quarter,*
> *are as brothers to one another,*
> *Why, then, do the winds and waves of strife*
> *rage so turbulently throughout the world?*

The Emperor's meaning was clear. All present were struck with awe, Konoye remembered, and there was silence throughout the hall. Nagano assured the Emperor that the whole Cabinet favored diplomacy first. The meeting adjourned in an atmosphere of unprecedented tension. . . .

The Call to Battle Stations

One could sense at the end of summer 1941 that the war was rushing toward another series of stupendous climacterics. German troops had isolated Leningrad and broken through Smolensk on the road to Moscow, had surrounded and overwhelmed four Russian armies in the Kiev sector; through the two-hundred-mile gap they had torn in the south the Nazis could see the grain of the eastern Ukraine and the oil of the Caucasus. Churchill was preparing a strong blow in North Africa and pressing for a bolder policy in Southeast Asia. Tokyo was vacillating between peace and war, under a dire timetable. Chungking's morale seemed to be ebbing away. Washington and London were stepping up the Battle of the Atlantic. And in Moscow, around the end of September, the first flakes of snow fell silently on the Kremlin walls.

Pressure from all these sectors converged on the man in the White House. Allies were stepping up their demands; enemies, their thrusts. His Cabinet war hawks battered him with conflicting advice. But Roosevelt under stress seemed only to grow calmer, steadier, more deliberate and even cautious. He joshed and jousted with the reporters even while artfully withholding news. He listened patiently while Ickes for the tenth time—or was it the hundredth?—maneuvered for the transfer of Forestry from Agriculture to Interior—an effort that the President might have found exquisitely irrelevant to the war except that he himself seemed excited by a plan to establish roe deer in Great Smoky Mountains National Park.

But Roosevelt was not impervious to the strain. More than ever before he seemed to retreat into his private world. He spent many weekends at Hyde Park, partly in settling his mother's estate. He devoted hours to planning a Key West fishing retreat for Hopkins and himself; he even roughed out a sketch for a hurricane-proof house. He found time to talk to the Roosevelt Home Club in Hyde Park, to Dutchess County schoolteachers, to a local grange. And always there were the long anecdotes about Washington during World War I days, about Campobello and Hyde Park.

Physically, too, the President was beginning to show the strain. Systolic hypertension had been noted four years earlier and not considered cause for concern; but—far more serious—diastolic hypertension was diagnosed during 1941. Dr. McIntire was no longer so rosily optimistic, though he said nothing publicly to temper his earlier statements. His patient was eating, exercising, and relaxing less, showing more strain, and carrying more worries to bed, than he had during the earlier years in the White House. But the President rarely complained and never seemed very curious about his health. Doubtless he felt that he had enough to worry about abroad.

Tension was rising, especially in the Far East. The imperial rebuke spurred Konoye to redoubled efforts at diplomacy even as the imperative timetable compelled generals and admirals to step up their war planning. The government seemed schizophrenic. All great powers employ military and diplomatic tactics at the same time; but in Japan the two thrusts were competitive and disjointed, with the diplomats trapped by a military schedule.

Subtly, almost imperceptibly, Konoye and the diplomats beat a retreat in the face of Washington's firm stand. Signals were confused: Nomura acted sometimes on his own; messages were also coming in via Grew and a number of unofficial channels; and Konoye and Toyoda had to veil possible concessions for fear extremists would hear of them and inflame the jingoes. The Japanese military continued to follow its own policies; amid the delicate negotiations, Washington learned that the Japanese Army was putting more troops into Indochina. The political chiefs in Tokyo, however, seemed willing to negotiate. On the three major issues Tokyo would: agree to follow an "independent" course under the Tripartite Pact—a crucial concession at this point, because America's widening confrontation with

Germany raised the fateful possibility that Tokyo would automatically side with Berlin if a hot war broke out; follow cooperative, nondiscriminatory economic policies, a concession that was as salve to Hull's breast; and be willing to let Washington mediate a settlement between Japan and China.

Day after day Hull listened to these proposals courteously, discussed them gravely—and refused to budge. He insisted that Tokyo be even more specific and make concessions in advance of a summit conference. By now the Secretary and his staff conceded that Konoye was "sincere." They simply doubted the Premier's capacity to bring the military into line. That doubt did not end after the war when historians looked at the evidence, which reflected such a shaky balance of power in Tokyo that Konoye's parley might have precipitated a crisis rather than have averted it. Konoye had neither the nerve nor the muscle for a supreme stroke. Much would have depended on the Emperor, and the administration did not fully appreciate in September either his desire for effective negotiations or his ability to make his soldiers accept their outcome.

The mystery lay not with Hull, who was sticking to his principles, but with Roosevelt, who was bent on *Realpolitik* as well as morality. The President still had one simple approach to Japan—to play for time—while he conducted the cold war with Germany. Why, then, did he not insist on a Pacific conference as an easy way to gain time? Partly because such a conference might bring a showdown *too* quickly; better, Roosevelt calculated, to let Hull do the thing he was so good at—talk and talk, without letting negotiations either lapse or come to a head. And partly because Roosevelt was succumbing to his own tendency to string things out. *He* had infinite time in the Far East; he did not realize that in Tokyo a different clock was ticking.

Amid the confusion and miscalculation there was one hard, unshakable issue: China. In all their sweeping proposals to pull out of China, the Japanese insisted, except toward the end, on leaving some troops as security, ostensibly at least, against the Chinese Communists. Even the Japanese diplomats' definite promises on China seemed idle; it was clear in Washington as in Tokyo that a withdrawal from a war to which Japan had given so much blood and treasure would cause a convulsion.

Washington was in almost as tight a bind on China as was Tokyo. During this period the administration was fearful of a Chinese collapse. Chungking was complaining about the paucity of American aid; some Kuomintang officials charged that Washington was interested only in Europe and hoped to leave China to deal with Japan. Madame Chiang at a dinner party accused Roosevelt and Churchill of ignoring China at their Atlantic meeting and trying to appease Japan; the Generalissimo chided his wife for her impulsive outburst but did not disagree. Every fragment of a report of a Japanese-American détente set off a paroxysm of fear in Chungking. Through all their myriad channels into the administration the Nationalists were maintaining steady pressure against compromise with Tokyo and for an immensely enlarged and hastened aid program to China.

Even the President's son James, as a Marine captain, urged his father to send bombers to China, in response to a letter from Soong stating that in fourteen months "not a single plane sufficiently supplied with armament and ammunition so that it could actually be used to fire has reached China." Chiang was literally receiving the run-around in Washington as requests bounced from department to department and from Americans to British and back again. Its very failure to aid China made the administration all the more sensitive to any act that might break Kuomintang morale.

So Roosevelt backed Hull's militant posture toward Tokyo. When the Secretary penciled a few lines at the end of September to the effect that the Japanese had hardened their position on the basic questions, Roosevelt said he wholly agreed with his conclusion—even though he must have known that Hull was oversimplifying the situation to the point of distortion. Increasingly anxious, Grew, in Tokyo, felt that he simply was not getting through to the President on the possibilities of a summit conference. On October 2 Hull again stated his principles and demanded specifics. The Konoye government in turn asked Washington just what it wanted Japan to do. Would not the Americans lay their cards on the table? Time was fleeting; the military now were pressing heavily on the diplomats. At this desperate moment the Japanese government offered flatly to "evacuate all its troops from China." But the military deadline had arrived. Was it too late?

Not often have two powers been in such close communication but with such faulty perceptions of each other. They were exchanging information and views through a dozen channels; they were both conducting effective espionage; there were countless long conversations, Hull having spent at least one hundred hours talking with Nomura. The problem was too much information, not too little—and too much that was irrelevant, confusing, and badly analyzed. The two nations grappled like clumsy giants, each with a dozen myopic eyes that saw too little and too much.

For some time Grew and others had been warning Washington that the Konoye Cabinet would fall unless diplomacy began to score; the administration seemed unmoved. On October 16 Konoye submitted his resignation to the Emperor. In his stead Hirohito appointed Minister of War Hideki Tojo. The news produced dismay in Washington, where Roosevelt canceled a regular Cabinet meeting to talk with his War Cabinet, and a near-panic in Chungking, which feared that the man of Manchuria would seek first of all to finish off the China incident. But reassurances came from Tokyo: Konoye indicated that the new Cabinet would continue to emphasize diplomacy, and the new Foreign Minister, Shigenori Togo, was a professional diplomat and not a fire-breathing militarist. As for Tojo, power ennobles as well as corrupts. Perhaps it had been a shrewd move of the Emperor, some of the more helpful Washingtonians reflected, to make Tojo responsible for holding his fellow militarists in check.

So for a couple of weeks the President marked time. Since he was still following the diplomacy of delay, he could only wait for the new regime in Tokyo to take the initiative—and to wonder when the next clash would occur in the Atlantic. . . .

That clash came on the night of October 16. About four hundred miles south of Iceland a slow convoy of forty ships, escorted by only four corvettes, ran into a pack of U-boats. After three ships were torpedoed and sunk, the convoy appealed to Reykjavik for help, and soon five American destroyers were racing to the scene. That evening the submarines, standing out two or three miles from the convoy and thus beyond the range of the destroyers' sound gear, picked off seven more ships. The destroyers, which had no radar, thrashed about in confusion in the pitch dark, dropping depth bombs; when the U.S.S. *Kearny* had to stop to allow a corvette to cross her bow, a torpedo struck her, knocked out her power for a time, and killed eleven of her crew. She struggled back to Iceland nursing some bitter lessons in night fighting.

At last the first blood had been drawn—and it was American blood (though the U-boat commander had not known the nationality of the destroyer he was firing at). News of the encounter reached Washington on the eve of a vote in the House on repealing the Neutrality Act's ban against the arming of merchant ships. Repeal passed by a handsome majority, 259 to 138. The bill had now to go to the Senate. On Navy Day, October 27, the President took up the incident. He reminded his listeners, packed into the grand ballroom of Washington's Mayflower Hotel, of the *Greer* and *Kearny* episodes.

"We have wished to avoid shooting. But the shooting has started. And history has recorded who fired the first shot. In the long run, however, all that will matter is who fired the last shot.

"America has been attacked. The U.S.S. *Kearny* is not just a Navy ship. She belongs to every man, woman, and child in this Nation. . . ."

The President said he had two documents in his possession: a Nazi map of South America and part of Central America realigning it into five vassal states; and a Nazi plan "to abolish all existing religions—Catholic, Protestant, Mohammedan, Hindu, Buddhist, and Jewish alike"—if Hitler won. "The God of Blood and Iron will take the place of the God of Love and Mercy." He denounced apologists for Hitler. "The Nazis have made up their own list of modern American heroes. It is, fortunately, a short list. I am glad that it does not contain my name." The President had never been more histrionic. He reverted to the clashes on the sea. "I say that we do not propose to take this lying down." He described steps in Congress to eliminate "hamstringing" provisions of the Neutrality Act. "That is the course of honesty and of realism.

"Our American merchant ships must be armed to defend themselves against the rattlesnakes of the sea.

"Our American merchant ships must be free to carry our American goods into the harbors of our friends.

"Our American merchant ships must be protected by our American Navy.

"In the light of a good many years of personal experience, I think that it can be said that it can never be doubted that the goods will be delivered by this Nation, whose Navy believes in the tradition of 'Damn the torpedoes; full speed ahead!' "

Some had said that Americans had grown fat and flabby and lazy. They had not; again and again they had overcome hard challenges.

"Today in the face of this newest and greatest challenge of them all, we Americans have cleared our decks and taken our battle stations. . . ."

It was one of Roosevelt's most importunate speeches, but it seemed to have little effect. After a week of furious attacks by Senate isolationists, neutrality revision cleared the upper chamber by only 50 to 37. In mid-November a turbulent House passed the Senate bill by a majority vote of 212 to 194. The President won less support from Democrats on this vote than he had on Lend-Lease. It was clear to all—and this was the key factor in Roosevelt's calculations—that if the administration could have such a close shave as this on the primitive question of arming cargo ships, the President could not depend on Congress at this point to vote through a declaration of war. Three days after Roosevelt's Navy Day speech the American destroyer *Reuben James* was torpedoed, with the loss of 115 of the crew, including all the officers; Congress and the people seemed to greet this heavy loss with fatalistic resignation.

It was inexplicable. In this looming crisis the United States seemed deadlocked—its President handcuffed, its Congress irresolute, its people divided and confused. There were reasons running back deep into American history, reasons embedded in the country's Constitution, habits, institutions, moods, and attitudes. But the immediate, proximate reason lay with the President of the United States. He had been following a middle course between the all-out interventionists and those who wanted more time; he had been stranded midway between his promise to keep America out of war and his excoriation of Nazism as a total threat to his nation. He had called Hitlerism inhuman, ruthless, cruel, barbarous, piratical, godless, pagan, brutal, tyrannical, and absolutely bent on world domination. He had even issued the ultimate warning: that if Hitler won in Europe, Americans would be forced into a war on their own soil "as costly and as devastating as that which now rages on the Russian front."

Now—by early November 1941—there seemed to be nothing more he could say. There seemed to be little more he could do. He had called his people to their battle stations—but there was no battle. "He had no more tricks left," Sherwood said later. "The bag from which he had pulled so many rabbits was empty." Always a master of mass influence and personal persuasion, Roosevelt had encountered a supreme crisis in which neither could do much good. A brilliant timer, improviser, and manipulator, he confronted a turgid balance of powers and strategies beyond his capacity to either steady or overturn. Since the heady days of August he had lost the initiative; now he could only wait on events. And events with the massive impact that would be decisive were still in the hands of Adolf Hitler.

The crisis of presidential leadership mirrored the dilemma of national strategy in the fall of 1941. According to long-laid plans, the

United States, in the event of war, would engage directly with Germany and stall off or conduct a holding action with Japan. Roosevelt was expecting a confrontation with Germany, probably triggered by some incident in the Atlantic, but he was evading a showdown with Japan. In his denunciations of Nazism he had been careful not to mention Nipponese aggression or imperialism. But Hitler still pointedly avoided final trouble in the Atlantic, while the Far Eastern front, instead of being tranquilized, was becoming the most critical one.

And if war did break out in the Pacific—what then? The chances seemed strong that the Japanese would strike directly at British or Dutch possessions, not American. Sherwood posed the question well. If French isolationists had raised the jeering cry "Why die for Danzig?" why should Americans die to protect the Kra Isthmus, or British imperialism in Singapore or Hong Kong, or Dutch imperialism in the East Indies, or Bolshevism in Vladivostok? It would no longer be enough for the United States to offer mere aid. Doubtless Roosevelt could ram through a declaration of war—but how effective would a bitter and divided nation be in the crucible of total war? And if the United States did not forcibly resist Japanese aggression against Britain and Holland, what would happen to Britain's defenses in the Far East while so heavily committed at home, in the Middle East, in North Africa, and on the seven seas?

The obvious answer was to stall Tokyo as long as possible. Eventually an open conflict with Germany must come; if Japan had not yet entered the war, perhaps it would stay out for the same reason it had kept clear of the Russo-German conflict. By November 1941 Roosevelt needed such a delay not only because of Atlantic First, but also as a result of a shift in plans for the Philippines. Earlier, the archipelago had been assumed to be indefensible against a strong enemy assault, and hence the War and Navy Departments had not made a heavy commitment there. Now, with General MacArthur's appointment as commander of U.S. forces in the Far East and the development of the B-17 heavy bomber, the Philippines were once again considered strategically viable. But time was needed, at least two or three months.

So early hostilities with Japan would mean the wrong war in the wrong ocean at the wrong time. Yet it was clear by November 1941 that the United States was faced with the growing probability of precisely this war. Why did not the President string the Japanese along further, taking care not to get close to a showdown?

This is what he did try, at least until November. It was not easy.

Every time reports spread that Washington had considered even a small compromise on the central issue of a Japanese withdrawal from China, frantic cries arose from Chungking. Churchill, too, pressed insistently for a harder line toward Tokyo. At home Roosevelt had to deal with public attitudes that turned more militantly against Japan than against Germany. In early August those opposing war with Japan outnumbered those favoring it by more than three to one, while by late November twice as many as not were *expecting* war between their country and Japan in the near future.

Doubtless the basic factor, though, was one of calculation, or analysis. Churchill, still responding to the bitter lessons of Munich, contended that a policy of firmness was precisely the way to earn peace; it was the democracies' vacillation that tempted aggressors to go to war. Roosevelt was not so sure that the Asiatic mind worked in just this way. Yet he went along with Churchill's theory of peace through firmness and with Hull's insistence on adherence to principles, rather than with Stimson's and Knox's urgent advice to stall the Japanese along in order not to be diverted from Atlantic First and in order to have time to prepare in the Pacific.

Later an odd notion would arise that the President, denied his direct war with Hitler, finally gained it through the "back door" of conflict with the Japanese. This is the opposite of what he was trying to do. He wanted to avoid war with Japan because—like all the grand strategists—he feared a two-front war, and American strategy was definitely set on fighting Hitler first. In another three or six months, after the Philippines and other Pacific outposts had been strengthened, the President might well have gone through the "back door" of war—but not in late 1941. Churchill's calculations, however, were more mixed. He could assume his stand-firm posture with far more equanimity than Roosevelt; the Prime Minister could reason that a Japanese-American break would probably bring the United States into the German war as well and thus realize London's burning hope of full American involvement. But much would depend on the strength of Berlin-Tokyo solidarity and on each nation's calculus of its interest. Churchill had to face the fearsome possibility that the United States might become involved *only* in the Pacific. Hence he, too, was following the Atlantic First strategy.

It was not Roosevelt's calculation that was at fault, but his miscalculation. And because he lacked the initiative, and was assuming the imperfect moral stand of condemning Hitlerism as utterly evil and bent on world domination without openly and totally combating it, he faced a thicket of secondary but irksome troubles. . . .

The whole anti-Axis coalition, indeed, was in strategic disarray by late fall of 1941, even while it was cooperating on a host of economic, military, and diplomatic matters. Churchill was almost desperate over Washington's stubborn noninvolvement. He still had serious doubts about Russia's capacity to hold out; he had to face the nightmarish possibility of Britain alone confronting a fully mobilized Wehrmacht. As it was, he had to share American aid with Russia, and while he was eager to do anything necessary to keep the Bear fighting, he found it surly, snarling, and grasping. He still feared a Nazi invasion of Britain in the spring, and he was trying to build up his North African strength for an attack to the west. Stalin was always a prickly associate. A mission to Moscow led by Lord Beaverbrook and Averell Harriman had established closer working relations with the Soviets, but no mission could solve the basic problem that Russia was taking enormous losses while only a thin trickle of supplies was arriving through Archangel, Vladivostok, and Iran. As for China, which was at best third on the waiting list for American aid, feeling in Chungking ranged between bitterness and defeatism.

So if Roosevelt was stranded in the shoals of war and diplomacy, he was no worse off than the other world leaders in 1941. All had seen their earlier hopes and plans crumble. Hitler had attacked Russia in the expectation of averting a long war on two fronts; now he was engaged in precisely that. Churchill had hoped to gain the United States as a full partner, but had gained Russia; he had wanted to take the strategic initiative long before, but had failed; he doubted that Japan would take on Britain and America at the same time, but events would prove him wrong. Stalin had played for time and lost; now the Germans, fifty miles west of Moscow, were preparing their final attack on it.

All the global forces generated by raw power and resistance, by grand strategies and counter-strategies, by sober staff studies and surprise blows—all were locked in a tremulous world balance. Only some mighty turn of events could upset that balance and release Franklin Roosevelt from his strategic plight.

Paul W. Schroeder

AN APPRAISAL

Professor Schroeder, in this summary passage from his The Axis Alliance
and Japanese-American Relations *(1958), carries on in the tradition of earlier
revisionists who criticized the policies that brought war with Japan. Unlike
them, however, he displays no personal bias against the Roosevelt administration. He differs also in accepting, as the revisionists did not, the basic
assumption that American policy was properly based on concern for the
treaty fabric in the Pacific, an obligation to protect China, and on national
interests. But in pursuit of these objectives the United States utilized the
wrong tactics, according to Schroeder. He contends that a shortsighted
moral stance and an unyielding "hard" policy drove Japan into a corner,
jeopardizing the very goals we sought and bringing on an undesired war for
which we were unprepared. In sharp disagreement with Feis, Schroeder
believes it was unwise and unnecessary to reject Japan's offer of a Konoye-
Roosevelt meeting. Note also his disagreement with Iriye about the importance of China in our Asian policy. Is Schroeder right in assuming that
moral principles, however mistakenly applied, were the proper basis for
United States policy?*

In judging American policy toward Japan in 1941, it might be well to
separate what is still controversial from what is not. There is no
longer any real doubt that the war came about over China. Even an
administration stalwart like Henry L. Stimson and a sympathetic critic
like Herbert Feis concur in this.[1] Nor is it necessary to speculate any
longer as to what could have induced Japan to launch such an
incredible attack upon the United States and Great Britain as occurred at Pearl Harbor and in the south Pacific. One need not, as
Winston Churchill did in wartime, characterize it as "an irrational
act" incompatible "with prudence or even with sanity."[2] The

[1] "If at any time the United States had been willing to concede Japan a free hand in
China, there would have been no war in the Pacific" (Stimson and Bundy, *On Active
Service*, 256). "Our full induction into this last World War followed our refusal to let
China fend for itself. We had rejected all proposals which would have allowed Japan to
remain in China and Manchuria. . . . Japan had struck—rather than accept frustration"
(Herbert Feis, *The China Tangle* [Princeton: Princeton University Press, 1953], 3).
[2] Speech to U.S. Congress, Washington, Dec. 26, 1941, *War Speeches of Churchill*, II,
150.

Japanese were realistic about their position throughout; they did not suddenly go insane. The attack was an act of desperation, not madness. Japan fought only when she had her back to the wall as a result of America's diplomatic and economic offensive.

The main point still at issue is whether the United States was wise in maintaining a "hard" program of diplomatic and economic pressure on Japan from July 1941 on. Along with this issue go two subsidiary questions: the first, whether it was wise to make the liberation of China the central aim of American policy and the immediate evacuation of Japanese troops a requirement for agreement; the second, whether it was wise to decline Premier Konoye's invitation to a meeting of leaders in the Pacific. On all these points, the policy which the United States carried out still has distinguished defenders. The paramount issue between Japan and the United States, they contend, always was the China problem. In her China policy, Japan showed that she was determined to secure domination over a large area of East Asia by force. Apart from the legitimate American commercial interests which would be ruined or excluded by this Japanese action, the United States, for reasons of her own security and of world peace, had sufficient stake in Far Eastern questions to oppose such aggression. Finally, after ten years of Japanese expansion, it was only sensible and prudent for the United States to demand that it come to an end and that Japan retreat. In order to meet the Japanese threat, the United States had a perfect right to use the economic power she possessed in order to compel the Japanese to evacuate their conquered territory. If Japan chose to make this a cause for war, the United States could not be held responsible.

A similar defense is offered on the decision to turn down Konoye's Leaders' Conference. Historians may concede, as do Langer and Gleason, that Konoye was probably sincere in wanting peace and that he "envisaged making additional concessions to Washington, including concessions on the crucial issue of the withdrawal of Japanese troops from China." But, they point out, Konoye could never have carried the Army with him on any such concession.[3] If the United States was right in requiring Japan to abandon the Co-Prosperity Sphere, then her leaders were equally right in declining to meet with a Japanese Premier who, however conciliatory he might

[3] Langer and Gleason, *Undeclared War*, 706–707.

have been personally, was bound by his own promises and the exigencies of Japanese politics to maintain this national aim. In addition, there was the serious possibility that much could be lost from such a meeting—the confidence of China, the cohesiveness of the coalition with Great Britain and Russia. In short, there was not enough prospect of gain to merit taking the chance.

This is a point of view which must be taken seriously. Any judgment on the wisdom or folly of the American policy, in fact, must be made with caution—there are no grounds for dogmatic certainty. The opinion here to be developed, nonetheless, is that the American policy from the end of July to December was a grave mistake. It should not be necessary to add that this does not make it treason. There is a "back door to war" theory, espoused in various forms by Charles A. Beard, George Morgenstern, Charles C. Tansill, and, most recently, Rear Admiral Robert A. Theobald, which holds that the President chose the Far East as a rear entrance to the war in Europe and to that end deliberately goaded the Japanese into an attack.[4] This theory is quite different and quite incredible. It is as impossible to accept as the idea that Japan attacked the United States in a spirit of overconfidence or that Hitler pushed the Japanese into war. Roosevelt's fault, if any, was not that of deliberately provoking the Japanese to attack, but of allowing Hull and others to talk him out of impulses and ideas which, had he pursued them, might have averted the conflict. Moreover, the mistake (assuming that it was a mistake) of a too hard and rigid policy with Japan was, as has been pointed out, a mistake shared by the whole nation, with causes that were deeply organic. Behind it was not sinister design or warlike intent, but a sincere and uncompromising adherence to moral principles and liberal doctrines.

This is going ahead too fast, however; one needs first of all to define the mistake with which American policy is charged. Briefly, it was this. In the attempt to gain everything at once, the United States lost her opportunity to secure immediately her essential requirements in the Far East and to continue to work toward her long-range goals. She succeeded instead only in making inevitable an unnecessary and avoidable war—an outcome which constitutes the ultimate failure of

---

[4] Charles A. Beard, *President Roosevelt and the Coming of the War, 1941* (New Haven: Yale University Press, 1948); George E. Morgenstern, *Pearl Harbor: The Story of the Secret War* (New York: Devin-Adair, 1947); Charles C. Tansill, *Back Door to War* (Chicago: Regnery, 1952); Rear Admiral Robert A. Theobald, *The Final Secret of Pearl Harbor* (New York: Devin-Adair, 1954).

diplomacy. Until July 1941, as already demonstrated, the United States consistently sought to attain two limited objectives in the Far East, those of splitting the Axis and of stopping Japan's advance southward. Both aims were in accordance with America's broad strategic interests; both were reasonable, attainable goals. Through a combination of favorable circumstance and forceful American action, the United States reached the position where the achievement of these two goals was within sight. At this very moment, on the verge of a major diplomatic victory, the United States abandoned her original goals and concentrated on a third, the liberation of China. This last aim was not in accord with American strategic interests, was not a limited objective, and, most important, was completely incapable of being achieved by peaceful means and doubtful of attainment even by war. Through her single-minded pursuit of this unattainable goal, the United States forfeited the diplomatic victory which she had already virtually won. The unrelenting application of extreme economic pressure on Japan, instead of compelling the evacuation of China, rendered war inevitable, drove Japan back into the arms of Germany for better or for worse, and precipitated the wholesale plunge by Japan into the South Seas. As it ultimately turned out, the United States succeeded in liberating China only at great cost and when it was too late to do the cause of the Nationalist Chinese much real good.

This is not, of course, a new viewpoint. It is in the main simply that of Ambassador Grew, who has held and defended it since 1941.The arguments he advances seem cogent and sensible in the light of present knowledge. Briefly summarized, they are the following: First is his insistence on the necessity of distinguishing between long-range and immediate goals in foreign policy and on the folly of demanding the immediate realization of both.[5] Second is his contention that governments are brought to abandon aggressive policies not by sudden conversion through moral lectures, but by the gradual recognition that the policy of aggression will not succeed. According to Grew, enough awareness of failure existed in the government of Japan in late 1941 to enable it to make a beginning in the process of reversal of policy—but not nearly enough to force Japan to a wholesale surrender of her conquests and aims.[6] Third was his conviction that what was needed on both sides was time—time in which

---

[5] Grew, *Turbulent Era*, II, 1255.
[6] Ibid., 1290.

the United States could grow stronger and in which the tide of war in Europe could be turned definitely against Germany, time in which the sense of failure could grow in Japan and in which moderates could gain better control of the situation. A victory in Europe, Grew observed, would either automatically solve the problem of Japan or make that problem, if necessary, much easier to solve by force.[7] Fourth was his belief that Japan would fight if backed to the wall (a view vindicated by events)[8] and that a war at this time with Japan could not possibly serve the interests of the United States. Even if one considered war as the only final answer to Japanese militarism, still, Grew would answer, the United States stood to gain nothing by seeking a decision in 1941. The time factor was entirely in America's favor. Japan could not hope to gain as much from a limited relaxation of the embargo as the United States could from time gained for mobilization; Roosevelt and the military strategists were in fact anxious to gain time by a modus vivendi.[9]

There is one real weakness in Grew's argument upon which his critics have always seized. This is his contention that Konoye, faced after July 26 with the two clear alternatives of war or a genuine peace move, which would of necessity include a settlement with China, had chosen the latter course and could have carried through a policy of peace had he been given the time. "We believed," he writes, "that Prince Konoye was in a position to carry the country with him in a program of peace" and to make commitments to the United States which would "eventually, if not immediately" meet the conditions of Hull's Four Points.[10] The answer of critics is that, even if one credits Konoye's sincerity and takes his assurances at face value, there is still no reason to believe that he could have carried even his own cabinet, much less the whole nation, with him on any program approximating that of Hull. In particular, as events show, he could not have persuaded the Army to evacuate China.[11]

[7] Ibid., 1268–1269, 1286.
[8] The opposite belief, that Japan would give way, not only was inconsonant with the best available political and military intelligence, but was also a bad estimate of Japanese national psychology and of expansionist psychology in general. F. C. Jones rightly criticizes it as "the folly of supposing that the rulers of a powerful nation, having committed themselves to an expansionist policy, will abandon or reverse that policy when confronted by the threat of war. So long as they see, or think they see, any possibility of success, they will elect to fight rather than face the humiliation and probable internal revolt which submission to the demands of their opponents would entail" (*Japan's New Order*, 461).
[9] Grew, *Turbulent Era*, II, 1276–1277.
[10] Ibid., 1263–1264.
[11] Feis, *Road to Pearl Harbor*, 275–77; Jones, *Japan's New Order*, 457–58.

The objection is well taken; Grew was undoubtedly over-optimistic about Konoye's capacity to carry through a peaceful policy. This one objection, however, does not ruin Grew's case. He countered it later with the argument that a settlement with Japan which allowed Japanese garrisons to remain in China on a temporary basis would not have been a bad idea. Although far from an ideal solution, it would have been better, for China as well, than the policy the United States actually followed. It would have brought China what was all-important—a cessation of fighting—without involving the United States, as many contended, in either a sacrifice of principle or a betrayal of China. The United States, Grew points out, had never committed herself to guaranteeing China's integrity. Further, it would not have been necessary to agree to anything other than temporary garrisons in North China which, in more favorable times, the United States could work to have removed. The great mistake was to allow American policy to be guided by a sentimental attitude toward China which in the long run could do neither the United States nor China any good. As Grew puts it:

> Japan's advance to the south, including her occupation of portions of China, constituted for us a real danger, and it was definitely in our national interest that it be stopped, by peaceful means if possible, by force of arms if necessary. American aid to China should have been regarded, as we believe it was regarded by our Government, as an indirect means to this end, and not from a sentimental viewpoint. The President's letter of January 21, 1941, shows that he then sensed the important issues in the Far East, and that he did not include China, purely for China's sake, among them. . . . The failure of the Washington Administration to seize the opportunity presented in August and September, 1941, to halt the southward advance by peaceful means, together with the paramount importance attached to the China question during the conversations in Washington, gives rise to the belief that not our Government but millions of quite understandably sympathetic but almost totally uninformed American citizens had assumed control of our Far Eastern policy.[12]

There remains the obvious objection that Grew's solution, however plausible it may now seem, was politically impracticable in 1941. No American government could then have treated China as expendable, just as no Japanese government could have written off the China Affair as a dead loss. This is in good measure true and goes a long way to explain, if not to justify, the hard American policy. Yet it is not

[12] Grew, *Turbulent Era*, II, 1367–68.

entirely certain that no solution could have been found which would both have averted war and have been accepted by the American people, had a determined effort been made to find one. As F. C. Jones points out, the United States and Japan were not faced in July 1941 with an absolute dilemma of peace or war, of complete settlement or open conflict. Hull believed that they were, of course; but his all-or-nothing attitude constituted one of his major shortcomings as a diplomat. Between the two extremes existed the possibility of a modus vivendi, an agreement settling some issues and leaving others in abeyance. Had Roosevelt and Konoye met, Jones argues, they might have been able to agree on a relaxation of the embargo in exchange for satisfactory assurances on the Tripartite Pact and southward expansion, with the China issue laid aside. The United States would not have had to cease aid, nor Japan to remove her troops. The final settlement of the Far Eastern question, Jones concludes,

> would then have depended upon the issue of the struggle in Europe. If Germany prevailed, then the United States would be in no position to oppose Japanese ambitions in Asia; if Germany were defeated, Japan would be in no position to persist in those ambitions in the face of the United States, the USSR, and the British Commonwealth.[13]

Such an agreement, limited and temporary in nature, would have involved no sacrifice of principle for either nation, yet would have removed the immediate danger of war. As a temporary expedient and as an alternative to otherwise inevitable and useless conflict, it could have been sold by determined effort to the public on both sides. Nor would it have been impossible, in the writer's opinion, to have accompanied or followed such an agreement with a simple truce or standstill in the China conflict through American mediation.

This appraisal, to be sure, is one based on realism. Grew's criticism of Hull's policy and the alternative he offers to it are both characterized by fundamental attention to what is practical and expedient at a given time and to limited objectives within the scope of the national interest. In general, the writer agrees with this point of view, believing that, as William A. Orton points out, it is foolish and disastrous to treat nations as morally responsible persons, "because their nature falls far short of personality," and that, as George F. Kennan contends, the right role for moral considerations in foreign

[13] Jones, *Japan's New Order*, 459.

affairs is not to determine policy, but rather to soften and ameliorate actions necessarily based on the realities of world politics.[14]

From this realistic standpoint, the policy of the State Department would seem to be open to other criticisms besides those of Grew. The criticisms, which may be briefly mentioned here, are those of inconsistency, blindness to reality, and futility. A notable example of the first would be the inconsistency of a strong no-compromise stand against Japan with the policy of broad accommodation to America's allies, especially Russia, both before and after the American entrance into the war.[15] The inconsistency may perhaps best be seen by comparing the American stand in 1941 on such questions as free trade, the Open Door in China, the territorial and administrative integrity of China, the maintenance of the prewar status quo in the Far East, and the sanctity of international agreements with the position taken on the same questions at the Yalta Conference in 1945.[16]

[14] William A. Orton, *The Liberal Tradition* (New Haven: Yale University Press, 1944), 239; George F. Kennan, *American Diplomacy, 1900–1950* (Chicago: University of Chicago Press, 1951), 95–103.

[15] One notes with interest, for example, a pre-Pearl Harbor statement by Senator Lister Hill of Alabama, a strong proponent of a radical anti-Japanese policy, as to America's attitude toward the Soviet Union: "It is not the business of this government to ask or to receive any assurance from Stalin about what he will do with regard to Finland after the war. . . . It is the business of this government to look out for and defend the vital interests of the United States" (*New York Times*, Nov. 5, 1941). If in the above quotation one reads "Tojo" for "Stalin" and "China" for "Finland," the result is a statement of the extreme isolationist position on the Far East which Hill and other supporters of the administration found so detestable.

[16] The writer has no desire to enter here into the controversy over the merits of the Yalta decisions, but only to draw a certain parallel. The standard defense for the Yalta policy on the Far East has been the contention that the United States conceded to Soviet Russia only what the USSR could and would have seized without American leave, that the only alternative to agreement would have been war with Russia, and that securing Russian entrance into the Far Eastern war was considered militarily necessary (George F. Lensen, "Yalta and the Far East," in John L. Snell, Forrest C. Pogue, Charles F. Delzell, and George F. Lensen, *The Meaning of Yalta: Big Three Diplomacy and the New Balance of Power* [Baton Rouge: Louisiana State University Press, 1956], 163–64). The argument may be quite sound, but surely it would serve equally well—indeed, much better, *mutatis mutandis*—to justify a policy of conciliation toward Japan in 1941. Applied to Japan, the argument would then read as follows: The United States would have conceded to Japan only the temporary possession of a part of what Japan had already seized without American leave; the only alternative to agreement would have been war with Japan; and preventing Japanese entrance into the European war was considered militarily necessary. The great difference between the two situations would seem to be that the concessions envisioned by Japan in 1941 were temporary and reversible; those gained by Russia in 1945 were not. The very necessity of pursuing the Yalta policy in 1945 casts doubt on the wisdom of the hard-and-fast stand of 1941. Felix Morley has put the parallel neatly: "To assert that the sudden and complete reversal of the long-established Far Eastern policy was justified was also to say, by implication, that the policy reversed was fundamentally faulty, that to fight a war with Japan in behalf of Chinese nationalism had been a dreadful mistake" (*The Foreign Policy of the United States* [New York: Alfred A. Knopf, 1951], 87–88). One may, as Morley does,

The blindness to reality may be seen in the apparent inability of American policymakers to take seriously into account the gravity of Japan's economic plight or the real exigencies of her military and strategic position, particularly as these factors would affect the United States over the long run.[17] Equally unrealistic and more fateful was the lack of appreciation on the part of many influential people and of wide sections of the public of the almost certain consequences to be expected from the pressure exerted on Japan—namely, American involvement in a war her military strategists considered highly undesirable. The attitude has been well termed by Robert Osgood, "this blind indifference toward the military and political consequences of a morally-inspired position."[18]

The charge of futility, finally, could be laid to the practice of insisting on a literal subscription to principles which, however noble, had no chance of general acceptance or practical application. The best example is the persistent demand that the Japanese pledge themselves to carrying out nineteenth-century principles of free trade and equal access to raw materials in a twentieth-century world where economic nationalism and autarchy, trade barriers and restrictions were everywhere the order of the day, and not the least in the United States under the New Deal. Not one of America's major allies would have subscribed wholeheartedly to Hull's free-trade formula; what good it could have done to pin the Japanese down to it is hard to determine.[19]

---

reject both the above premise and the conclusion, or one may accept both; but it is difficult to see how one may affirm the premise and deny the conclusion. For those who believe that a vital moral difference existed between the two cases, the problem would seem to be how to show that it is morally unjustifiable to violate principle in order to keep a potential enemy out of a war, yet morally justifiable to sacrifice principle in order to get a potential ally into it. The dilemma appears insoluble.

[17] In his very interesting book, *America's Strategy in World Politics* (New York: Harcourt, Brace, 1942), Nicholas Spykman displays some of the insights which seem to have been lacking in the American policy of the time. He points out, for example, that Japan's economic and geographic position was essentially the same as that of Great Britain; that her position vis-à-vis the United States was also roughly equivalent to England's; that therefore it made little sense for America to aid Great Britain in maintaining a European balance of power, while at the same time trying to force Japan to give up all her buffer states in Asia; that the Japanese war potential could not compare to that of a revivified and unified China; and that one day (a striking prediction in 1942!) the United States would have to undertake to protect Japan from Soviet Russia and China (pp. 135–37, 469–70). Spykman saw then what is today so painfully evident—that without a Japanese foothold on the Asiatic mainland no real balance of power is possible in Asia.

[18] Robert E. Osgood, *Ideals and Self-Interest in America's Foreign Relations* (Chicago: University of Chicago Press, 1953), 361.

[19] A memorandum by the Chief of the State Department Division of Commercial Policy

But these are all criticisms based on a realistic point of view, and to judge the American policy solely from this point of view is to judge it unfairly and by a standard inappropriate to it. The policy of the United States was avowedly not one of realism, but of principle. If then it is to be understood on its own grounds and judged by its own standards, the main question will be whether the policy was morally right—that is, in accord with principles of peace and international justice. Here, according to its defenders, the American policy stands vindicated. For any other policy, any settlement with Japan at the expense of China, would have meant a betrayal not only of China, but also of vital principles and of America's moral task in the world.

This, as we know, was the position of Hull and his coworkers. It has been stated more recently by Basil Rauch, who writes:

> No one but an absolute pacifist would argue that the danger of war is a greater evil than violation of principle. . . . The isolationist believes that appeasement of Japan without China's consent violated no principle worth a risk of war. The internationalist must believe that the principle did justify a risk of war.[20]

This is not an argument to be dismissed lightly. The contention that the United States had a duty to fulfill in 1941, and that this duty consisted in holding to justice and morality in a world given to international lawlessness and barbarism and in standing on principle against an unprincipled and ruthless aggressor, commands respect. It is not answered by dismissing it as unrealistic or by proscribing all moral considerations in foreign policy. An answer may be found, however, in a closer definition of America's moral duty in 1941. According to Hull, and apparently also Rauch, the task was primarily one of upholding principle. This is not the only possible definition. It may well be contended that the moral duty was rather one of doing the most practical good possible in a chaotic world situation and, further, that this was the main task President Roosevelt and the administration had in mind at least till the end of July 1941.

If the moral task of the United States in the Far East was to uphold a principle of absolute moral value, the principle of nonappeasement of aggressors, then the American policy was entirely successful in

and Agreements (Hawkins) to Ballantine, Washington, Nov. 10, 1941, offers interesting comments on the extent and nature of the trade discriminations then being practiced against Japan by nations throughout the world, including the United States (*Foreign Relations, 1941*, IV, 576–77).
[20] Rauch, *Roosevelt*, 472.

fulfilling it. The American diplomats proved that the United States was capable of holding to its position in disregard and even in defiance of national interests narrowly conceived. If, however, the task was one of doing concrete good and giving practical help where needed, especially to China, then the American policy falls fatally short. For it can easily be seen not only that the policy followed did not in practice help China, but also that it could not have been expected to. Although it was a pro-China and even a China-first policy in principle, it was not in practical fact designed to give China the kind of help needed.

What China required above all by late 1941 was clearly an end to the fighting, a chance to recoup her strength. Her chaotic financial condition, a disastrous inflation, civil strife with the Communists, severe hunger and privation, and falling morale all enfeebled and endangered her further resistance. Chiang Kai-shek, who knew this, could hope only for an end to the war through the massive intervention of American forces and the consequent liberation of China. It was in this hope that he pleaded so strongly for a hard American policy toward Japan. Chiang's hopes, however, were wholly unrealistic. For though the United States was willing to risk war for China's sake, and finally did incur it over the China issue, the Washington government never intended in case of war to throw America's full weight against Japan in order to liberate China. The American strategy always was to concentrate on Europe first, fighting a defensive naval war in the Far East and aiding China, as before, in order to keep the Japanese bogged down. The possibility was faced and accepted that the Chinese might have to go on fighting for some years before eventual liberation through the defeat of Japan. The vehement Chinese protests over this policy were unavailing, and the bitter disillusionment suffered by the Chinese only helped to bring on in 1942 the virtual collapse of the Chinese war effort during the latter years of the war.[21]

As a realistic appraisal of America's military capabilities and of her world-wide strategic interests, the Europe-first policy has a great deal to recommend it. But the combination of this realistic strategy with a moralistic diplomacy led to the noteworthy paradox of a war incurred

[21] Levi, *Modern China's Foreign Policy*, 229–37. On the danger of internal collapse in China as early as 1940, see U.S. Department of State, *Foreign Relations of the United States: 1940*, vol. IV, *The Far East* (Washington: Government Printing Office, 1955), 672–77.

for the sake of China which could not then be fought for the sake of China and whose practical value for China at the time was, to say the least, dubious. The plain fact is that the United States in 1941 was not capable of forcing Japan out of China by means short of war and was neither willing nor, under existing circumstances, able to throw the Japanese out by war. The American government could conceivably have told the Chinese this and tried to work out the best possible program of help for China under these limitations. Instead, it yielded to Chinese importunities and followed a policy almost sure to eventuate in war, knowing that if the Japanese did attack, China and her deliverance would have to take a back seat. It is difficult to conceive of such a policy as a program of practical aid to China.

The main, though not the only, reason why this policy was followed is clearly the overwhelming importance of principle in American diplomacy, particularly the principle of nonappeasement of aggressors. Once most leaders in the administration and wide sections of the public became convinced that it was America's prime moral duty to stand hard and fast against aggressors, whatever the consequences, and once this conviction became decisive in the formulation of policy, the end result was almost inevitable: a policy designed to uphold principle and to punish the aggressor, but not to save the victim.[22]

It is this conviction as to America's moral duty, however sincere and understandable, which the writer believes constitutes a fundamental misreading of America's moral task. The policy it gave rise to

[22] It is Secretary of War Henry L. Stimson who gives evidence on how strong was the role of avenging justice in the prevailing picture of America's moral duty. He displays a striking anxiety to acquit the administration of the charge of being "soft" on Japan and to prove that the administration was always fully aware of the Japanese crimes and morally aroused by them. The nation's leaders, he insists in one place, were "as well aware as their critics of the wickedness of the Japanese." Avenging justice, too, plays an important role in the defense he makes of the postwar Nuremberg and Tokyo war crimes trials. These trials, he claims, fulfilled a vital moral task. The main trouble with the Kellogg Pact and the policy of nonrecognition and moral sanctions, according to Stimson, was that they named the international law-breakers but failed to capture and punish them. The United States, along with other nations in the prewar world, had neglected "a duty to catch the criminal. . . . Our offense was thus that of the man who passed by on the other side." Now, this is a curious revision of the parable of the Good Samaritan, to which the Secretary here alludes. According to the Stimson version, the Good Samaritan should not have stopped to bind up the victim's wounds, put him on his beast of burden, and arrange for his care. Had he been cognizant of his real moral duty, he would rather have mounted his steed and rode off in hot pursuit of the robbers, to bring them to justice. This is only an illustration, but an apt one, of the prevailing concept of America's moral duty, with its emphasis on meting out justice rather than doing good (Stimson and Bundy, *On Active Service*, 384, 262).

was bad not simply because it was moralistic but because it was obsessed with the wrong kind of morality—with that abstract "Let justice be done though the heavens fall" kind which so often, when relentlessly pursued, does more harm than good. It would be interesting to investigate the role which this conception of America's moral task played in the formulation of the American war aims in the Far East, with their twin goals of unconditional surrender and the destruction of Japan as a major power, especially after the desire to vindicate American principles and to punish the aggressor was intensified a hundredfold by the attack on Pearl Harbor.[23] To pursue the later implications of this kind of morality in foreign policy, with its attendant legalistic and vindictive overtones, would, however, be a task for another volume.

In contrast, the different kind of policy which Grew advocated and toward which Roosevelt so long inclined need not really be considered immoral or unprincipled, however much it undoubtedly would have been denounced as such. A limited modus vivendi agreement would not have required the United States in any way to sanction Japanese aggression or to abandon her stand on Chinese integrity and independence. It would have constituted only a recognition that the American government was not then in a position to enforce its principles, reserving for America full freedom of action at some later, more favorable time. Nor would it have meant the abandonment and betrayal of China. Rather it would have involved the frank recognition that the kind of help the Chinese wanted was impossible for the United States to give at that time. It would in no way have precluded giving China the best kind of help then possible—in the author's opinion, the offer of American mediation for a truce in the war and the grant of fuller economic aid to try to help the Chinese recover—and promising China greater assistance once the crucial European situation was settled. Only that kind of morality which sees every sort of dealing with an aggressor, every instance of accommodation or conciliation, as appeasement and therefore criminal would find the policy immoral.[24]

[23] Admiral William D. Leahy (*I Was There* [New York: McGraw-Hill, 1950], 81) expresses his view of America's war aims in dubious Latin but with admirable forthrightness: "*Delenda est Japanico.*" He was, of course, not the only American leader to want to emulate Cato.
[24] See the introductory remarks on the possibilities of appeasement, under certain circumstances, as a useful diplomatic tool, along with an excellent case study in the wrong use of it, in J. W. Wheeler-Bennett, *Munich: Prologue to Tragedy* (London: Macmillan, 1948), 3–8.

What the practical results of such a policy, if attempted, would have been is of course a matter for conjecture. It would be rash to claim that it would have saved China, either from her wartime collapse or from the final victory of communism. It may well be that already in 1941 the situation in China was out of control. Nor can one assert with confidence that, had this policy enabled her to keep out of war with Japan, the United States would have been able to bring greater forces to bear in Europe much earlier, thus shortening the war and saving more of Europe from communism. Since the major part of the American armed forces were always concentrated in Europe and since in any case a certain proportion would have had to stand guard in the Pacific, it is possible that the avoidance of war with Japan, however desirable in itself, would not have made a decisive difference in the duration of the European conflict. The writer does, however, permit himself the modest conclusions that the kind of policy advocated by Grew presented real possibilities of success entirely closed to the policy actually followed and that it was by no means so immoral and unprincipled that it could not have been pursued by the United States with decency and honor.

Norman A. Graebner

ROOSEVELT AND THE JAPANESE

The following selection is taken from an impressive volume of collected papers presented at a bi-national conference held in Japan in 1969, when Japanese and American scholars joined to review the many factors that played a part in plunging the two nations into war. Graebner's essay maintains that Roosevelt did not expect Japan to fight if Britain and the United States stood firm. Should the President have listened to moderates like Ambassador Grew? Although Japanese leaders accepted war as an alternative if diplomatic efforts failed, Roosevelt hoped to avoid a war that appeared beyond our means at that time. Should the United States have revised its view of our Asian interests? Did the country have anything to gain by preventing Japan from becoming the dominant power in Asia?

By mid-1940 it was clear that Roosevelt's defense of principles in the Far East had failed to bring peace. Nevertheless United States officials still assumed that a combination of Chinese resistance and the mere threat of economic sanctions would stop Japan without any recognition of Japanese gains in China. They were wrong. The Japanese, unable to negotiate an acceptable agreement with China, now moved to consolidate their Asian position by controlling the southern approaches to China. At the same time the threat of an American embargo, especially on oil, focused Japanese attention on the oil resources of the Netherlands East Indies. The German offensive against Holland, Belgium, and France in May-June 1940 rendered the Dutch and French empires in Asia vulnerable to Japanese expansion. During June the Japanese Foreign Ministry extorted the promise of a million tons of oil from the Dutch authorities in the Indies and pressed France for the right to blockade the Indochinese border with China.

For Washington the Japanese move into Southeast Asia shifted the issue from concern for the treaty structure in China to defense of the East Asian balance of power. Immediately United States policy began to harden as the Roosevelt administration began anew its search for the elusive deterrent. Admiral Harold Stark, chief of naval operations, explained that the continued presence of the fleet at

From Norman A. Graebner, "Hoover, Roosevelt, and the Japanese," in D. Borg and S. Okamoto, eds., *Pearl Harbor as History* (New York: Columbia University Press, 1973), pp. 44–52, footnotes omitted. Reprinted by permission of the publisher.

Pearl Harbor "would serve as a deterrent, even if the U.S. were not in fact prepared to take action if the Japanese attacked the Dutch Indies. The mere uncertainty as to U.S. intentions would hold them back." Then on July 2 the new National Defense Act gave the president authority to place under license arms, munitions, critical and strategic raw materials, airplane parts, optical instruments, and metal working machinery. But this new order omitted the two items Japan needed most urgently—oil and scrap iron. The moderates in the State Department, led by Hamilton, were still determined to avoid a showdown with Japan and the encouragement of a Japanese invasion of the East Indies. Grew warned the administration in July that the continuing hard line on negotiations would soon compel Japan to join the Axis.

Still convinced that Japan could be stopped without war, the hard-line faction around Roosevelt pressed for an embargo and no compromise. In July Roosevelt himself strengthened this group immeasurably by naming Stimson secretary of war and Knox secretary of the navy, two men who shared Hornbeck's long-standing opposition to Japanese policy. "The only way to treat Japan," declared Stimson shortly after taking office, "is not to give her anything." On July 20 the president signed a bill to create a two-ocean navy. In time, the administration hoped, the United States would be able to confront Japan in the Pacific without deserting Britain in the Atlantic. At this point, under increased insistence from Stimson, Knox, and Morgenthau, Roosevelt ignored Sumner Welles' warning that further pressure would provoke a Japanese advance into Southeast Asia and on July 25, 1940 signed an order to include oil and scrap iron in the export license system. Subsequently, however, the State Department moderates forced a compromise that limited export restrictions to aviation motor fuel and lubricants and heavy iron and steel scrap. Japan countered with further thrusts into Indochina and increased demands for East Indian oil. The president responded to a Japanese ultimatum regarding Indochina in September by terminating the export of scrap iron and steel to Japan, but it seemed clear that further economic pressures on Japan would encourage not submission but a more rapid advance to the south and possibly war with the United States. Grew's prediction of July proved correct. On September 27, 1940 Japan signed the Tripartite Pact with Germany and Italy.

Still the illusion of Japanese vulnerability and momentary collapse did not die. Those who favored a stronger policy to restrain

Japan—whether through economic sanctions, a show of naval might in the western Pacific, or aid to China—assumed that United States resistance would produce the desired result without direct United States military involvement in the Pacific. Early in October 1940, in a letter which Roosevelt distributed to his key advisers, Enoch Walter Earle, a New York attorney, urged the administration to grant a large and immediate loan to China, reinforce the Asiatic squadron, impose an absolute embargo on Japan, and increase American aid to Britain. "Japan," he warned, "must be stopped sooner or later." Later that month Ickes urged the president to impose an oil embargo on Japan. It would not stop Japanese expansion into Southeast Asia, he admitted, but shortages of oil would render an attack on the Dutch East Indies more difficult. The more optimistic Stimson urged a display of United States military power in the East Indies to prevent a Japanese invasion. As Stimson declared in a memorandum of October 2, Japan "has also historically shown that when the United States indicates by clear language and bold actions that she intends to carry out a clear and affirmative policy in the Far East, Japan will yield to that policy even though it conflicts with her own Asiatic policy and conceived interest. But Admirals Stark and James O. Richardson, commander of the United States Fleet, opposed any American naval presence in Southeast Asia. With this judgment Roosevelt and Hull agreed. During November a secret naval report made clear that the United States was not prepared for war in the Pacific. Whereas with Britian's collapse, ran the report, "we might not *lose everywhere,* we might, possibly, not *win anywhere."* The United States, with its deep interest in the Far Eastern balance of power, the report warned, dared not reduce Japan to a second-class power.

Roosevelt continued to move cautiously. On November 30 he placed another $100 million at Chiang's disposal and promised China fifty modern pursuit planes immediately. In December a State Department memorandum assured the president that China was inflicting heavy casualties on the Japanese and further aid to China, including the establishment of a Chinese air force, would permit China to dispose of the Japanese invasion without further risk to the United States. Roosevelt dispatched some ships and planes to the Philippines under the principle, as explained by Hull, of "letting them [the Japanese] guess as to when and in what set of circumstances we would fight. While Japan continued to guess, we continued to get ready for anything she might do." Unfortunately the vagueness of

Roosevelt's policy kept the British guessing no less than the Japanese. As Harry Hopkins reported to Roosevelt from London in December 1940, "Eden asked me repeatedly what our country would do if Japan attacked Singapore or the Dutch East Indies, saying it was essential to their policy to know." Roosevelt refused to answer. Three weeks later he explained his dilemma to Grew: "The problems which we face are so vast and so interrelated that any attempt even to state them compels one to think of five continents and seven seas." The United States, he admitted, was on the defensive. It could not establish hard and fast plans; it could only determine its course as circumstances permitted. If United States policy in the Pacific continued to perform on a "twenty-four hour" basis, the reason is clear. Roosevelt was never able to establish goals in the Far East which reflected the nation's limited interests, its lack of available strength, and its desire to avoid war. Nor could he, at any price, create a world which conformed to established American principles. No available policy, in short, could bridge the gulf between the nation's limited power and its unlimited objectives in the Orient.

Long before Admiral Nomura Kichisaburō reached Washington as Japanese ambassador in February 1941 to reopen conversations amid a crisis atmosphere, the character of United States-Japanese relations, as well as their diplomatic hopelessness, was well established. The Japanese challenge appeared obvious enough. As Hull reminded the House Foreign Affairs Committee in January: "It has been clear throughout that Japan has been actuated . . . by broad and ambitious plans for establishing herself in a dominant position in the entire region of the Western Pacific. Her leaders have openly declared their determination to achieve and maintain that position by force of arms." Still the administration, while rejecting any thought of compromise, hoped to counter Japan on all Asian fronts by exerting moral and, if necessary, economic pressure. At stake was less the defense of China than the nation's capacity to establish the principle of peaceful change. Hull spelled out United States purposes in a note to Roosevelt in March 1941: "We wish to be friends . . . with any nation in the world—but in our concept real friendship and real cooperation can prevail only between and among nations each and all of which want peace, justice, and security for all." Japan scarcely conformed to such standards.

Roosevelt greeted Nomura on February 14. Earlier the State Department had advised the president, in his conversations with the

Japanese ambassador, to adopt the tactics of Theodore Roosevelt: to "speak softly" without any hint of compromise "while simultaneously giving by our acts in the Pacific new glimpses of diplomatic, economic, and naval 'big sticks.' " Roosevelt addressed Nomura as an old friend but reminded him that the American people were troubled over Japanese aggression in the Far East. Because United States-Japanese relations were strained, Roosevelt suggested that Nomura "sit down with the Secretary of State and other State Department officials and review and reexamine the important phases of the relations between the two countries, . . . to see if our relations could not be improved."

Nomura awaited specific instructions from Tokyo. On March 8 he opened conversations with Hull which were to continue until December. From the beginning the disagreements were profound. Hull made it clear that the United States would accept no settlement until Japan abandoned its aggression and agreed to negotiate on the basis of the established treaty structure. Nomura responded that Japan's expansionism resulted not from a desire for conquest but to counter Western pressures and advantages in the Far East. He assured Hull as well as other Washington officials that his country did not want war with the United States but warned that embargoes would force Japan to take additional military steps. During subsequent meetings the two negotiators extended and embroidered their arguments; they never approached an agreement.

On April 16 Hull presented Nomura the four-point demands that became the final stand of the United States government:

> *(1) Respect for the territorial integrity and the sovereignty of each and all nations; (2) support of the principle of noninterference in the internal affairs of other countries; (3) support of the principle of equality, including equality of commercial opportunity; (4) nondisturbance of the status quo in the Pacific except as the status quo may be altered by peaceful means.*

There could be no negotiation, Hull declared, until Japan agreed to these four principles. He suggested that Japan adopt the principle of the good neighbor and establish mutually beneficial relations with its Far Eastern neighbors as the United States had done in Latin America. Nomura replied that the United States enjoyed special privileges in South America and the Caribbean which the Western powers would never grant Japan in the Orient. Nomura's dispatch to

Tokyo scarcely revealed the full extent of Hull's demands, for he wanted the conversations to continue. Yet so bitter and pervasive were the disputes in Tokyo that the Japanese government did not respond for another month.

If Japan wanted peace, the Japanese reply of May 12 rejected totally the capitulation that Hull's principles demanded. It asked Roosevelt to compel Chiang to negotiate a peace with Japan (under threat of a cessation of all United States aid to China) in accordance with principles that would leave China independent but obligated to cooperate with Japan in the future. Hull distrusted the Japanese formula, for it failed to state precisely what terms Japan intended to impose. In exchange for peace in China, moreover, Japan demanded a resumption of normal trade relations with the United States. Hull found the proposal completely unacceptable.

To break this deadlock, both Japan and the United States began to escalate the means of policy available to them. To conserve shipping space in the Atlantic, Washington on June 20, 1941 terminated all shipments of oil from Atlantic ports except to the fighting British empire and the western hemisphere. But Ickes was not satisfied. He addressed Roosevelt on June 23: "There will never be so good a time to stop the shipment of oil to Japan as we now have. Japan is so occupied with what is happening in Russia and what may happen in Siberia that she won't venture a hostile move against the Dutch East Indies." An embargo on oil, wrote Ickes, would enjoy popular approval throughout the United States. Roosevelt asked Ickes if he would favor an embargo if this were "to tip the delicate scales and cause Japan to decide either to attack Russia or to attack the Dutch East Indies." To Ickes, who now tendered his resignation from the cabinet, such possible Japanese decisions were immaterial. "Foreign wars," he wrote on June 25, "cannot be fought without oil and gasoline, and we are furnishing Japan with this sine qua non in order to fight against what we are fighting for." Roosevelt reminded Ickes on July 1 that Japan was experiencing a deep internal struggle in its attempt to decide whether to invade Siberia, attack the Indies, or sit on the fence and be more friendly to the United States. "No one knows," he concluded, "what the decision will be but, as you know, it is terribly important for the control of the Atlantic for us to help to keep peace in the Pacific. I simply have not got enough Navy to go round—and every little episode in the Pacific means fewer ships in the Atlantic."

Unable to reach agreement with either the United States or China, the Japanese government at an Imperial Conference on July 2 decided to establish the Greater East Asia Coprosperity Sphere and achieve a settlement of the China Incident with an invasion of Indochina, whatever the obstacles encountered. Whereas the Konoye government still hoped to avoid war with the United States, it was now determined to choke off further Chinese resistance before the United States crippled Japan with economic sanctions. On July 10 Acting Secretary of State Welles notified the British ambassador of Roosevelt's decision to counter any Japanese thrust into Southeast Asia with economic and financial embargoes. Several days later General George C. Marshall informed Roosevelt that a decoded Japanese message contained an ultimatum to France for the Japanese occupation of naval and air bases in Indochina. But in Washington the Japanese embassy denied any knowledge of an intended Japanese occupation of Indochina. On July 20 Nomura called on Admiral Richmond Kelly Turner, who reported the conversation to Admiral Stark. Turner warned that an embargo would drive Japan toward the East Indies and possibly into war with the United States. He recommended that existing trade with Japan continue. Stark on July 21 sent this report to Roosevelt with the notation, "I concur in general." For him the navy faced enough challenges in the Atlantic.

On July 23 Nomura asked for a meeting with Welles. He admitted that the Japanese government had concluded an agreement with the French Vichy regime for the occupation of southern Indochina. Nothing less, he explained, would guarantee the flow of rice to Japan and terminate the overland flow of supplies to China. He warned again that an oil embargo would enflame Japanese opinion but assured Welles that his government wanted an agreement with the United States based on Hull's four principles. Welles retorted that the Japanese invasion of Indochina was a clear violation of the letter and spirit of those principles and rendered any further conversations pointless. On July 24 Roosevelt received Nomura and warned him that any Japanese move against the Dutch East Indies would provoke Dutch-British resistance and bring a general war to the Far East. He then offered a proposal. If Japan refrained from occupying Indochina, he would "do everything within his power to obtain from the Governments of China, Great Britain, the Netherlands, and of course the United States itself a binding and solemn declaration, provided Japan would undertake the same commitment, to regard Indochina as a neutralized country."

Finally on July 26 Roosevelt, having received no response from Tokyo, issued an executive order freezing Japanese assets in the United States and thus effectively terminating all United States commercial and financial relations with Japan. Roosevelt, unlike Stark, was convinced that Japan would not fight the United States and the British empire simultaneously. This judgement was fundamental to his decisions after July 1941. But Roosevelt, in effect, had given the Japanese the immediate alternative of capitulating or committing more of their strength to the Far Eastern struggle. Again the warnings of the moderates in Washington proved accurate. The Japanese accelerated their move into Southeast Asia while they still had enough oil. The final crisis in United States-Japanese relations was but a matter of time.

No Japanese effort at negotiation after July 1941, despite that nation's narrow choice between prolonged scrimping and expanded war, held any promise of success. Konoye's proposal of August 6 met with immediate rejection in Washington, for he sought to trade Japanese withdrawal from Indochina for restoration of normal trade relations with the United States. The United States, in addition, was to initiate direct Japanese-Chinese negotiations and recognize Japan's special status in Indochina even after the withdrawal of troops. Nor did Konoye's subsequent request for a personal meeting with Roosevelt assure any greater compliance with United States principles. Roosevelt reminded Nomura on August 17 that his administration was standing firmly on the principles laid down by Hull. When Hull in September suggested how the president might explain his past refusal to meet Konoye, Roosevelt replied: "I wholly agree with your pencilled note—to recite the more liberal original attitude of the Japanese when they first sought the meeting, point out their narrowed position now, earnestly ask if they cannot go back to their original attitude, start discussions again on agreement in principle, and reemphasize my hope for a meeting." Still Roosevelt's firmness appeared to Americans as a guarantee of peace. "Any sign of weakness, backing down, or palliation," wrote one Washington attorney in mid-August, "will certainly bring war. The Japanese military officers will consider it due to timidity. If they ever form that opinion, we will certainly have war. . . . There is a chance to avoid a conflict if the present policy is continued."

Confronted by almost universal assumptions of invincibility within the United States, Japan's choices became desperate. Unless Japan returned to its position of 1937, it could never hope to come to terms with Washington. Such a retreat would require fundamental, gradual adjustments, but time was running out. Konoye could not sustain his own or his country's position any longer without an immediate settlement. On October 7 the prime minister's secretary informed the American embassy in Tokyo that private Konoye-Roosevelt negotiations comprised the last hope for peace. "Prince Konoye," he said, "was at a loss to know what further he could do. . . . When Prince Konoye had taken that responsibility [for starting the talks], the Army gave him full and unqualified support, and if his high hopes are not fulfilled he will have to 'assume responsibility,' and there would be no one who would have the courage to take the risks which the Prince has taken or with sufficient prestige and political position to gain the support of the Army."

With the negotiations deadlocked and the two nations standing at the edge of war, the Konoye government fell on October 18. United States-Japanese relations had reached an impasse, not because Tokyo's demands had become greater—indeed, the Japanese, under intense economic pressure, would have accepted less after September than they would have earlier—but because the Roosevelt administration had made it increasingly clear that Tokyo could anticipate no compromise. Thus the final Japanese proposals of November 1941 sought only a modus vivendi—a temporary agreement—not a permanent settlement. That month an Imperial Conference made the fateful decision to fight beginning in December if the United States still refused to compromise on the tangential issues of Indochina and oil sanctions.

Standing firm on principle, the Roosevelt administration in November looked to the nation's defenses. Early that month Chiang warned the president and Churchill that Japan, if it succeeded in closing the Burma Road, would sever China's transportation with the outside world and perhaps force China out of the war. Hull and Roosevelt, reluctant to issue any further warnings unless the United States were prepared to act, turned to the army and navy. Both Marshall and Stark said that the United States should avoid any immediate involvement in the Far East. Already the movement of Flying Fortresses and mechanized equipment to the Philippines was under way. These heavy bombers, with an operating radius of 1500 miles, could reach Japanese cities and hopefully the Japanese positions in Indochina. Stimson had reported to the president on October 21: "A strategic opportunity of the utmost importance has suddenly arisen in the southwestern Pacific. . . . From being impotent to influence events in that area, we suddenly find ourselves vested with the possibility of great effective power . . . even this imperfect threat, if not promptly called by the Japanese, bids fair to stop Japan's march to the south and secure the safety of Singapore." Churchill was equally gratified at the growing United States military presence in the Pacific. He cabled Roosevelt on November 2: "The firmer your attitude and ours, the less chance of their taking the plunge."

No more than Japan did the United States want war. But Roosevelt and his advisers preferred war to recognition of any successful assault on the treaty structure of the Far East. They would fight, not for China, but for the principle of peaceful change and ultimately for the East Asian balance of power. In his press conference of November 28, 1941 Roosevelt declared that United States policy in the Pacific had been based on infinite patience. The situation was serious, he admitted, "because our one desire has been peace in the Pacific, and the taking of no steps to alter the prospects of peace, which of course has meant nonaggression. It really boils down to that." On both China and Indochina United States policy was set, he told the newsmen. There would be no compromise. Nor did Roosevelt's eleventh-hour message to the Japanese emperor on December 6 contain any suggestion of compromise. It was a moving appeal to reason and peace, but ultimately on American terms.

Roosevelt's dilemma in confronting a clearly definable Japanese challenge was understandable. Through two administrations he refused to alter, on the basis of independent advice and judgment, the Far Eastern policy that had been inherited from Hoover and perpetuated by the nation's dominant foreign policy elite. Unwilling to modify the ends of United States policy—the complete unraveling of the Japanese empire—Roosevelt moved cautiously but unerringly toward the acceptance of those judgments which promised victory in Asia without compromise or direct United States involvement. The result was a policy of escalation anchored to economic sanctions and a limited show of force. With each major increment of pressure, the administration sought and anticipated a Japanese capitulation.

Washington officials anchored their optimism to two assumptions. First, they believed Japan so vulnerable to United States economic policy that its government would ultimately be compelled to relent in its defiance of the Far Eastern status quo. Stimson himself informed a cabinet meeting on October 4 that "in the autumn of 1919 President Wilson got his dander up and put on an embargo on all cotton going to Japan and a boycott on her silk, with the result that she crawled down within two months and brought all of her troops out from Siberia like whipped puppies." Whatever the truth of Stimson's observation, no Japanese government would submit to economic and moral sanctions in 1941.

Second, Hornbeck and others assured Roosevelt repeatedly that Japan would avoid war with the United States, especially if the nation remained resolute. In January 1941 Hornbeck developed the thesis that Japan always went to war suddenly and with a minimum of warning. Japan's open belligerence, he concluded, was evidence that Tokyo was engaged in a campaign of bluff. As late as November 27, 1941 Hornbeck declared that in his opinion "the Japanese Government does not intend or expect to have forthwith armed conflict with the United States. The Japanese Government, while launching new offensive operations at some point or points in the Far East will endeavor to avoid attacking or being attacked by the United States." The disparity between Japanese and United States power was profound, but those who controlled Japanese policy, facing the simple choice between total capitulation or an interminable war in China, chose the most drastic solution available—a direct attack on the United States Asiatic Fleet. As Prime Minister Tojo Hideki once phrased it, "sometimes a man has to jump with his eyes closed from the temple of Kiyomizu into the ravine below." Roosevelt no less than Hoover had identified the American interest in the Pacific with the moral defense of existing treaties. Unfortunately, as Stimson observed so clearly ten years earlier, the old treaty structure no longer had much relationship to the political and military realities of the Far East.

Akira Iriye

TOWARD PEARL HARBOR

In this selection from Across the Pacific *(1967), Akira Iriye deals with the images the United States, Japan, and China had of each other. Born in Japan, educated at Haverford and Harvard University, Iriye is uniquely equipped to understand the thinking of these three peoples and to read their languages in the original. Unlike earlier historians who wrote to justify policies or condemn them, Iriye is representative of more recent scholarship engaged in analyzing factors that determined events the better to understand them. His view, that war came in the Pacific because of misguided or mistaken notions on both sides, is similar to the position of James Mac-Gregor Burns, author of one of the best biographies of Roosevelt, an excerpt of which is reprinted earlier in this volume. Why does Iriye differ with Schroeder about the importance of China in our policy formulation? Does Iriye's analysis suggest comparisons with views of recent presidents and their advisers concerning our national interest?*

For about ten years after 1938, Sino-American cooperation against Japan defined both East Asian politics and what the three peoples thought of their relations as they faced each other. For most Chinese the American alliance was merely a fulfillment of what they had foreseen; for most Japanese the Sino-American coalition signaled a final obstacle in the way of their attempt to establish a new Asian order; while for Americans the new tripartite drama dissipated the tension that had existed between their moral universalism and political parochialism. By 1948, however, Chinese were denouncing the United States for interference in their domestic politics and for trying to resurrect Japanese militarism; Americans were becoming upset over the Chinese civil war; and Japanese were turning almost exclusively to America for help and advice, material and spiritual.

It is a measure of the superficial nature of American-Chinese-Japanese contact that such drastic transformations should have taken place in their mutual perceptions in less than ten years. Looked at historically, however, it also becomes evident that these changes were not as unnatural as might appear. For Americans, China had become a moral question. If sentiment dictated support of a tragic China during the war, it also called for rejection of a hostile

China after the war. Security considerations, on the other hand, had necessitated the policy of American resistance to Japanese expansionism; after Japan's defeat the same considerations would result in a policy of containing China. In the long drama of Sino-American confrontation, it was the brief moment of cooperation that was exceptional, rather than the mutual antagonism that followed the war. For this very reason, the years of direct American involvement in China merit serious study as an extraordinary interlude in otherwise friction-ridden relations.

American Policy and Global Security

The American-Japanese war was brought about by Japan's decision to extend its control over Southeast Asia and by America's determination to prevent it. Beginning in 1938, the Japanese military pushed their China campaign southward to offshore islands and eventually to French Indochina. Their undisguised aim was to achieve the control of the Dutch East Indies as well as Singapore. The inclusion of all these regions would enable Japan to form a gigantic Asian bloc, presumably an impregnable fortress and a source of most raw materials that were needed for national defense. It was such moves that ran counter to the American policy of defending the status quo in Southeast Asia. The survival of the British, Dutch, and French colonies in Asia necessitated America's involvement in that part of the world and led directly to war with Japan. It is obvious that Southeast Asia became a crucial factor in American-Japanese relations because of developments in Europe after 1938. Japanese penetration, actual and premeditated, of Southeast Asia was prompted by the German victories and the expectation of further victories in Europe, while America's opposition to Japanese "southern advance" was designed to prevent the collapse of the British empire, which was, Americans thought, essential to the survival of England itself. A Japanese victory over China would release resources for southern expansion, whereas a prolonged Sino-Japanese war would tie the Japanese military down on the continent of Asia and prevent them from penetrating the colonial empires to the south.

Thus, ultimately as a result of the European war, the Sino-Japanese war developed into a Pacific war via southeast Asia. The United States became involved in the East Asian conflict because the survival of Britain in Europe and in Asia was considered vital to

America's own security. Seen from such a perspective, it is clear that no single road led to Pearl Harbor. Without the German-British war there might not have been a Japanese-American war, and without the collapse of France in Europe there might not have developed a Southeast Asian Crisis. The Sino-Japanese war did not automatically result in war between the United States and Japan. There had, after all, been no war between the latter before 1941, and no grave crisis before 1938. From new situations in Europe and in southeast Asia grew distinct possibilities of armed conflict in the Pacific.

But if those were the realities of prewar American–East Asian relations, what was perceived was very different. There still exists the myth, shared by many scholars in the three countries, that the United States and Japan went to war over China, and that, whether for moral, economic, or other motives, the United States was determined to prevent Japanese domination of China. Such a view of the recent past is convenient on many counts. For Americans it gives a psychologically satisfactory explanation for the origin of the Pacific war: America had gone to the rescue of the beleaguered Chinese. It is just a step from that to the corollary that the Chinese have betrayed American generosity, that they have bitten the hands that fed them. For the Chinese, also from the postwar perspective, the Pacific war appears as the beginning of America's unmistakable intervention in Asia, leading up to the postwar policy of interference in Chinese domestic politics. Many American, Chinese, and Japanese historians picture Japan as intent on establishing a predominant position in China ever since the Russo-Japanese War, and the United States as countering this intent with the policy of the Open Door. In fact, many still see in the Pacific war a culmination of the American-Japanese conflict in China that emerged after 1905.

Some contemporaries in the United States, China, and Japan, however, clearly saw the key issues in the late 1930s. In America, there is no doubt that, beginning in 1938, the conviction grew that the East Asian crisis was no longer an isolated phenomenon but was part of a developing world crisis. Italy and Germany had revealed their intention of altering the status quo by force even before 1936, but there was a time lag between these developments and the realization in the United States of the seriousness of the crisis. The crucial factor seems to have been the series of diplomatic crises in Europe in 1938, culminating in the Munich fiasco. It was in this connection that Japanese action in China throughout 1938, conquer-

ing Hankow and Canton and enunciating the principle of a new order
in East Asia, appeared particularly ominous. In the minds of American policymakers, a clear link was established between the developments in Europe and in East Asia. There emerged the possibility, as
they saw it, that the aggressive nations, in particular Germany and
Japan, might band together and collectively menace the status quo
and peace in the whole world. It seemed imperative to respond to the
challenge if America's security and its concomitant, peace in the
world, were to be maintained. Aggression in Asia must be resisted to
discourage lawless action in Europe. Moral globalism was given official status by security considerations.

A few examples will illustrate the new language of global security.
In July 1939 Secretary of State Hull told the Japanese ambassador,

> *We consider the preservation of peace so supremely important to the*
> *future of all nations that we draw the line between honest, law-abiding,*
> *peaceful countries and peoples, without reference to their form of Gov-*
> *ernment, on the one hand, and those who are flouting law and order and*
> *officially threatening military conquest without limit as to time or ex-*
> *tent; . . . we will work in a friendly spirit with every peaceful nation to*
> *promote and preserve peace, without serious thought as to who they are.*

In this unusually strong language Secretary Hull, the symbol of caution before 1938, put forth the philosophy of globalism in its simplest
form. It is to be noted that he stressed the division of the world into
peace-loving countries and aggressors "without serious thought as
to who they are." It did not matter whether the aggressor or the
victim of aggression was in Europe or in Asia, a democracy or a
socialist state. What mattered was the distinction between the party
of order and that standing for forceful alteration of the status quo.

From Hull's and his colleagues' point of view, Japan's self-styled
new order in East Asia was the epitome of lawlessness. At the end of
December 1938, the United States openly rejected the Japanese contention that a new situation had arisen in East Asia, necessitating
changes in the principles of international conduct. The United States
government did not admit, it declared, "that there is need or warrant
for any one Power to take upon itself to prescribe what shall be the
terms and conditions of a 'new order' in areas not under its
sovereignty and to constitute itself the repository of authority and the
agent of destiny in regard thereto." In a similar vein Ambassador
Grew made his famous speech at an America-Japan Society meeting

in Tokyo in October 1939. He reiterated the belief that international peace was dependent on law and order; this was particularly the case, he said, since nations were economically interdependent. Grew reminded the Japanese that "the present trend in the Far East, if continued, will be destructive of the hopes which [the American people] sincerely cherish of the development of an orderly world." The new order in East Asia ran counter to the American aspiration for "security, stability, and progress not only for themselves but for all other nations in every quarter of the world."

As often happens, military strategists perceived most clearly the trend toward global conflict. Before 1938 American naval and army planning vis-à-vis Japan had been conceived in terms of an "Orange war"—war in the Pacific against Japan. After 1938, however, strategic thinking was centered around a "Rainbow war," that is, war involving the Atlantic as well as the Pacific, Germany and Italy as well as Japan. Various possibilities were considered, depending on the timing of the war, capabilities of the belligerents, and geographical distribution of armed strengths. There was little doubt, after 1939, that the United States would cooperate with Britain to fight against an Axis alliance. Here the question of priority had to be raised; should the United States concentrate its resources first in the Atlantic or in the Pacific? Much depended on specific situations, and of the five Rainbow plans that were drafted in 1939, three envisaged a strategic defensive in the Pacific, while two specified an offensive. In the end the strategy of defeating the enemy first in Europe and then in Asia was adopted, but the tradition of global strategy had been firmly established by the end of the 1930s.

Now that Japan was identified with Germany, the psychological transition was made to identify China with the democracies in Europe. As Hull's statement indicates, the United States was to assist the victims of aggression regardless of their form of government. America would help China resist Japan just as it would encourage British and French opposition to German militarism. Before 1938 the United States had not been moved to come to the aid of China in any substantial degree, and had rationalized its passivity in numerous ways. Now a sudden turn to positive action was accompanied by the image of the world divided between two camps. Without the awareness of the global crisis, one suspects, there would not have been a shift of attitude toward China. One notices, for instance, that American business publications began denouncing Japan and expressing support of China only after 1940. Some of them, in fact, maintained an awkward silence on the East Asian situation throughout 1940 and then began attacking Japan in 1941. It is obvious that the shift was due to the awareness of the European war and its implications for East Asia. Opinion polls, too, began to show signs that the American public was now willing not only to express themselves unequivocally in sympathy with China but to approve of certain measures short of war to restrain Japan. The feeling was that the crisis in China was closely related to America's own security problems, now that Germany and Japan were emerging as the twin threat to the peace of the world. It is interesting to note, too, that such specialists on American East Asian policy as Paul W. Clyde and A. Whitney Griswold were subtly changing their attitude toward the East Asian question. Earlier they had expressed the view that America's basic interest in Asia was economic and that whatever Japan did in China was not America's business. Griswold's classic *Far Eastern Policy of the United States,* published in 1938, may be regarded as characteristic of the era of isolationist writings on the subject. He eloquently pled for America's noninvolvement in East Asia so long as its essential economic interests were not injured. For him the whole adventure in Asian politics, begun in the 1890s, had been misplaced politically and confused morally. Clyde had written much in a similar vein. By early 1941, however, they were talking of the relevance of the East Asian crisis to America's security. In an extremely lucid analysis, Griswold pointed out that the East Asian crisis and the European crisis had been merged and that America's and Britain's security had become menaced. The best safeguard for Anglo-American security seemed to lie in an undeclared peace in East Asia and an undeclared war in Europe. The idea was that the United States should do all it could to assist the British effort at survival, and to this end it seemed best to take a cautious stand toward Japan. Clyde declared that Japan's new order rested upon "a system which, whatever its merits may be, is the antithesis of every ideal represented by a century of American policy in China." Although he had tended to be sympathetic toward Japan's aspirations in China and critical of America's unilateral adherence to the Open Door policy, he now came around to a solid denunciation of Japanese action.

Since they were predisposed to thinking in terms of global security, it was natural that Americans should find Japan's alliance with Germany, consummated in September 1940, final evidence that the

two arch-aggressors had combined forces to challenge the democracies and conquer the world. In American thinking a point of no
return seemed to have been reached when the Japanese recklessly,
as it appeared, entered into a pact for universal aggression. The
spectacle of Japan and Germany subjugating the weak nations and
dominating the Atlantic and the Pacific was frightening. Should England and the British empire fall, their rich resources and naval power
would have been at the service of Germany and Japan. The United
States would be surrounded by a formidable combination of hostile
forces. The only safeguard, then, was to prevent the collapse of the
British empire. "The United States is isolated except for one great
power and that's the British Commonwealth," Secretary of War Stimson wrote down in his diary, "and I already see signs of a realization
of this among the thoughtless." He had long realized the need for
cooperation with Britain, but even the "thoughtless" isolationists
were slowly coming around to such a view. Perhaps the clearest
exposition of the new state of American–East Asian relations was
made by Ambassador Grew in his "green light message" of September 1940, a few days before the signing of the Axis alliance. In the
telegram Grew, who had tried to understand the Japanese side of the
East Asian question for nearly a decade, explicitly castigated Japan
as "one of the predatory powers." He went on,

> American interests in the Pacific are definitely threatened by her policy of
> southward expansion, which is a thrust at the British Empire in the East.
> Admittedly America's security has depended in a measure upon the
> British Fleet, which has been in turn and could only have been supported
> by the British Empire. If the support of the British Empire in this her hour
> of travail is conceived to be in our interest, and most emphatically do I
> so conceive it, we must strive by every means to preserve the status quo
> in the Pacific, at least until the war in Europe has been won or lost.

Here was a clear rationale for new action to deter Japan in Southeast
Asia. Stripped to essentials, Grew's message bespoke the fundamental truth, as he saw it, that American and British security were interdependent. That belief became the guiding principle of American
policy and strategy, as well as of popular thinking from this time on.

The New Order in Asia

The Japanese, too, perceived that Japan's new order was a threat to
British and American security, although few at first were willing to

accept the logical connection between the new order in Asia and the possibility of conflict with the United States. Even those who did accept it disagreed as to which stage of Japanese expansion in Southeast Asia would provoke forceful American intervention. This, however, was a question of military strategy, not of policy.

Southern advance was a basic Japanese policy after 1938. Partly this was a military move, an aspect of the new definition of national security. The military had explained their acts in Manchuria and China as an attempt to create an economically self-sufficient and militarily impregnable "defense state." The bloc embracing Japan, Manchukuo, and China was obviously far from being self-sufficient. From this point of view there was a logical necessity to include Southeast Asia, with its rich mineral and vegetable resources, in the Japanese empire. Such a new order would help reduce Japan's dependence on American supplies of oil, iron, and other materials. Thus from a military standpoint the new order was often conceived of as an alternative to Japanese-American trade. The navy in particular, with its absolute need for fuel oil, came to view a southern advance as an inevitable choice forced upon Japan by America's policy. Since, in naval reasoning, unrestricted trade with America was being endangered by America's policy of opposing Japan in Asia, the latter would have no choice but to strike southward. By 1940, when southern advance was made a national policy, top naval circles had also come to the conclusion that Japanese action in Southeast Asia would bring about conflict not only with Britain but also with the United States. This was because of the view, held by the navy, that Britain and America could not be separated; once Japan struck at British colonies, the United States would be bound to intervene. The question, therefore, was whether war with these two powers justified the policy of southern advance. By late 1940 section chiefs of the Navy Ministry and the Naval General Staff came to the belief that since war with America was sooner or later inevitable, Japan should take the initiative and advance into southern Indochina and the Dutch East Indies to secure naval bases and strategic raw materials. Circular reasoning here is notable. For naval strategists, the policy of southern advance would make conflict with the United States inevitable; since war was bound to occur, Japan should advance southward to prepare itself for the conflict.

The idea of a new order in Asia, however, was not totally a military notion. More and more civilian officials became believers in "pan-regions," several blocs into which the world was to be divided. Each bloc would be dominated by one or two super-powers, and all blocs would coexist harmoniously among themselves. World peace would be maintained on the basis of a balance of power among them. Japan was obviously to be the overlord of Asia, the term that came to include not only China but Southeast Asia. The "expulsion of Anglo-American influence" from Asia, to use an oft-employed phrase, was clearly a first step toward realizing this end. Already at the end of 1938 the Tokyo government had explicitly enunciated its new policy when Foreign Minister Arita Hachirō stated, in a note to the United States, that Japan was building a new order in East Asia and that the old ideas and principles of diplomacy would no longer serve to establish permanent peace there. At the same time, Japan's policymakers believed that the pan-Asian order was compatible with peaceful relations between Japan and the United States, once the latter recognized the new order.

How it was felt that Japan could go on building a new order while avoiding open conflict with America, provides a clue to Japanese thinking. According to Matsuoka Yōsuke, who as foreign minister in 1940–1941 was the major ideologue behind Japanese policy, Japanese-American relations would form part of the global system in which Japan predominated in Asia, Germany and Italy in Europe, the Soviet Union would remain neutral, and the United States would keep its hegemony in the Western Hemisphere. As he wrote in January 1941, "The world is to be divided into the great East Asian zone, the European zone (including Africa), the American zone, and the Soviet zone (including India and Iran), though Australia and New Zealand may be left to England, to be treated in a similar manner as Holland." Matsuoka seems to have been completely sincere in stating again and again that the Axis alliance and Japan's nonaggression pact with Russia, both part of the bloc policy, were designed to prevent war between Japan and the United States. America's influence in Asia and hostility to Japan were such, he thought, that only by presenting a determined stand would America be deterred from entering the war against Japan. Matsuoka's view of America is revealed in an informal statement he made in September 1940 at a government conference. He remarked that Japan was confronted with a choice between the United States and Germany. To choose understanding and coopera-tion with the former would entail a settlement of the China war in accordance with America's dictates, abandonment of the new order idea, and submission to Anglo-American influence for at least half a century. Amity with America and Britain would bring material benefits to Japan, he conceded, but the Japanese should remember what happened after the First World War, when Japan was their ally. Moreover, the Chiang Kai-shek regime would be emboldened and openly insult Japan. Thus Matsuoka justified the Axis alliance as essential to the completion of the new order. Japan would force American acquiescence in the new order by its very existence and splendor. From Matsuoka's and his supporters' point of view, the crisis with America had progressed to such an extent that only a bold new stroke of policy would work in maintaining Japanese-American peace. They were so captivated by their own logic that they did not note the primitive circularity of their reasoning. Nevertheless, their perception of America was realistic in that Americans, too, had come to view their relations with Japan in the light of the new order in East Asia.

Outside of the military and the government, there was in Japan a great deal of theorizing about what was called the Great East Asian Co-Prosperity Sphere. It is remarkable that the Japanese, who had developed few ideas of international relations, suddenly poured forth treatise after treatise about the meaning of East Asian conflict. A good example of Japanese thinking after 1938 is an article by Ozaki Hotsumi, a Marxist thinker, entitled "The Idea of the 'East Asian Co-operative System' and the Objective Bases of its Formation," which appeared in the January 1939 issue of *Chūōkōron*. Although he had China specifically in mind rather than the whole of Asia, the author wrote that nationalism was a basis of the new order. The cooperative state system in Asia would be a "regional, racial, cultural, economic, and defensive combination," which would shield itself against the West's imperialistic expansionism. There must be genuine cooperation among the member states, although it would be justifiable for Japan to assert its special status within the combination. The new order seemed economically inevitable, as an increase in productive power in Asia was destroying the equilibrium in the colonial societies. Their liberation and welfare would be promoted by economic cooperation within the East Asian bloc. This was also the best way for Japanese capitalism to survive in competition with Western capitalist nations. At the same time, Ozaki emphasized the need for Japan's internal economic and political transformation so as to enable it truly to play a central and leading role in the new order.

Here an avowed Marxist was justifying Japanese policy while advocating internal reform, a response common to a vast number of Japanese liberals and leftists at this time. There was something appealing in the idea of a new Asian order, liberated from Western influence and truly integrated economically and politically. Such an image of Japan's mission was shared by a whole range of Japanese writers, from traditional ultranationalists to Marxist intellectuals. They had come to interpret the history of modern Asia as a story of Western capitalist exploitation. Japan was leading a crusade to free Asia. In the new dispensation the language of harmony would replace that of force, and the principle of co-prosperity would take the place of capitalism, materialism, and individualism. America was the symbol of the West, and the establishment of a new order necessarily meant rejection of America's role in Asia. It goes without saying that much ink was spent rationalizing the alliance with Germany and Italy while theoretically rejecting the West. Somehow these countries were seen as an antithesis of the United States and other democracies and therefore as more "Japanese." Such were the extremes to which the ideology of the new order led Japanese thinking. At any rate, the image of Western exploitation of Asia lay behind Japanese policy toward China, Southeast Asia, and the United States.

China: The Expectation of American Aid

The Chinese, too, believed that Western imperialism had been a key factor in China's deterioration. But they saw an even greater foe in Japan. A few of them, in particular those that joined Wang Ching-wei's Nanking government under Japanese sponsorship and control, were ideologically motivated by anticommunism; but they were far from enthusiastic about the Japanese-proclaimed new order in Asia. They seem to have reasoned that the United States would not intervene in the East Asian war and therefore Japan would subjugate Chungking. It seemed best, therefore, to salvage what was left of China if the only alternative was continued desolation of the land or an increase in Communist strength. By the last years of the 1930s, however, the vast majority of Chinese were confident of American support. Though they had been disappointed by America's passivity before 1937, they were encouraged by the gathering clouds in Europe which, in their view, were bound to involve the United States in East Asia. The critical situation in Europe after 1938 afforded evidence that they had been right in predicting the coming of a world war as a result of Japanese aggression. Chiang Kai-shek was only reiterating a popular and long-standing conviction when he declared, in January 1939, that international conditions were favorable to the defense of peace and justice; people in Europe and America, he said, were more and more loudly denouncing aggression.

There was particular reason for the Chungking government to desire American help. With Germany approaching Japan, and Britain adopting an appeasement policy, Nationalist China's only substantial friend before 1939 was the Soviet Union. For obvious reasons Chiang Kai-shek was unwilling to rely solely on Soviet assistance, no matter how valuable and timely it had proved. If he was to resist Japan and at the same time forestall Communist subversion, the only avenue of help had to be the United States. If no American aid could be obtained, China would either have to continue a hopeless war against Japan, inviting further internal chaos and deterioration, a condition favorable for Communist subversion, or it would find itself more and more deeply tied to the Soviet Union, with the same probable result. Close ties with the United States would help solve both the external and domestic problems.

It was no coincidence, then, that the view of America as China's closest ally emerged after 1939, the year of crisis in Europe and resumption of Kuomintang-Communist rift in China. It is undeniable that there was an element of "self-fulfilling prophecy" in Chungking's image of the United States. It was psychologically imperative to believe that moral commitment as well as strategic interest moved Americans to support Kuomintang China; believing that, the government could ask for more and more help, hinting at China's defeat by Japan or take-over by the Communists unless it was given. Because the Nationalist leaders were confident of obtaining American assistance, they could play with time, making a gesture of seeking settlement with Japan or preparing themselves for an eventual showdown with the Communists.

Chinese Communists, on their part, never departed from the theoretical framework of Marxism-Leninism, to which was being added "Maoism," through Mao Tse-tung's idea of "the people's new democracy." According to Mao, China was defined as a semi-colony ruled by a collective dictatorship of all revolutionary classes. The country was neither a bourgeois state nor a proletarian dictatorship, the two types of states that Lenin had identified. Advanced capitalist countries of the West as well as Japan belonged to the former, while only the Soviet Union qualified for the second category. Between the two there were a host of colonies and semi-colonies, which went through a transition stage of "new democracy" on their way to proletarian dictatorship. These societies could not immediately transform themselves into socialist republics but had to go through the stage of collective government by revolutionary classes under the leadership of the proletariat. "Revolutionary classes" were defined tautologically; they were anti-imperialist and anti-feudal, such as proletariat, peasants, intelligentsia, petty bourgeoisie, and national bourgeoisie. These classes would bring about a "new bourgeois democratic revolution" as a necessary stage in China's ultimate development as a socialist state under proletarian dictatorship.

Internally, this theory was at least consistent; all anticommunist groups could simply be branded as feudal and therefore outside the pale of the revolutionary struggle. Externally, strain existed as soon as the imperialists fought not only among themselves but often in alliance with semi-colonial states. So long as the United States and Japan, for instance, clashed over their rights and possessions, such a conflict could be regarded as a purely imperialist power struggle. Actually, some imperialists were more friendly to China than others; and some were closer to the Soviet Union, the only socialist state, than others. The Chinese Communists had to explain away within the framework of "new democracy" such disparate phenomena as the German-British war, the German-Soviet neutrality pact, to be followed by Germany's invasion of Russia, and the Japanese-Soviet nonaggression pact. The theory of coalescence of all revolutionary classes could justify the view that the democratic imperialists, such as the United States, Britain, and France, would come to the aid of China against fascist aggressors. These bourgeois nations might cooperate with the socialist Soviet Union to help China, just as petty and national bourgeoisie in China worked together with the peasants and proletariat to eradicate feudalism. The fact remained, however, that the bourgeois nations were by definition imperialists. The war in Europe was inevitably characterized as the "second imperialist war," fought among imperialists who were alike motivated by anti-Soviet and anti-revolutionary principles. Soviet overtures for temporary rapprochement with Germany and with Japan were defended as necessary tactics to strengthen the socialist state by taking advantage of imperialist politics. These two views of the Western democracies, as imperialist and as anti-fascist, could be reconciled by a view of the state that distinguished between the ruling (bourgeois) class and the masses. Though a bourgeois society was by definition imperialistic, there were the "people," other classes in society, that remained democratic and potentially revolutionary. They could be expected to be in sympathy with the revolutionary struggle abroad. Thus the United States, too, was imperialistic but its people were opposed to imperialism; they were sympathetic to the Chinese as they fought against the Japanese aggressor and against feudal elements at home. Nevertheless, so long as the class structure in a capitalist state remained unchanged, the only reliable ally for the Chinese people was the Soviet Union. It is not surprising, then, that in 1940, in the middle of crisis at home and abroad, Mao Tse-tung should reassert the need to "lean to one side." He wrote, "As the conflict between the socialist Soviet Union and the imperialist Great Britain and the United States becomes further intensified, it is inevitable that China must stand either on one side or on the other." It was simply impossible to be neutral.

It is very difficult to evaluate general Chinese thinking on the United States apart from Kuomintang or Communist party dogma. Many pamphlets and articles written at this time reflected either one of these dogmas. Nevertheless, the two views were not wholly contradictory. All were agreed that the United States was an imperialist power and also that it stood in the way of Japanese aggression. It remained the task of publicists and general writers to apply such theories to concrete situations and somehow present a coherent picture of American policy in East Asia. Chou Chi-ch'üan's *American Far Eastern Policy,* a hundred-page tract published in Changsha in 1940, offers a good example. The book reiterated the clichés about America's Open Door policy as an expression of the country's economic interests and as the antithesis of Japan's policy of monopolistic control over China. But he also emphasized the fact that the United States had developed as a Pacific power, with influence and interests in the western Pacific and East Asia. Japan was challenging this role played by America. As the author saw it, the question was soon to be settled whether American influence would be expelled from Asia. So long as the United States persisted in the policy of the Open Door, such an outcome seemed unlikely. America would resist with all its force Japan's threat to its interests in Asia. However, if it was to continue to play a role in East Asia, it must recognize the mistake of continuing trade with Japan and resolutely come to the aid of China. Americans, the author concluded, should clearly determine what destiny they sought to obtain in Asia. As revealed in such an outline of American–East Asian relations, the Chinese were aware that the United States was confronted with two aspects of the East Asian conflict, one in China and one in the Pacific. The United States was pictured as a naval power in the Pacific whose policy In China had been that of insisting on tho Open Door. Japan's aggression in China compromised the second principle, while its southern advance would threaten the former position. Like the Japanese and the Americans, the Chinese saw that the war in China was becoming part of a Pacific struggle for power, which in turn was an aspect of the global crisis. American policy in China, they felt, would be determined by global considerations. On the whole it is fair to say that pro-Kuomintang writers tended to play up the China aspect of American policy, emphasizing the absolute incompatibility of Japanese and American policies in China. The United States had traditionally opposed the ambitions of a third power to dominate China, and such a long-standing principle could not be surrendered without a fight.

Communist-oriented writings, on the other hand, tended to emphasize the Pacific and international aspects of United States policy. They also agreed that Japan and America stood opposed in China, but Communist and pro-Communist writers put all of this in a Leninist framework. According to Chin Chung-hua, editor of *World Culture,* American involvement in the East Asian crisis was inevitable because the question was being decided as to who was to control the large market of China and who was to dominate the Pacific Ocean. Due to the war in Europe, American capitalists were being forced to turn their attention more and more seriously to the potential market of China. Not that the Japanese market was unimportant. As so many Chinese writers noted uneasily at this time, even after 1940, when the United States repudiated the commercial treaty with Japan, the trade between the two countries went on. A writer bluntly predicted that the United States would come to the aid of China only when its ruling capitalist circles judged that the loss of trade in China due to Japanese aggression outweighed the advantages of continued trade with Japan. However, most authors agreed that trade with Asia was but a part of America's global strategy. More fundamentally, the United States was challenging Japan's bid to establish a new Asian order, with itself as the overlord of the Pacific. As Marxist writers saw the Pacific struggle, there was also a third party, the Soviet Union, which complicated the picture. China's struggle, Chin noted, "is one aspect of the three-cornered struggle in East Asia, involving Japan, the Soviet Union, and the Anglo-Saxon powers." Reflecting Soviet dogma, Chinese Communist writers on occasion expressed anxiety over a great imperialist collaboration against the socialist state. The United States was pictured as oscillating between its hostility toward Japan and toward Russia while trying to prevent rapprochement beween them. At any event, from the Chinese Communist point of view, America's opposition to Japan in the Pacific and in China was of great help to the Chinese people, but they should not delude themselves that such help was selfless. They should try to understand America's global policy and utilize it wherever possible so as to make it serve their struggle for national liberation. In the end only the Chinese people had the key to the future of their country.

Toward War

Despite the theorizing of all concerned, the road to Pearl Harbor was basically a military road. On the American side, of the five Rainbow plans considered after 1939, Rainbow Five was eventually adopted, with its emphasis on the defense of Britain in Europe. The crucial decision was made by the highest authorities in the winter of 1940–1941, based on the recommendation of Admiral Harold R. Stark, chief of naval operations. Called Plan Dog, his proposal called for an offensive in Europe and a defensive in the Pacific. Until British survival was ensured, it was considered best to delay decisive action vis-à-vis Japan. At the same time, Japan's southern advance must be prevented, as it would threaten the British empire, and necessary measures would have to be taken in order to prepare for an eventual conflict with Japan. More specifically, while diplomatic delaying tactics should be employed so as not to provoke Japan, Pacific islands should be fortified, the United States fleet should be retained at Pearl Harbor, and staff conversations should be held with British and Dutch commanders in Southeast Asia with a view to joint defense. These measures would serve as deterrents against rash Japanese action, while diplomatic action would postpone final confrontation. There was, of course, a fine distinction between military measures as deterrents and as stimulants. Certain steps might actually involve the United States precipitously in war with Japan instead of serving the aim of postponing the showdown. In retrospect it appears that while military leaders in America generally sought to concentrate on the Atlantic theater of war, specific measures were taken in the Pacific which did not help postpone war with Japan. After July, when Japan sent troops to southern Indochina, the United States stepped up joint strategic planning with Britain, the Commonwealth, and the Dutch East Indies, and these countries were implicitly assured of American intervention should Japan attack Singapore or the East Indies. Meanwhile Japanese funds in the United States were frozen, bringing about a cessation of trade and cutting off the supply of fuel oil, vital to the Japanese navy. The bulk of the United States fleet was still kept in Hawaii despite the urgency of the struggle in the Atlantic.

American action in the Pacific prior to December 1941 reveals a view of Japan that was a product of wishful thinking. There was the idea that strong determination on the part of the United States would keep Japan in check, that force was the only language the Japanese understood and that concessions would encourage further aggression. Since Japan was pictured as inferior militarily and economically to the United States, it was not expected to risk American retaliation by precipitous action. At the same time, delaying diplomatic action would serve to gain time for the United States and keep Japan from becoming desperate. In other words, the Japanese would behave as Americans would if placed in a similar situation. America's show of determination, backed up by superior economic resources and military potential, would moderate Japan and prevent it from challenging the United States. There is no question that here was an element of self-complacency. American military leaders as well as American policymakers wanted to believe that the measures they were taking would suffice to hold Japan in check. Some, notably Ambassador Grew, tried to warn that the Japanese could be extremely erratic and irrational, that out of desperation they might resort to extreme measures. President Roosevelt and his senior advisers, however, held to the view that war could be avoided or at least postponed through military preparedness coupled with diplomatic talks.

It was such a view of Japan that was put to a severe test as months went by in the year 1941. As seen already, some in Japan, particularly naval officers, had come to believe in the inevitability of war with the United States. The point of no return had been reached in Japanese-American relations, they argued; therefore Japan should worry only about how to wage war against the United States most effectively. Advocated most forcefully by the navy's section chiefs, such a view came to be accepted by their superiors as well as by army strategists. After the spring of 1941 both the armed services were in virtual agreement on the inevitable logic of coming events; Japan would strike southward, the United States would retaliate by imposing a total embargo on exports to Japan, and Japan would finally decide on war with America. The Japanese military became so captivated by their own logic, which, it must be admitted, was not far wrong, that it became more and more difficult for them to transcend it and think of alternatives. The only logical alternative they could accept would have been restoration of normal trade with the United States, which would ensure the navy of continued oil supply and render unnecessary the forceful seizure of Southeast Asia. It was this alternative that the civilian government in Tokyo sought to pursue in the peace talks in Washington. Put simply, Japan's leaders embraced a clear formula of choosing between American oil and Southeast Asian oil. Believing that the United States would welcome a deal, they carried on their last-minute negotiations with Secretary of State Hull and sought to hold a leaders' conference in Honolulu. The burden of the Japanese offer was that Japan would give up its southern advance if the United States would consent to the resumption of trade. The Japanese, too, were guided by military considerations. Even the navy advocates of war admitted that it was doubtful if Japan could win an American war; war, however, was considered preferable to the continuation of the stalemate, with the stock of oil running out. If war had to be faced, the decision must be made quickly. It would be impossible to wait past the end of November 1941.

The Japanese attitude throughout 1941, like the American, reveals an image of its potential antagonist. That the Japanese prepared for war against the United States as they advanced southward indicated that they could not separate America from Britain and the Dutch East Indies. The United States, they realized, was to enter the scene as soon as Japan attacked British and Dutch possessions in Southeast Asia. At the same time, they recognized that America desired peace in the Pacific in order to concentrate on the Atlantic. Furthermore, in the Japanese view, the United States would be ready to buy peace with oil and iron; it would be willing to resume trade if Japan refrained from attacking Southeast Asia. Such a view of America persuaded the Japanese government that it was worthwhile pursuing a

modus vivendi with Washington. The idea that the United States
really did not want war with Japan encouraged some optimism. Thus
the Japanese tended to read into America's policy statements what
they wanted to find there, as revealed for instance when Ambassador
Nomura Kichisaburō misrepresented Hull's remarks to Tokyo. Though
the secretary's tone was always uncompromising if not belligerent,
the ambassador desperately sought in it some indication of a conciliatory spirit. The conviction that the United States in the end would
compromise explains why the Japanese regarded Hull's November 26
note as an ultimatum and decided on war.

The "Hull note" visualized the return to the status quo, not of
1940, 1939, or even of 1937, but virtually of 1931, by demanding that
Japanese troops be withdrawn from Indochina and China in return
for resumption of trade with the United States. The presentation of
the note signaled the end not only of negotiations in Washington but
also of the fiction of peace between the two countries. This was well
recognized by leaders in Tokyo as well as in Washington. What is
crucial, however, is the intrusion of the China question at the very
last moment. American and Japanese military planning, as well as
Japan's civilian diplomacy, had visualized the alternative of war or
peace in terms of Southeast Asia, not of China. The Japanese had
hoped for a compromise on the issue of oil, and the American
military had sought to prevent Japan's southern advance. In the fall
of 1941, as the sense of crisis heightened on both sides of the
Pacific, serious thought was given to averting war on the basis of the
resumption of limited trade in return for Japan's abstention from a
southern thrust. In Washington the military planners felt such a bargain was worthwhile, in order to gain time and wait for the outcome
of the European conflict. It was considered imperative to prevent
Japan's advance into Malaya and elsewhere and this could be done,
it was felt, only by agreeing to the resumption of trade. It was at this
point that the question of China assumed decisive proportions. Par-
tially it was a military question. Japan might refrain from advancing
into Southeast Asia and even to withdraw forces from Indochina, but
it would still be predominant in China. There was no assurance that
Japanese troops might not again attempt to thrust southward.
Moreover, the British were adamant on the question of China.
Winston Churchill believed that the collapse of China would menace
the British position in Southeast Asia. Thus he would have the United
States insist on total evacuation of Japanese troops from Indochina,

and he also opposed concessions in China. The United States, committed to joint defense with Britain and the Dutch, had to consider such views.

More fundamentally, however, there was American revulsion at the idea of sacrificing China in order to arrive at a deal with Japan merely to gain time. Here was, as Americans saw it, a moral question. It seemed morally wrong to compromise with Japan without considering China's destiny. Harry Dexter White, assistant secretary of the Treasury, was expressing a commonly held opinion when he wrote, in August 1941, "To sell China to her enemies . . . will not only weaken our national policy in Europe as well as in the Far East, but will dim the bright luster of America's world leadership in the great democratic fight against Fascism." The dualism in American thinking, dividing the world into fascist aggressors and peace-loving peoples, dictated the conclusion that the destinies of America and China were bound closely together, as two free, democratic nations fighting against totalitarianism. When the State Department considered accepting a temporary modus vivendi with Japan in November, Treasury Secretary Henry Morgenthau wrote a note, drafted by White, opposing such moves. "No matter what explanation is offered the public of a 'truce' with Japan," the note asserted, "the American people, the Chinese people, and the oppressed peoples of Europe, as well as those forces in Britain and Russia who are with us in this fight, will regard it as a confession of American weakness and vacillation." From Chunking, Owen Lattimore, advisor to Chiang Kai-shek, telegraphed, "A relaxation of American pressure while Japan has its forces in China would dismay the Chinese. Any modus vivendi now arrived at with [Japan] would be disastrous to Chinese belief in America and analogous to the closing of the Burma Road, which permanently destroyed British prestige."

Similar statements can be multiplied. Here was moral concern with the destiny of China, or rather with an image of Chinese-American relations. America was pictured as having built up good will in China; Free China, a phrase that began to be used in official documents, looked to the United States for support and cooperation. Any compromise with Japan would do irreparable damage to the state of Sino-American relations. It was simply unthinkable to betray the Chinese trust in America. In the light of what we now know about Chinese Communist thinking at the time, the American image of China appears hollow, a product of the liberal American imagination.

There is no question that America's view of China was part of its global picture, a picture in which the democracies of the world were seen as fighting against dictatorships.

Some, undoubtedly, were unhappy with such a characterization of American–East Asian relations. Ambassador Grew, while absolutely opposed to Japan's southern advance, remained unconvinced that the United States should take up China's cause against Japan with military force. As he wrote in September 1941, "I question whether it is in our own interest to see an impoverished Japan reduced to the position of a third-rate Power." He would have liked to see Japan continue as a stabilizer in East Asia, especially against the Soviet Union. Grew's colleague in China, Ambassador Clarence E. Gauss, wrote to the president in November, "it is important that we bear in mind that the defeat of Japanese aggression does not necessarily entail, as many Chinese think, our crushing Japan militarily. The complete elimination of Japan as a force in the Far East would not be conducive either to order or prosperity in this area." Both Grew and Gauss were thinking in the framework of power, rather than of morality, and were championing a cause that was daily becoming unpopular with the administration in Washington. "Japan has no friends in this country, but China has," wrote Secretary of Interior Harold Ickes. America's friendship with China was not on account of any consideration of power politics but was by then a moral concern for China's plight and heroic struggle against odds. Given an image of the Chinese placing their trust in American friendship, and an image of the American people eager to help the Chinese, there was no psychological possiblity of coming to terms with Japan, however temporarily, if it meant sacrificing China. Unlike the Soviet leaders, who cavalierly entered into a nonaggression pact with Japan for their own national interest and later thought of reasons to justify it, American leaders were psychologically bound to an idealistic image of Chinese-American relations.

In view of the American attitude what is striking is not that no compromise with Japan was possible because of American-Chinese ties, but that there was any thought at all of such a compromise. A temporary modus vivendi with Japan was basically a military idea; it seemed imperative from the military point of view to postpone war with Japan, if only for three months. In the end military considerations were subordinated to moral principles, reinforced by concern for British security in Southeast Asia. These two strategic and moral concerns remained the basis of American thinking as the United States entered war with Japan. Subsequent developments, however, were to demonstrate the tension between military objectives and more political and ideological concern with the fate of China.

The Chinese, too, had an image of friendship with America, but, as earlier, their view of Sino-American relations was by no means uniform or unqualified. Communist writers had a difficult time adjusting themselves to rapidly changing conditions in international relations—the Axis alliance, the Soviet-Japanese nonaggression pact, the German invasion of Russia, Japanese-American negotiations in Washington, and other developments. As expected there was less emphasis now on the alleged machinations of imperialist countries to collaborate against the Soviet Union. America was pictured as having emerged as the leader of the global war, determined to assert prominence in the world. In particular, the United States was perceived as stiffening its attitude toward Japan and willing to step up assistance to China. The Japanese-Soviet pact was hailed as encouraging to China; now that there was no immediate prospect of war in the north, the Japanese imperialists would surely strike southward, thus inviting conflict with the United States. Such a situation would undoubtedly induce the latter to increase its aid to China, paralleling Soviet help to China. Though Communist writers initially warned that despite such help the Chinese people must in the end rely upon their own effort for national salvation, after the German invasion of Russia in June there emerged an unequivocal image of an international anti-fascist front against Germany, Italy and Japan. An author noted that the Soviet Union was the leader of the anti-fascist coalition, America was in its front line, and China was its pillar in the East. The United States, Britain, and the Soviet Union were termed the three greatest nations of the world, jointly defending humanity against the aggression of the fascist states. Throughout the summer and fall of 1941 there was a note of uneasiness concerning Japanese-American negotiations, but it is remarkable that few openly referred to United States imperialism and monopoly capitalism. A minority expressed the view that the United States might come to terms with Japan because the former would need the latter's assistance in a postwar struggle against socialism. But even these writers remained confident that America would not sacrifice China entirely. Huang Yao-mien, writing for *World Culture* in mid-November, perhaps offered a psychologically most acceptable explanation of American policy by picturing the United States as divided between fascist-oriented isolationists and the anti-fascist majority of the population. The former were finance capitalists, and the latter democrats. The government's policy was swayed by the tug of war between the two, but some influential leaders seemed to take a compromising course, trying to take advantage of the global anti-fascist coalition in order to establish American hegemony in the postwar world. The implication here was that the United States would remain in the democratic camp so long as its policies reflected the aspirations of the people, but that there always remained reactionary propensity. Such a theory would explain almost anything, and for the time being the apparently uncompromising stand of the Washington government toward Japan satisfied Communist writers that the world coalition of democratic peoples was still secure and would in the end triumph over the forces of fascism and militarism.

Pro-Kuomintang writers naturally underplayed the role of the Soviet Union in the East Asian conflict. They expressed their regret at the signing of the Soviet-Japanese nonaggression pact as a betrayal of Sino-Soviet friendship. Still, most writers remained convinced that the United States would step up aid to China and that sooner or later Japan would advance southward, thus inviting a clash with America. There was an optimistic image of America as economically and militarily a far superior nation to Japan; these writers believed, therefore, that no matter what happened in areas outside East Asia, an eventual Pacific war would bring about Japan's downfall and China's salvation. In contrast to Communist-oriented writers, official and semi-official Kuomintang spokesmen held to an image of Sino-American friendship as a basic factor in the way of Japanese ambitions. In their view China was a member of a democratic alliance in the world, and the United States was its leader. There was every reason why the two should cooperate in Asia. The German invasion of the Soviet Union at first gave rise to the fear that by reducing pressure on Britain the new situation might delay America's intervention in the war. Soon, however, the Chinese recognized the emergence of a coalition among the United States, Britain, and Russia, and expressed the hope that the alliance would function as effectively in Asia as in Europe. Throughout the fall of 1941 Kuomintang opinion remained confident that the tides were changing in favor of China and that by determined economic and military cooperation Japan would be isolated in the Pacific. The Chunking regime naturally opposed the modus vivendi proposal discussed between Tokyo and Washington late in November, but it does not seem that the Chinese leaders really believed compromise was possible between Japan and the United States. They had come to view America's commitment to assist China as axiomatic; China's survival was considered vital to American security, and there could be no compromise between an aggressive, fascist Japan and the democratic United States.

Nationalist thinking on the United States in 1941 may further be illustrated by a speech made by Sun Fo, son of Sun Yat-sen and a high Kuomintang official, to a meeting of college students. He pointed out that for many years China alone, under the National government, had shouldered responsibility for fighting against aggression and defending human justice and world peace. America, Britain, and other nations, he said, had failed to comprehend the historical significance of the Manchurian incident, regarding it as an isolated occurrence in East Asia. It was only after the outbreak of war in Europe, in particular since 1940, that the friendly powers came to realize that China's struggle against aggression was intimately linked to world peace. Now they recognized the truth that only through supporting China could peace be maintained in Asia and in the world. America, in particular, was determined to extend all necessary help to China. Such friendly support had been won by the Chinese people's persistent effort and perseverance. After the war China would emerge as one of the four major powers, in addition to America, Britain, and the Soviet Union. Unequal treaties would be abolished, the humiliating status as a semi-colony would disappear, and China would gain complete equality as one of the strongest nations in the world. Though the enemy disseminated the propaganda that China was not a democracy and did not deserve help from democracies, this was complete nonsense. China was a state governed by the "three people's principles" under the leadership of the Kuomintang, and there was no doubt that the nation was marching toward a democratic form of government.

Finally, for the Japanese, too, the developing crisis with the United States had more than a purely military meaning. At bottom was the image of Japan as the leader in Asia, opposed to the policies of the United States which stood for "the maintenance of the status quo, the conquest of the world, and the protection of democracy," as a General Staff memorandum noted. Under the circumstances,

Japanese-American conflict was a "historical inevitability." As the Imperial rescript on the declaration of war stated, the United States and Britain had created chaos and confusion in Asia by supporting the Chunking regime, interfered in Japan's peaceful foreign commerce, and seriously menaced the nation's existence. Japanese existence was so defined as to include domination over Asia. Acceptance of the Hull note would have been tantamount to the rejection of the ideology that had underlined Japanese policy for a decade.

In the end, the Japanese navy's strategic decision to attack Hawaii, as well as the European colonies in Southeast Asia, demonstrated the failure of American policy, a policy that had been unable to imagine either the degree of Japanese military recklessness or the irrationality of pan-Asianism. For the Japanese, the ensuing attack on Pearl Harbor was a symbol of Asia's revolt against the West. Only the Chinese saw no need to reorient their thinking after the Pearl Harbor attack; they had foreseen it for a decade.

III SOURCES OF AMERICAN POLICY

James C. Thomson, Jr.
THE ROLE OF THE DEPARTMENT OF STATE

In the two brief essays that follow, the authors consider the influence, respectively, of men in the State Department's Far Eastern Division, and of U.S. Navy planning. On the whole historians seem to agree that Roosevelt's position toward Japan was not affected by some of the influences one might traditionally expect. For instance, Mira Wilkins concludes in an essay in Pearl Harbor as History *that business leaders exerted little influence. The President was not noticeably partial to business, and businessmen shared widespread distrust of Japanese aggression rather than being influenced by specific economic interests.*

In the same work, Wayne S. Cole finds few defenders of Japan in Congress, which was increasingly critical of Japan's southern expansion and even impatient with the cautious measures of Roosevelt and Hull. Legislators, reflecting a general American dislike of the Japanese, supported measures of economic coercion.

Warren I. Cohen's study of public opinion and private interest groups, in the collection edited by Borg and Okamoto, indicates that Roosevelt was influenced by events more than by public attitudes. Isolationists who opposed increasing intervention in the Atlantic made little protest against Roosevelt's Asian policy. Public opinion, moreover, was contradictory, opposing war but supporting the freeze on Japan's assets in the United States; advocating no change in policy even when it appeared to be taking us toward war.

The role of the press has been surveyed by Ernest R. May. His essay in the same volume of papers indicates that the press failed to present the problems of those Japanese leaders who sought to avoid conflict, playing up, instead, the military movements that confirmed America's adverse view of Japan. The press notably failed to provide the public with a sense of the imminence of war with Japan.

How, then, was policy determined? Thomson's account of influential people in the Department of State, especially Stanley Hornbeck, indicates the extent to which career men—area experts—contributed to Administration decisions. Was Hornbeck right in concluding that neither the American government nor its people were prepared to make the concessions Japan required?

The Far Eastern policy of the United States will undergo neither a rapid nor a gradual 'reorientation' unless and until . . . the whole world be-

From James C. Thomson, Jr., "The Role of the Department of State," in D. Borg and S. Okamoto, eds., *Pearl Harbor as History* (New York: Columbia University Press, 1973), pp. 81–84, 101–104, 106, footnotes omitted. Reprinted by permission of the publisher.

comes an utterly different *world from that which it has been ever since the Pilgrims landed at Plymouth and the Cavaliers at Jamestown.—* Stanley K. Hornbeck to Sumner Welles, May 18, 1940.

In his eightieth year of life, Stanley Kuhl Hornbeck was asked by a friend on the Department of State's Policy Planning Council what America should "do" to meet the challenges of the 1960s in foreign affairs. "Well, I am sure about some things," the old man responded. "Our national concern for and regarding principles and practices of freedom, independence, justice and security is greater than is that of any other nation. . . . We should be prepared to go further and to make greater efforts in defense of those principles and practices than is to be expected of any other country."

About the same time, Hornbeck filed a note to posterity in a box marked "Pearl Harbor": "Did I underestimate Japan's strength? The answer is: Yes, both in absolute terms and in comparative terms, and so did practically everyone else in the United States, both in the Government and out of the Government, in varying degrees. The strength of any country is relative."

In these two separate reflections lies one central dilemma of Stanley Hornbeck and his department in the decade of the thirties: how to "go further" than other nations in defense of "principles and practices" when other nations are strong, perhaps stronger than we suspect—and perhaps zealous, one might add, to defend their own "principles and practices."

Stanley K. Hornbeck presided over the making of Far Eastern policy at the Department of State from 1928 to 1941, and beyond. The Hornbeck story is not the full story of State. But it is a good place to begin. . . .

Within the division Foreign Service officers came and went. But continuity was present in the person of Stanley Hornbeck. It was also present in the two chief deputies he acquired over the years.

In June 1930 Hornbeck had requested the appointment of an assistant chief, and by the following April his candidate, Maxwell M. Hamilton, was named to the job, a post Hamilton held until he himself became chief at the time of Hornbeck's promotion. For the next ten years, under two secretaries of state, assorted undersecretaries, and others, Hornbeck and Hamilton worked in close tandem—indeed *were* the Far East Division in the eyes of those above.

Maxwell Hamilton was a Princetonian from Sioux City, a Chinese language officer who had served during the twenties as a vice con-

sul in Canton and assessor on the Shanghai Mixed Court. He had
been in FE since the summer of 1927. Thirteen years younger than
Hornbeck and milder of disposition, he was, as a colleague recalls,
"a man essentially trained to point out why we should do nothing
ever lest we rock the boat." He is said to have chafed against his
boss and judged the world less sternly. Others also chafed; the chief
ran a "cantankerous ship," one officer remembers, and required
attendance at Saturday morning staff meetings at which he delivered
extended public rebukes to those who had failed to meet his standards of diligence and precision during the previous seven days.
With his FE "family" (as another aide recalls) he was avuncular but
fierce, evoking fear; yet his bluntness and rudeness "were directed at
the idea, not the person."

The second of Hornbeck's deputies was a later arrival. Joseph W.
Ballantine, the son of missionaries to India, was an Amherst graduate
and Japanese language officer. From 1909 on he had served in
Japan, as well as Formosa and Dairen. He worked under Hornbeck in
1928–30, then, after six more years abroad, spent in Canton, Mukden,
and Tokyo, he returned to FE and became Hamilton's assistant chief
a year later. Described by one who knew him as "frightfully timid, a
broken-spirited clerk," Ballantine was nonetheless a man whose
overseas experience made him a good deal more sympathetic to
Japan's sensed needs and aspirations than Hornbeck or even Hamilton.

As the decade wore on and the Far East crisis deepened, it was
Hornbeck, Hamilton, and Ballantine who pressed the division's views,
fended off the critics, and protected the evolving policy. If there were
serious substantive divisions among them, they are hard to detect
until late in the decade. Most likely they were usually submerged in
the strength of Hornbeck's personality. The August 1937
reorganization—Hornbeck's shift to political adviser—only added
another layer between FE and the secretary. Although the new structure was designed to release Hornbeck and his counterparts in the
other regional divisions from day-to-day responsibilities and give
them "time to think," this objective, according to Hornbeck, "was
soon lost in the shuffle." The former chief, now elevated, continued
to preside; all significant FE documents required his clearance
and/or comment.

The triumvirate, then, was not without cohesiveness. Nor was it
without influence. When Cordell Hull chose to remember the names of

"my principal associates" (some think the recurrent phrase suggests his misty distance from all who served under him), he would invariably list "my three ranking Far Eastern experts," naming Hornbeck, Hamilton, and Ballantine as men who "had had long experience and training in oriental affairs and were especially equipped for the work they performed in the Department." The threesome, Hull attests in his memoirs, were responsible for State's meticulous performance during the fateful talks with Nomura at the end of the decade: "This was owing to Dr. Hornbeck's precise draftsmanship and analysis of documents, Hamilton's infinite capacity for detail, and Ballantine's skillful industry in returning to the State Department after my night talks . . . and putting down on paper precisely what had been said."

In style, however, the three men had their differences. As Herbert Feis reports the Hull-Nomura dialogues: "Hornbeck was seldom present. . . . A confirmed foe of compromise, inclined to lay down the law, he was little suited for this touchy and circuitous business. In the background his incisive analysis caused many vague Japanese proposals to crumble into dust. Any tendency to bypass some disputed point or to leave it in the mists of language was routed by him." By contrast, Hamilton, sometimes present, was "patient, gentle, and eagerly on the search for something in the Japanese proposals which might form the basis for a settlement. Within him the Japanese plight aroused worry, sympathy, rather than reproof—which led to a wish to give them all the chance possible to amend their course." As for Ballantine, Feis sees in him "the language scholar and the industrious draftsman. Behind the pale impassive face, a nimble mind kept account of every corner of the talk. His drafts were monotonous and exhaustive. They left no spaces in which the Japanese might hide their intentions. There was a dull evenness in his speech which made him a good interpreter."

With such a crew, Feis concludes, "the Secretary of State could have worn out even the voluble Matsuoka, had he been there." . . .

In early November 1941 a junior Foreign Service officer, just back from a tour of duty in Tokyo, paid a courtesy call on the Far East political adviser. Hornbeck asked the young man about the mood of the embassy staff. They were worried, was the answer, deeply worried about the imminence of war between Japan and the United States, a war that Japan might well initiate out of sheer desperation. Hornbeck was incredulous and disdainful. "Tell me," he said, "of one case in history when a nation went to war out of desperation." The flustered Foreign Service officer could think at the moment of none, and the interview was soon terminated.

A year earlier a more senior colleague, Jay Pierrepont Moffat, who was Grew's son-in-law, had called on Hornbeck during a brief home leave from Ottawa. He found the political adviser convinced that America was "already at war" with Japan, "though if we adopted a firm and uncompromising stand we might yet avoid being dragged into a 'combat war.' " Moffat's wry comment was that "Stanley regarded Japan as the sun around which its satellites, Germany and Italy, were revolving."

A further glimpse of Hornbeck comes from a memorandum he sent to Sumner Welles on July 23, 1941. "I submit," he wrote, "that under existing circumstances it is altogether improbable that Japan would deliberately take action in response to any action which the United States is likely to take in the Pacific which action if taken by Japan would mean war between that country and this country."

How is one to understand the Hornbeck position during the critical months of 1941? He talked of war—indeed claimed to have predicted collision to Hull as early as 1938—and yet he seemed convinced that war could be avoided. He urged that increased pressure, increased force, be brought to bear on Japan; and yet he regarded a warlike response, whether out of despair or deliberation, as improbable.

The basis for the Hornbeck view seems threefold. In the first place, he was deeply convinced that the Japanese were bluffing or, at least, that they desperately wanted to avoid war with the United States and would back down under the threat of war. Second, he was haunted by the memory of the Anglo-American failure to stand up to Japan during the Manchurian episode,[1] was convinced, in retrospect, that the weakness of Hoover and of Sir John Simon had sown the seeds of the present crisis. And third, he was contemptuous of Japan's military strength, which, he judged, was severely reduced by the long China War.

If, in fact, Japan was bluffing, it was vital to call its bluff. If, in fact, the U.S. response to Manchuria had communicated a permissive signal, it was high time to communicate something tougher. As for Tokyo's capacity to fight a war, "Japan, whatever may have been four years ago her rightful rating, on the basis of military strength and

[1] The Manchurian episode was the military takeover of Manchuria by Japanese troops in 1931 that resulted in erection of the Japanese-dominated state of Manchukuo.—Ed.

capacity, as a major power, is today very tired and comparatively weak." Indeed, Hornbeck saw "more than a good chance" of Japan's collapse from overexertion before Germany's defeat, to be followed by "changes in Japanese leadership and Japanese psychology," after which the United States could "do business with Japan."

Given such assumptions, and given Hornbeck's conviction as early as 1935 that "no conceivable concessions on the part of the Government and people of the United States would have any conclusive effect" on Japan, it is little wonder that the political adviser devoted his energies tirelessly during the months of 1941 to the propagation of the diplomacy of force and to the defeat of its bureaucratic opponents. Never had his sturdy pen been wielded more confidently or polemically.

It was Hornbeck within the department who pressed hardest for a freezing of Japanese assets in July 1941: "If we have any intention of freezing them and do not freeze them now, we should give ourselves pretty good reasons for not doing so." It was Hornbeck who argued for additional pressures in a forceful July 16 memorandum and then again in a follow-up one month later in which he underlined in blue those things from his previous paper that had been done and in red those that had not. The latter included: "a new disposal of armed force . . . the only thing that really impresses and tends to restrain the Japanese at this point is evidence of armed capacity and intention; . . . keep open the line of communication into China at Rangoon; . . . make a new show of force in the western Pacific; . . . additional aid should be sent to China immediately; . . . additional planes . . . should be sent immediately to Manila" and "a cruiser squadron" to the Philippines, the Dutch East Indies, or Singapore.

It was Hornbeck, as well, who fought hardest against the Konoye proposal for a summit meeting with Roosevelt. "Mr. Hull viewed it with suspicion," he recalled. "I viewed it from the outset with suspicion and disfavor. . . . Mr. Grew was both disappointed and greatly vexed." To Hornbeck, Grew was now advocating "appeasement."

As for the Hull-Nomura conversations, the political adviser observed the long process with watchful distaste. He had no hope for the talks, and indeed they clearly posed some danger to his formula of pressures. Hornbeck did not attend but studied the transcripts and did what he could to keep the more conciliatory Maxwell Hamilton firmly in line. "Mr. Hull and I completely and expressly agreed that participation by me in the conversations would not be profitable . . .

and that I should play the role, in the background and off-stage, of observer, analyst and counselor." Others recall a different Hornbeck, one who deeply resented his exclusion from the talks by a secretary of state who now distrusted him as a "firebrand."

Hornbeck's rigidity, while more consistent than most, was not, of course, unique. Even the patient Cordell Hull felt his heart hardening as the "Magic"[2] intercepts seemed to document Japanese duplicity. "Nothing will stop them except force," he told Welles on August 4. Stimson felt Hull had "made up his mind that we have reached the end of any possible appeasement with Japan and there is nothing further that can be done with that country except by a firm policy."

As the autumn wore on and the crisis deepened, Maxwell Hamilton still hoped for a way out of the impasse. On November 17 Morgenthau passed on to State and the White House an extraordinary memorandum by Harry Dexter White proposing a "creative economic policy"—an imaginative regional settlement scheme—to arrest the drift toward war. Hamilton judged the memorandum a "most constructive one" and the services posed no objection. But the hour was very late and the document died in the bureaucracy.

Ten days later Hull presented a proposal to the Japanese envoys that was "comprehensive, uncompromising, and entirely unresponsive to all Japanese drafts." In this circumstance, on the 27th Hull met with Hornbeck, Hamilton, and Ballantine to plan for the president's meeting with the Japanese that afternoon. The talks had clearly failed. Hornbeck, reports A. A. Berle, "was urging determination to act by force of arms. The Secretary was pointing out that the Army felt it would not be ready for another three weeks, that the Navy wanted another three months. Hornbeck pointed out that the Navy had asked for six months last February and the Secretary, through his negotiations, had got them that six months. Now they wanted three more. Hornbeck's idea was that the President ought to stop asking the Navy, and tell it. The Secretary, rather wearily, passed it aside."

Hornbeck's energy, his confidence, indeed his exhilaration that day were unbounded. He went so far as to write a memorandum whose opening sentence read, "In the opinion of the undersigned, the Japanese Government does not desire or intend or expect to have forthwith armed conflict with the United States." Not content

[2] Magic was the code name for material gathered by United States intelligence efforts that was deemed most important and circulated only to a selected list of officials.—Ed.

with this assertion, he was in a wagering mood. His "bets," the memo continued, were five to one "that the United States and Japan will not be at 'war' on or before December 15," three to one against war by January 15, and "even money" against war by March 1. "Stated briefly," he concluded, "the undersigned does not believe that this country is now on the immediate verge of 'war' in the Pacific.

Such uncustomary and ill-timed flamboyance requires some explanation, and Hornbeck has one for the student of history: "I made the mistake," he writes, "of yielding to an emotional urge and committing myself on the record in terms of wishful thinking and gratuitous predicting." But he was careful to add that "both my thinking and my predicting were, however, based on my scrutiny of materials which emanated from 'intelligence' services, some British and some American"—specifically, with regard to the strength of Singapore and the current position of the Japanese main fleet.

Ten days after Hornbeck's confident predictions, the Japanese bombed Pearl Harbor. Did he foresee the attack? A candid answer to this very question may be found neatly typed In his private papers: "No, and so far as I am aware neither did any other American. The Secretary of State came nearer to it, in my opinion, than did any other American." And did he underestimate the strength of Japan? Again the candid answer—with which we commenced this paper—is to be found in his files.

But did Stanley K. Hornbeck understand *why* it all happened—the Japanese-American crisis and impasse, the Pearl Harbor attack, the war itself? His answer, twenty years later: "Japan's attack . . . came *not,* as is often affirmed, of our China policy but of (a) the commitment of Japan's leaders to their program of conquest and (b) American opposition to aggression in general and to Japan's and her Axis allies' aggressions in particular." And as a further elaboration he wrote that throughout the Far Eastern crisis in the decade of the thirties, Americans "were on the defensive. They were thinking and they argued in terms of principles. They were in effect saying to the Japanese that what had been, presumably, good for the United States, would be good for Japan and for each and all lands. To and for Japan's rulers that thinking, those principles and that contention had no meaning: they were committed to a program; they were engaged in and they intended to persevere in operations of conquest; as they saw it, what would be good for Japan would be good for Japan's neighbors."

The struggle, then, was between America's "principles" and Japan's "program," the one universal and benevolent, the other particularist and self-serving. Principles were abstractions, perhaps—abstractions learned in the household of a Methodist minister, taught in college classrooms, applied to the people and promise of China, and practiced under the aegis of Stimson and Hull. But still potent abstractions, rooted, Hornbeck believed, in the American Experiment—and therefore abstractions to which all men must eventually pay homage, by persuasion if possible, by force if necessary.

Waldo H. Heinrichs, Jr.

UNITED STATES NAVY PLANNING

By late 1941 the U.S. Navy faced a real war in the Atlantic. In the following study by Waldo H. Heinrichs, Jr. the author makes it clear what capabilities the navy had, what it knew it could or could not do in the event of a two-ocean war. Did the navy's well-understood limitations make Roosevelt and Hull more patient in their negotiations? Why did the navy's need for time not weigh more heavily in favor of a conference with Konoye or acceptance of a modus vivendi?

The shock effect of the fall of France greatly accelerated the process of change in the navy. It radically altered the security picture and ushered in a period of rapid flux in the navy's planning and preparation for war. One result was an immediate, gigantic increase in the projected size of the navy. The third Vinson program, authorizing an 11 percent increase, was already out of date when it became law in June 1940. The following month a fourth program called for an expansion of 70 percent. Now the cliché was not "treaty navy" but "two-ocean navy."

The projected composition of the fleet reflected the new waves of change. In November 1939 Admiral Stark pleaded with a reluctant

From Waldo H. Heinrichs, Jr., "The Role of the United States Navy," in D. Borg and S. Okamoto, eds., *Pearl Harbor as History* (New York: Columbia University Press, 1973), pp. 218–23, footnotes omitted. Reprinted by permission of the publisher.

president for two more 45,000-ton battleships and gained approval. These with the ones authorized or building made a total of twelve new battleships. The General Board expressed its concern over reports that Japan was building eight battleships and urged faster construction. Intelligence estimated eight as a conservative figure. Meanwhile carrier building lagged: only one keel was laid between April 1936 and April 1941. The trend was reversed under the impact of air war in Europe. Eleven *Essex*-type attack carriers were ordered in July and September 1940. At the same time, the navy added no more battleships and ultimately canceled two.

The fall of France also hastened a gradual reorientation of navy strategy and dispositions from the Pacific to the Atlantic. The first trace of this shift is detectable early in 1938 when the administration presented the second Vinson bill as a measure for the defense of both coasts. According to a naval officer closely involved in the legislation, the worsening situation in Europe during debate on the bill gave it a boost toward passage. In July 1938 the president decided to send the fleet to the opening of the New York World's Fair in 1939. This visit to the East Coast after a long absence was to provide tangible evidence of the fleet's covering role in the Atlantic, but in fact a real European crisis forced the fleet back to its usual position in the Pacific. Nevertheless, the Atlantic could not be left bare. The Atlantic Squadron, United States Fleet, was formed in October 1938 in part as a "politico-diplomatic gesture aimed at the totalitarian powers on the eve of the Munich Crisis." By September 1939 it consisted of four old battleships, four new heavy cruisers, an aircraft carrier, and a destroyer squadron. Atlantic responsibilities continued to assist naval growth: Admiral Stark noted in September 1939 that the European war gave him "leverage" in securing additional appropriations. These responsibilities steadily expanded. In February 1941 the Atlantic force attained fleet status and its commander, Ernest J. King, the rank of vice admiral. The president had desired a higher rank for the Atlantic commander for over a year. Thenceforth the Atlantic Fleet never had enough ships and the aggressive King regarded any warship on either coast not otherwise attached as "legitimate prey."

The Pacific tugged at American naval strength too. After German victory in the West, Japan joined the Axis alliance and moved into northern Indochina. Events pointed toward a climax as Roosevelt responded with a scrap iron embargo and the British by opening the

Burma Road. Since May 1939 Britain had repeatedly urged the sending of an American naval force to Singapore to stand in for the fleet Britain itself was unable to send. Predominant opinion within the administration regarded the Singapore venture as wholly impractical, but in October 1940 the president seriously considered reinforcing the Asiatic Fleet. The navy was dubious and finally reduced the allotment to ten submarines, vessels able to do their damage and escape. Meanwhile the president reverted to the containment thesis in contemplating moves in case of a further Japanese advance southward. In that case he would place a total embargo on Japanese trade and set up a long-range blockade. He toyed with the idea of setting up two lines of patrol vessels, one from Samoa to the Dutch East Indies and another from Hawaii to the Philippines, to intercept Japanese commerce, along the lines of Yarnell's recommendation of 1937. The thought of war measures with the fleet still unprepared and of such a blithe dispersion of naval forces in dangerous waters horrified Admiral Richardson, who managed to dissuade the president. But U.S. policy was now drifting steadily toward active opposition to Japan in the Far East and the navy, the traditional exponent of a firm Far Eastern policy, found itself the voice of caution and restraint.

In the middle, pulled both ways, was the United States Fleet. It had been conducting maneuvers in Hawaiian waters at the time of the German invasion of France and the president ordered it to remain at Pearl Harbor indefinitely as a deterrent to Japan. At the moment some in the navy would have preferred to withdraw it to the Atlantic to guard against loss of the British and French fleets. Richardson argued for return to the West Coast on the ground that congestion in Hawaii made training difficult. But the president, strongly supported by the State Department, refused, saying he would first need a statement convincing to the American people and the Japanese government that such a move would not be a step backward. During the summer of 1940 the governing condition was Rainbow 4, hemispheric defense, which precluded westward movement of the fleet in case of war; but in October, with fears for Britain easing slightly and American policy toward Japan hardening, the door to Pacific strategies reopened. Richardson, perhaps for no other reason than to save himself from the president's strategic notions, drew up a plan that was a hybrid of Rainbow 2, 3, and 4. In the event of an American embargo, the fleet would move west, but not beyond recall to the

Atlantic. This was a convenient restriction since venturing as far as Truk was regarded as too hazardous in any event. Instead Richardson proposed to attack the nearby Marshalls and "if possible" to send a single-carrier task force to join the Asiatic Fleet, which would retire southward to assist in the defense of the Malay Barrier. This was less a plan than a recognition of the failure of planning.

This was a painful moment for the American navy and no one expressed the mood of uncertainty and frustration better than the commander-in-chief of the fleet. In communications to Knox and Stark, Richardson bitterly reflected on the awkward position of his fleet, posed as a deterrent, yet inadequately manned and trained, lacking sufficient superiority in ships, and consequently unready to fight if deterrence failed. He wondered whether the navy had presented its views forcibly and frankly to the rest of the government so that there could be no misunderstanding about what it could and could not do, and whether coordination between the State, War, and Navy departments was adequate. Above all he pointed out the anachronism of naval thinking. Waging transpacific war had been a budgetary strategy that was unrealistic now. There was always a danger of overemphasizing the point of view of staff corps officers whose long removal from sea duty distorted their priorities. He inveighed against the public image the navy cultivated of a fleet ready to fight, big enough to keep America out of war, to impose the nation's will on others, or, if war came, to provide a "mobile Maginot line" behind which the citizenry could reside in peace. Such publicity lulled the public into believing the United States could "risk war without danger or wage war without risk." The time had come for the nation to decide what the objectives of a Pacific war might be and to compare its costs and value. And the navy must formulate "sound plans" based on "present realities."

Richardson's views arrived in time for a major reassessment of American naval strategy directed by Admiral Stark that culminated on November 4, 1940 in the well-known Stark Memorandum, otherwise known as the Plan D or, in military parlance, Plan Dog Memorandum, a document that played a vital part in crystallizing American strategy in favor of prosecution of war on Germany first. The awkward position of the fleet in the Pacific was one of a number of factors contributing to the reassessment and the result, another being the obvious threats in and across the Atlantic. Others factors were the passing of Hitler's opportunity to invade Britain until spring, making long-term plans for assisting the British worthwhile, and the passing of the election season in America, promising undivided presidential attention to problems of national defense. The memorandum reflected the growing influence of the professional side of the navy as war approached. Prominent on the Stark planning team was Captain Richard Kelly Turner, director of War Plans, who had been in charge of the advanced course at the Naval War College in 1938-39. The revamped course dealt with war in a broad social, political, and economic context. An estimate prepared by the staff in 1939, for example, had deliberately ignored the Orange plan and concluded that the correct employment of the fleet at the beginning of war was in protection of the assembly and preparation of the nation's forces for maximum effort. The correct location of the fleet, according to a study of April 1940, was the Caribbean. Other factors contributing to Plan Dog can be surmised. One was certainly the fact that it would be several years before completion of the "two-ocean navy" and realization of the nation's full potential naval strength. Also, an Atlantic war was a familiar war. The staff could proceed according to precedents of World War I, when Stark had been flag secretary to Admiral Sims at London. At the same time, with reentry to Europe necessary now, the navy could anticipate a more significant role.

The main premise of the Plan Dog Memorandum was that the vital interest of the United States lay in the continued existence of Britain and the British empire. To defend that interest the United States should direct its concentrated effort toward Europe, even to the point of waging war on the Continent for the defeat of Germany. The memorandum measured alternative strategies against the imperative of European concentration and rejected them. Plan A, hemispheric defense, and Plan B, the Orange or Rainbow 3 war, ruled out American influence on the outcome in Europe. Plan C, the Rainbow 2 concept of limited war in the Pacific presented similar difficulties. The memorandum raised the question whether Japan was necessarily committed to military action against British and Dutch territories. Given the hope of long-term economic influence in those territories and assurance of trade with Britain and the United States, Japan might bide its time. If it did attack, a Plan C war might be waged in two ways, both involving an economic blockade. The first involved dispatching forces to assist the British and Dutch in defense of the Malay Barrier, and the second operations against the Marshall Islands to divert the Japanese from pursuing the southward advance.

The memorandum raised the question of the extent to which the British and Dutch were willing or able to resist Japan and ruled out the possibility of sending the battle fleet to Singapore. But even sending a smaller force or raiding the Marshalls would drain American strength from Europe. Limited war in the Far East in cooperation with Britain would probably mean war against Germany as well. Reverses in the Pacific might lead to popular clamor for escalation, to the detriment of the European theater. Thus limited war could develop an irreversible dynamic of its own.

A strategy of Europe first meant a strict defensive in the Pacific. The memorandum did not entirely reject the possibility of a limited war with Japan. Rather it insisted that any decision on joint defense with the British and Dutch must depend on a clear understanding of the strength and extent of their commitment to the defense of the Malay Barrier, keeping in mind the priority of Europe. For the moment the fleet should remain at Hawaii. Meanwhile "positive efforts" should be made to prevent war with Japan and between Japan and the British and Dutch. The memorandum was obscure about the cost of avoiding war, but its acceptance of the necessity of paying some cost illustrates how naval thinking had changed.

The containment thesis survived despite the severe doubts of the naval planners. The Plan Dog concept gained broad acceptance in the government but strong opinion, particularly in the State Department, still favored some sort of assistance to the British and Dutch in the Far East. A note in the margin of the Stark Memorandum illustrates the persistence of the idea. The text at that point read: "Under Plan (D) we would be unable to exert strong pressure against Japan, and would necessarily gradually reorient our policy in the Far East." Next to that statement Secretary Knox, who approved Plan Dog, scribbled: "In combination with Dutch and British could contain Jap. fleet + prevent army transport to Dutch E. Indies." Stark himself continued to hope some force might be sent. He wrote the commander of the Asiatic Fleet that a reinforcement, probably to Soerabaja or Singapore, could be counted on, but he warned that its size and composition would be influenced by the necessity of holding the fleet at mid-Pacific for possible recall to the Atlantic.

The hope lingered on into 1941. On seeing the Stark Memorandum the British urged, without success, the sending of nine American battleships to Singapore. A British naval representative saw Stark in December and explained in great detail the importance of Singapore to the defense of Britain and the British empire as well as to the interests of the United States, thereby seeking to redirect the Plan D assumption of defense of the British empire toward a Plan C limited-war solution. In January 1941, as reports circulated of an imminent Japanese move southward, the question arose of sending four heavy cruisers to Singapore and Secretary Knox called a meeting to discuss it, attended by Eugene Dooman, counselor of embassy in Tokyo, who was home on furlough. Dooman pointed out that the Japanese would not tolerate the presence of major American fleet units in the South China Sea and that sending lesser ships would be a futile gesture. Knox disagreed, Stark agreed, and, according to Dooman, the discussion became heated. Ultimately the president, who was never enthusiastic about the Singapore project, sent four cruisers to New Zealand and Australia instead. With no better success, the British continued to press the issue at the staff conversations in Washington early in 1941 that led to the basic British-American strategic agreement known as ABC-1.

Specific decisions succeeding the Stark Memorandum hardened theoretical misgivings into final rejection of the Singapore reinforcement project. An important consideration was the unsatisfactory state of British defenses. As the chairman of the British staff delegation in Washington admitted:

> On the one hand we shall say to the Americans that the whole safety of the Far East depends on the arrival of their battle fleet at Singapore. On the other hand we shall also have to say that we have not placed a garrison in Malaya sufficiently powerful to ensure that the base at Singapore will be intact when the United States fleet arrives. . . .

At a crucial point in the staff discussions the British admitted that Singapore could not repair capital ships. Other factors contributed too: the political awkwardness of defending a British imperial bastion, the great distance of the supply route, the violation of the naval maxim of concentration, and the fear of losing the ships sent. By 1941 the United States had virtually conceded control of the western Pacific to Japan. The ABC-1 staff agreement assigned the United States defense responsibility to the international date line north of the equator and to the line of the Solomons south of it, still one thousand miles short of the Malay Barrier. Henceforth Barrier defense and Pacific defense would be considered as distinct problems.

The final moves to resolve the Singapore problem were like chess:

American warships would move from the Pacific to the Atlantic and an equivalent force of British warships would move to the Far East. Atlantic needs alone argued for the transfer. Admiral King was beginning escort of convoys and planning landings at strategic points in the Atlantic to forestall the Germans. The move had the added virtue of getting at least part of the fleet at Pearl Harbor unstuck without seeming to step backward. At first the idea was to switch roughly half the fleet including six battleships. Both service secretaries and both service chiefs supported the move, but the State Department strongly objected to losing its deterrent and the commander-in-chief of the Pacific Fleet to losing half his command. According to Secretary of War Stimson, Admiral Stark wavered under these contradictory pressures and the president finally decided to move no more than about one-quarter of the fleet. This was still a major force, consisting of three battleships, an aircraft carrier, four new cruisers, sixteen new destroyers, and auxiliaries. The British may have doubted the equivalent value of nonbelligerent battleships but in the end ordered three capital ships to Singapore. The carrier went aground and did not go: the fate of the two vessels that did arrive, the *Repulse* and *Prince of Wales,* is well known.[3]

By June 1941 the navy had moved about as far in planning and dispositions as it would go before December 7. It was operating under Rainbow 5, a forward policy in the Atlantic and strict defense in the Pacific. It was also somewhat reluctantly operating under a limited containment strategy, maintaining the Pacific Fleet as a deterrent against a Japanese southward advance. No early decisive action was expected of that fleet in the event of war. The president talked of hit-and-run raids, interdicting enemy commerce, and protecting American commerce and home territory. He doubted any seizure of the Marshalls or Carolines until the second or third year of war. Interallied arrangements for the defense of the Malay Barrier were the responsibility of the commander of the Asiatic Fleet. He would have to make do with light forces.

The events of July 1941 changed the situation in the Pacific, but the navy stayed on course. Admiral Stark opposed the application of an embargo on the ground that it would probably result in an early Japanese attack on Malaya and the Dutch East Indies. The navy's build-up in the Philippines—more patrol planes and submarines—was

[3] The *Repulse* and *Prince of Wales* sailed from Singapore without air cover to intercept an expected Japanese attack and were both sunk by Japanese air attack.—Ed.

relatively modest compared with the army's, particularly the army's deployment of a long-range bomber force. The two services in fact switched roles on containment of Japan, the navy hanging back and the army pressing forward. With the embargo economic war began in the Pacific. For the navy real war was beginning in the Atlantic.

IV PEARL HARBOR ATTACK

Ladislas Farago

SPIES AND CODEBREAKERS

The controversial subject of why American forces were caught by surprise when Japan attacked Pearl Harbor and adjacent military and air bases on December 7, 1941 is subsidiary to the main issue of United States Asian policy but intimately connected with it. What the diplomats learned from our intelligence sources played a primary role in shaping the decisions they made. In the following selections from Ladislas Farago's book, The Broken Seal, *the author traces Japan's success in masking the forthcoming attack and the extent to which United States intelligence services succeeded in knowing ahead of time what Japan was doing in contrast to what Japanese negotiators were saying. "Magic" was the code name for all the most important and most secret disclosures obtained by American intelligence. This material was circulated to a very limited group. "Purple" was the designation given to the top Japanese diplomatic code which American experts had managed to break.*

A single spy at large is like the proverbial needle in a haystack—he is very difficult to find. Ensign Yoshikawa was such an elusive loner in espionage.

At the consulate, only Kita and Okuda were aware of his true identity, and even they knew nothing of his background and very little about the exact nature of his work. To all others, he was a brash, indolent probationary consul of the eighth rank, the lowest man in the hierarchy, who was falling down badly on his job.

His associates considered him an upstart, the worthless protegé of someone influential at the Foreign Ministry. To Yoshie Kikkawa, his personal maid, he was something of a mystery man whom she knew only as Vice-Consul Morimura. He kept one of his rooms at his quarters permanently locked and would not even let her in to clean it.

His behavior naturally caused much comment among the consulate's secretaries and clerks. Some of them suspected that Yoshikawa was an officer of the Imperial Navy on a secret mission. But Yokichi Seki, who had had a year in the navy and fancied himself an expert in naval matters, doubted this. "I know how our naval officers behave," he told the others, "and Morimura definitely doesn't conduct himself as an officer. As a matter of fact," he added, for he resented the new man who had replaced him at his clandestine sideline, "he doesn't really know what he's doing."

As for Yoshikawa himself, he seemed to be enjoying himself hugely, playing much harder than he worked. A handsome, outgoing man of twenty-eight with a good sense of humor and a certain rough charm, he was, as consumptive people often are, highly sensuous and a lover of life. The budget of his mission was by no means generous—the *joho kyoku* kept a very thrifty house—but it enabled him to indulge in certain of the luxuries he had had to forgo before. And apparently he was determined to make the most of this windfall.

He had made many friends in Honolulu even in this short time, and had become a fixture at the Venice Café and the Seaview Inn, and especially at the tea houses where the service was enhanced by accommodating geisha girls. He taught *kendo* fencing at the Dai Nippon athletic club, which had a sprinkling of American servicemen among its members, took his girl friends on sightseeing trips to Kaneohe Bay in the glass-bottom boat, and over Pearl Harbor in a Piper Cub he rented at John Rodgers Airport; played golf (badly but dutifully with the consul general) and baseball on the consulate grounds; gossiped in the City Room of the *Nippu Ji Ji,* a local Japanese–English newspaper; joked easily, drank heavily, stayed up late at night; courted a prim little schoolteacher from Wahiawa and wrote sentimental poems to Tomoyoka, a lovely geisha at the Muchizoki tea house.

In between he put in brief appearances at the office (where he had a desk in Okuda's room) but spent most of his time roaming about Oahu or going on tours to Maui or Kauai islands. He bought picture postcards of volcanos and exotic plants, like any proper tourist captivated by the scenic splendor of the islands.

On the rare nights when he stayed home, he gave *sake* parties to the girls from the tea houses or tried to learn English (which he understood but could not speak well) by listening to the radio for hours or struggling with such books as Beth Proun's *For Men Only* and *Wife for Sale* by Kathleen Norris. He kept a notebook in which he jotted down idiomatic phrases that happened to strike his fancy— such as "boisterous merrymaking" and "both my feet had gone to sleep"[1]—but he had no intellectual pretenses. He did not strike people as being very bright.

Actually, Yoshikawa was neither the simpleton nor the sybarite he appeared to be. His casual approach to espionage was calculated—in fact, it was his own shrewdly chosen cover. The man who could be exasperatingly indiscreet in his private affairs was a paragon of discretion in his professional pursuits.

Technically competent both as a naval officer and a secret agent, he was indefatigable, conscientious, and an excellent judge of men. He suffered from none of the usual delusions of espionage operatives and eschewed the hoary melodrama of their craft. He regarded his mission fatalistically, with the stoic submission of an officer doing his duty. As he himself later put it, "I, who was reared as a naval officer, never came to serve in action, but look back on my single top-secret assignment as the *raison d'être* of the long years of training in my youth and early manhood."

Yoshikawa once said that when he first arrived in Honolulu the only useful information he had about the place was that the Seaview Inn served an excellent balloon-fish soup. In only a few months, however, he learned everything one could find out about Hawaii—from trivial rumors abroad in the taverns and barber shops to such crucial details of Pearl Harbor's defenses as underwater obstructions, beach gradients, the protective net in the entrance channel, and the exact schedule and range of the American patrol planes.

He thoroughly familiarized himself with the topography of Oahu during his first fortnight in Hawaii, pinpointed the places of special interest to him and chose vantage points from which they could be observed best. He returned to these spots again and again, sometimes driven by Mikami or Kotoshirodo, but often by himself, covering enormous distances on foot.

On one of his set tours (which usually lasted from two to four hours) he would board a jitney bus at the Kalihi junction, get off at Aiea just below the sugar refinery, look down on Pearl Harbor, then walk back all the way to the gate of the Submarine Base in the Southeast Loch. On the return hike he would observe the submarines

---

[1] A few entries in the notebook were more suggestive of other interests. He once jotted down the word "observe" and underlined it four times. On another occasion he put down the sentence: "If there is any problem that you like to have explained, please feel free to call upon us." But the next entry was: "The man has committed single adultery, double adultery."

from a favored spot between Aiea and Makalapa. Sometimes he would ride with Mikami around Diamond Head and Koko Head, passing Hanauma and Waimanalo beaches on the windward side of the island, to the Kailua Beach Pavilion, dismiss the driver and walk along the road past the Kaneohe Naval Air Station. He went bathing at the Haleiwa and Waianae beaches on the west side of Oahu, potential landing spots for invasion forces, or walked to Wailupe for a look at the Naval Radio Station.

He never spent more than a few minutes at any one point, but would rather return a next time for another look. There was a certain spot on Aiea Heights which he visited thirty times in a two-month period because it was what he considered the best spot from which to view Pearl Harbor.

Yoshikawa carried out his mission with remarkable decorum. Except for having entered Hawaii under assumed name and diplomatic cover, he did all his spying without violating any American laws. His primary rule was "not to get caught." He never went out of his way to get information. Even when he could not see his objective from a nearby highway he never asked questions about it, nor did he ever leave the road to get a better view.

He carried a cheap little camera hanging from his shoulder on his sightseeing excursions, but mainly as a "prop" to aid his pose as a tourist, for he would have been conspicuous without it. Only once did he take pictures. The maps he used during his tours were issued by the Hawaii Visitors Bureau. He never made any notes or sketches on his wanderings, he had trained himself to memorize the things in which he was interested. Once in a while he took a pair of field glasses along, but nobody ever saw him using them. And though he had several acquaintances who could have been developed as intelligence sources (including the chief yeoman in the office of the Navy's Cable Censor and two young draftsmen at the Navy Yard to whom he gave *kendo* lessons), he never pumped them for any information.

Not a single individual was later found by the FBI or the Navy's District Intelligence Office whom Yoshikawa had involved in his clandestine activities—except for the two men the consulate had enlisted prior to his arrival—Dick Kotoshirodo and Johnny Mikami. Yoshikawa needed them to chauffeur him around on Oahu; this remarkable secret agent did not know how to drive an automobile.

For all his informality, however, and his smart security precautions, Yoshikawa's existence in Hawaii was precarious. The special nature of his mission projected him more than any other member of the consular staff into a strange and highly distrustful environment, and made him a fifth wheel even within the consulate (where he was supposed to handle repatriation cases).

The American counterintelligence agencies—of which there was no shortage in Hawaii[2]—kept elaborate suspect lists in which people were graded "A," "B" and "C," according to the degree of danger they were presumed to represent. Otto Kühn, the "sleeper spy" Captain Ogawa had planted on Oahu in 1936, was an "A" suspect on the FBI's list, as was the intelligence officer who posed as a chemist at the Honolulu Sake Brewery. But Yoshikawa was on none of the lists.

The Japanese consulate general was under close surveillance. Both the FBI and the DIO had several "contacts" who reported periodically on most of the goings-on in its offices, including Consul General Kita's visitors. Since 1940 the DIO had taps on six of the consulate's business phones, another on Okuda's private line, and still another on the phone in Kita's residence. An average of sixty conversations were recorded daily by Chief Ships Clerk Theodore Emanual in the DIO's office. They were translated by Lieutenant Commander Denzel Carr, and circulated to Colonel Bicknell's Contact Office and the FBI. Okuda was thus overheard in December 1940, when he asked the Reverend Unji Hirayama to observe the ships at Lahaina and found out from him that they had abandoned this anchorage.

But no amount of tapping developed even a scintilla of derogatory information about Yoshikawa. He was, in fact, the only Japanese official at the consulate who was never as much as suspected of espionage activities by the American authorities. They accepted him implicitly for what he pretended to be—a mere vice-consul who was having a corking good time in Hawaii. Nobody among the American counterspies was prepared to believe that the Japanese intelligence service would entrust as important a spot as Hawaii to the care of a single bibulous spy. . . .[3]

---

[2] Counterespionage in Hawaii was split three ways: (1) the Navy (the District Intelligence Office of the 14th Naval District headed by Captain Mayfield); (2) the Army (the so-called Contact Office of the Hawaiian Department G-2 under Lieutenant Colonel George W. Bicknell, the Criminal Investigation Division at Fort Shafter headed by Lieutenant Colonel Byron M. Meurlott, and the G-2 of the Hawaiian Air Force under Lieutenant Colonel Edward W. Raley); and (3) the FBI Field Office, with Special Agent Robert L. Shivers in charge. Together, they had a personnel of about a hundred officers and full-time investigators, and several hundred "special agents" and "confidential informants" in a dense web that covered the Islands.

[3] It was only on February 15, 1942—seventy days after Pearl Harbor, in an investigation

At nine o'clock in the morning on November 1 the *Taiyo Maru* docked at Pier 8 in Honolulu Harbor. This voyage reflected the deepening crisis. Since all Japanese shipping to America had been suspended, the *Taiyo Maru* had been especially chartered to make the trip so that people who had been stranded in Japan or in Hawaii could go home under the gathering war clouds.

A little army of immigration and customs officials greeted the passengers instead of the usual hula troops and carnival atmosphere. Mingling among them were all of Colonel Bicknell's Contact agents and Shivers' G-men. Passports and baggage were thoroughly inspected, but no suspicious persons were found among the passengers, and no papers of any importance from the standpoint of national security were discovered in the suitcases.

And yet, the *Taiyo Maru* was on a crucial secret mission. Disguised as stewards in her crew were two young men whose presence on the trip made this a momentous voyage—nothing less than a test cruise to chart the course of Admiral Yamamoto's striking force to Hawaiian waters. One of them was Suguru Suzuki, the youngest lieutenant commander in the Imperial Navy, now serving on the staff of Admiral Chuichi Nagumo's air fleet getting ready for "Operation Z." The other was Lieutenant Commander Toshihide Maejima, staff officer of Vice-Admiral Gunichi Mikawa's support force of battleships, cruisers and submarines.

On instructions from the Naval General Staff, the *Taiyo Maru* had altered her regular course outward bound and taken a northern

---

Report prepared by the 14th Naval District—that "Secretary Tadasi [*sic*] Morimura" was first mentioned at all. And it was not until June 15, 1942, that "Morimura" was identified as "the chief collector of facts for the consulate concerning the movements of U.S. Navy vessels in and out of Pearl Harbor." His true identity was never established by any of the American counterintelligence agencies.

In December 1953 the *Ehime Shimbun,* a provincial Japanese newspaper, published an interview with a former officer of the Imperial Navy who stated that "an ensign named Takeo Yoshikawa" had been "assigned as intelligence officer to the Japanese consulate at Honolulu prior to the Pearl Harbor attack on December 7, 1941." The interview was reprinted in the *New York Times* on December 9, 1953. In the wake of this publicity, Yoshikawa received several offers from newspapers and magazines to tell his own story. He did not accept these invitations.

However, in the summer of 1960 Lieutenant Colonel Norman Stanford, USMC, the American assistant naval attaché in Tokyo, managed to track him down at Matsuyama on Shikoku Island, where Yoshikawa was managing a gasoline station. The Japanese, who are still anxious to hide their espionage effort before Pearl Harbor, never rewarded him with a promotion or decoration for his extraordinary service.

Yoshikawa himself views his fate philosophically.

"I am older now," he told Colonel Stanford, "and dwelling more in the past as the years go by. Some things are certainly ordained. . . . In truth, if only for a moment in time, I held history in the palm of my hand."

route, crossing over between Midway and the Aleutians, then cutting south to Honolulu. Suzuki and Maejima had been assigned to check the winds and atmospheric pressures during the crossing, observe how the liner behaved in heavy weather, and record how many ships they encountered. Not a single one was sighted during the entire voyage.

On November 2, when the crew was allowed to go ashore, Suzuki drove to the consulate compound and demanded to be taken to Kita, who had been alerted to his arrival in a telegram from Ogawa on October 19. Closeted with the consul general, he revealed his identity and told Kita that "the day is rapidly approaching." He asked him in Captain Ogawa's name to instruct Ensign Yoshikawa to intensify his surveillance of Pearl Harbor.

During the meeting Suzuki gave Kita a ball of crumpled rice paper. It was a list with ninety-seven specific questions about the defenses of Pearl Harbor. When Suzuki had left, Kita called in Yoshikawa and passed the list to him. That same day Kita boarded the *Taiyo Maru,* going in his official capacity as consul general and pretending to supervise the repatriation cases. He sought out Suzuki and handed him Yoshikawa's answers to most of the questions, including the one that topped the list:

"This is the most important question: On what day of the week would the most ships be in Pearl Harbor on normal occasions?"

"Sunday" was Yoshikawa's reply.

He also smuggled a package to Suzuki containing a collection of intelligence documents which Yoshikawa had assembled—sketches, a map he had drawn of Pearl Harbor with the berthing plan and another on which he had marked the airfields on Oahu, with a special report describing the structural details of the hangars at Hickam and Wheeler fields. Included in the package was a set of aerial photographs—the only such pictures Yoshikawa had taken with his little "prop" camera during his mission. He had made them only twelve days before, on October 21, on a flight in a small plane he had chartered at John Rodgers.

"We knew then," he later wrote, "that things were building to a climax and that my work was almost done."

The ship was held in Honolulu for five days to give the American authorities ample time to make a thorough inspection of the departing passengers. Suzuki and Maejima used the long stopover to advantage. From information they picked up by interviewing certain

visitors, they corroborated Okuda's previous intelligence that the
Pacific Fleet was no longer using the Lahaina Anchorage as an
assembly point. They picked up some additional data about the
hangars at Hickam and Wheeler, and purchased picture post cards of
Oahu and Pearl Harbor.

In one of the gift shops in downtown Honolulu they discovered a
Laporello set of post cards showing a panoramic view of Pearl Harbor from the air. It sold for one dollar a set, and Suzuki purchased
several sets. (Less than five weeks later, photo copies of the set were
in the cockpits of the Japanese planes attacking Pearl Harbor. The
panorama of the harbor was divided into numbered squares. Each
bombardier knew which square was his target and what ships he
would find there.) . . .

. . . The Japanese had begun to camouflage their fleets. Promptly
at 0000 hours on November 1, all radio call signs of the forces afloat
were changed. This was unusual. Service calls were normally revised
only every six months, but this change occurred a whole month
before the end of the current period. The Japanese sought to conceal
the purport of the change by leaving shore-station calls, shore addresses and some of their tactical calls unaltered, and using their old
garble tables, to give the impression that the revision amounted
merely to a re-assignment of old calls. In the immediate wake of the
change, moreover, they held traffic volume below normal to make it
more difficult for American radio intelligence to "line up" the new
calls.[4]

This was a severe blow to the American intelligence effort at this
crucial juncture. Fleets are usually kept under surveillance either by
so-called naval observers or by radio intelligence. In Japan, the United
States Navy had only a tiny group of "fleet watchers," partly because
the maintenance of observers on the scale which the surveillance of
Yamamoto's mercurial fleet needed would have been too difficult and
costly, but mainly because it was not deemed necessary. Communications intelligence had proved more than adequate to ascertain the
missions and positions of Japanese fleets and ships.

For a long time the compromised FLAG OFFICERS code had
supplied most of the intelligence the United States Navy needed

---

[4] In the scheme of naval communications, each facility, command, authority or unit is
assigned a call sign of its own. One of the functions of radio intelligence is "traffic
analysis"—the recovery ("line-up") of these calls to identify the agencies or units which
use them. The location of the sender is established by means of goniometric direction
finding.

about its Japanese adversary. In addition, a relatively well-staffed and well-endowed radio intelligence organization was maintained in Washington, Hawaii and the Philippines.[5] By the late fall of 1941, however, huge gaps had developed in this coverage. The FLAG OFFICERS code was lost and Rochefort's team of cryptanalysts was making no headway whatsoever in its effort to solve its replacement. Op-20-G did succeed in keeping the old JN series open and was, in fact, using its twenty-fifth variant, solved a few months before. But it was yielding only routine information, mostly of an administrative nature, with very little operational or tactical intelligence.

Under these circumstances, dependence on traffic intelligence had become crucial. At about this time Lieutenant Commander Wilfred J. Holmes, a communications expert specializing in traffic intelligence, joined Rochefort's staff in Hawaii to plot the movements of Japanese ships by sifting and collating their radio calls. He was confronted with a major emergency even before he could settle down in his new job.

"Greatest effort is being made," he wrote on November 7 in the Unit's daily Communication Intelligence Summary, "to increase the number of identified calls to facilitate analysis of the traffic but Orange changes in methods of handling fleet traffic renders this more difficult than had been hoped." Even a week later he had to concede that "the large number of alternate calls used by major forces renders analysis of traffic headings very slow and difficult."

For a brief moment in this race it seemed, nevertheless, that Holmes had stumbled upon Yamamoto's big secret. On November 3 he discovered what he described as "an entirely new organization of the naval air force" and identified it as "the First Air Fleet." It was, indeed, Nagumo's task force, exercising at Saeki Bay for the Pearl Harbor attack. But no sooner was it spotted and identified than it was lost again.

Most of the intelligence that traffic analysis produced during these weeks proved not only woefully erroneous but fatally misleading. Thus, on November 17—when Admiral Nagumo's fleet was at sea, en route to Tankan Bay in the Kuriles—Holmes reported that "the carriers are mostly in the Kure-Sasebo area." On November 27—when

[5] In Hawaii, Commander Rochefort's Communications Intelligence Unit was composed of a decryption section, an interception section, a traffic intelligence section and the mid-Pacific direction-finder net, with stations at Dutch Harbor in Alaska, Samoa, Pearl Harbor and Midway. Rochefort had a total of twenty officers and about eighty enlisted men working in his C/I Unit on various "missions," one of which was traffic analysis.

the striking force with its six carriers was a day out of Etorofu, steaming toward Hawaii—traffic analysis located the carriers "in home waters" and the submarines "in Chichijima area."

After that Commander Holmes gave up this guessing game. He admitted that he had lost both groups. From then on to the bitter end, the refrain of his Communication Intelligence Summaries was: "No information on submarines or carriers."

Yet, Admiral Yamamoto's supposedly ironclad communications security had a "leak" after all. Through a narrow opening his aides had overlooked, a channel to his big secret had opened up. This channel was the Foreign Ministry's line of confidential communications. It had been used for some time by the Third Bureau of the Naval General Staff, but the intelligence reports this circuit carried until the middle of November were neither important nor urgent. Now, however, it suddenly became the main link in Japan's most vital intelligence operation—Ensign Yoshikawa's watch at Pearl Harbor.

During the whole first half of November, Yashikawa had sent only two ship-movement reports to Captain Ogawa in the Third Bureau— one on the 10th, the other on the 14th. But he knew from Commander Suzuki's mission to Hawaii that "things were building to a climax," and was awaiting direct word from Tokyo to accelerate his espionage effort.

It came on November 15, in a radiogram from Ogawa. "As relations between Japan and the United States are most critical," it read, "make your 'ships-in-harbor' reports irregularly but at a rate of twice a week. Although you already are no doubt aware, please take extra care to observe secrecy."

This was Y-Day for Yoshikawa's operation in Hawaii. The cadre of "inside agents" at the consulate received its own call to action. Dick Kotoshirodo was now given the assignment of "counting" the destroyers in Pearl Harbor. He motored daily to the harbor area, driving at a speed of 25 miles an hour on Kamehameha Highway along the perimeter of the Navy Yard, observing the destroyers as he drove. Secretary Seki, back in the secret fold, was to report on the cruisers. He became a regular customer at old Eto's soft-drink stand and a daily visitor at the Pan American Landing in Pearl City, whence the cruisers could be seen best. Johnny Mikami was asked to obtain whatever information he could about the defenses of the harbor. Otto Kühn was told to complete his visual signal system and submit it as soon as possible so that it could be forwarded to Ogawa.

Ensign Yoshikawa observed the battleships and carriers, and coordinated the effort. On November 18 he filed his first report under the new schedule. No. 222 in the series of intelligence dispatches sent in the consulate's code, it read:

1. *The warships at anchor in the Harbor on [Saturday] the 15th were as I told you in my No. 219 on that day:*
   Area A—A battleship of the Oklahoma-*class entered and one tanker left port.*
   Area C—3 warships of the heavy-cruiser class were at anchor.
2. *On the 17th, the* Saratoga *was not in the Harbor. The carrier* Enterprise *(or some other vessel) was in Area C. Two heavy cruisers of the* Chicago-*class, one of the* Pensacola-*class were tied up at docks KS. Four merchant vessels were at anchor in Area D.*
3. *At 1000 on the 17th, 8 destroyers were observed entering the Harbor. Their course was as follows: In a single file at a distance of 1000 meters apart at a speed of 3 knots, they moved into Pearl Harbor. From the entrance of the Harbor through Area B to the buoys in Area C, to which they were moored, they changed course five times, each time roughly 30 degrees. The elapsed time was one hour. However, one of these destroyers entered Area A after passing the water reservoir on the eastern side.*

For the next eighteen days, until the night of December 6, Yoshikawa filed twenty-four telegrams, a list of which will show by itself the intensity and scope of his effort in this final phase of his secret mission:

November
18th—ship-movement report
  report that the customary announcements of ship sailings had been suspended
  arrival in Honolulu of American technicians en route to the Burma Road
19th—two ship-movement reports
22nd—departure of an American convoy bound for Singapore
  two ship-movement reports
23rd—ship-movement report[6]
24th—report on the Pacific Fleet's training areas
25th—ship-movement report
26th—ship-movement report
28th—miscellaneous military information
29th—two ship-movement reports

---

[6] It was on this day that Yoshikawa entered in his diary the word "observe," underlining it four times.

December
1st—ship-movement report
2nd—ship-movement report
3rd—three ship-movement reports
  submission of Kühn's signal system
4th—two ship-movement reports
5th—ship-movement report
6th—the last two ship-movement reports

In the meantime Captain Ogawa sent a number of triple-priority telegrams to Yoshikawa asking him to report on specific features of Pearl Harbor's defenses. On November 18, for instance, he asked the ensign to report on vessels in Honolulu's Mamala Bay and "the area adjacent thereto"; on the 20th he instructed Yoshikawa to "investigate thoroughly the fleet air bases in the vicinity of the Hawaiian military reservation"; on the 29th he asked him to report henceforth "even when there are no movements of ships." And he repeated the admonition: "Make your investigations with great secrecy."

At the diplomatic end, the Foreign Ministry was now liquidating the peace and preparing the war, and this whole hectic business was reflected fully in the telegrams. Foreign Minister Shigenori Togo's dispatches to Ambassadors Nomura in Washington, Oshima in Berlin and Horikiri in Rome resounded with impatience, exasperation and alarm. The telegrams carried increasingly broader hints that the critical moment of the crisis was at hand. The Foreign Ministry's dispatches to Japanese missions abroad had the unmistakable tone of a supreme emergency.

A sequence of urgent dispatches to Washington in particular made clear that Japan had set a time limit on the negotiations and would take "drastic action" after that. The series began with three telegrams on November 4—the eve of the imperial conference—in which Togo told Nomura bluntly that the Empire had reached the crossroads. "Conditions both within and without Japan are so tense," Toto wrote in the first telegram of this day, "that no longer is procrastination possible. This is our last effort. The success or failure of the pending discussions will have an immense effect on the destiny of our Empire."

His second and third telegrams of the day reemphasized this theme. "Our internal situation makes it impossible for us to make any further compromise," he wrote in one; then added in the other, as a footnote to the Tojo government's "final proposals" for a "truce" sent to Nomura in the same dispatch: "This is the last effort to prevent something from happening."

On November 5 Togo advised Nomura of the ominous decision of the imperial conference. "Because of various circumstances," he wrote, "it is imperative that all arrangements for the signing of this agreement be completed by the 25th of this month. I realize that this is a difficult order, but it is unavoidable under the circumstances. Please understand this fully and do your utmost to save Japanese-American relations from falling into a chaotic condition. Do so with great resolve and with unstinted labor, I beg of you. This information is to be kept strictly to yourself only."

For the first time a deadline was explicitly set and Nomura, who apparently regained some of his equilibrium, responded by advising the Foreign Minister to be more circumspect and discreet in his telegrams. "There is danger," he wrote, "that America will see through our proposals. If we have made up our minds on a final course of action, it would be the part of wisdom to keep quiet about it."

But Togo had implicit faith in the absolute security of his communications. In his next telegram he spoke of "the exceeding seriousness of the moment," and told Nomura: "The situation is nearing the climax. Time is indeed becoming short."

On November 14 Nomura sent a long dispatch to Tokyo, which Commander Safford aptly described as the ambassador's swan song. The policy of the American government in the Pacific, he told the Foreign Minister, is to stop any further move on Japan's part, "either southward or northward." The Americans, he wrote, "are contriving by every possible means" to prepare for war if need be; it was not Washington's intention to see Munich repeated. The United States would never grant Japan preferential treatment over China. A war resulting from the crisis would be a long one. Whoever had the power to hold out would win. "I would like to counsel patience for one or two months," Nomura concluded his passionate plea, "to get a clear view of the world situation. This would be our best plan."

Togo's answer was curt. The fate of the Empire hangs by the slender thread of a few days, he wrote. I set the deadline, not you! There will be no change in our policies!

The threat had become explicit. On November 22 Togo wrote to

Nomura as bluntly as he could afford: "There are reasons beyond your ability to guess why we want to settle Japanese-American relations by November 25, but if the signing [of an agreement] could be completed by the 29th, we would be willing to wait until that date."

Then he added: "This time we mean it that the deadline absolutely cannot be changed. After that things are automatically going to happen."

Like a man condemned to be hanged in the morning, Nomura was now fighting for every precious hour. Togo had set the new deadline as November 29. But the 29th in Tokyo would only be the 28th in Washington. Perhaps Togo had meant Washington time. Here was the prospect of gaining a whole day's reprive. Nomura eagerly queried the Foreign Minister, only to have his last hope promptly squashed. "The time limit set in my telegram No. 812," Togo wrote back, "is in Tokyo time."

Simultaneously Admiral Yamamoto sent another "Top-Secret Operations Order," this one to Admiral Nagumo with the striking force at Tankan Bay. "The task force will depart Hitokappu Wan [Bay] on November 26," he wrote, "and proceed without being detected to rendezvous set for December 3.

"X-Day will be December 8."

Yamamoto's signal went out in the impregnable new code on a masked circuit and was completely missed by "Magic." But the Togo-Nomura exchange was in the B system (Purple) and moved in the usual way, by radio via the commercial cable companies. Togo had betrayed the hidden hand of Japan, and "Magic" caught him in the act.

Every single one in the Togo-Nomura exchange of telegrams was intercepted and processed promptly and fully. The dispatches—all of them in translations whose English even exaggerated the furor of their tone—were before the American policymakers by the morning of November 25.

Mr. Hull recognized them for what they were. He concluded from their tone and contents that the military in Japan were chafing at the passage of time and that Tokyo regarded the "proposals" as the last bargain—"the hinge on the breach of the cannon." He knew that the alternative was war.

At this time the President, too, was getting the intercepts. He was no longer denied access to the " 'magics' in the raw," but it had taken a presidential order issued in no uncertain terms to bring this about. From June to the end of September, no intercept had been shown to Mr. Roosevelt: Bratton had simply ignored the procedure during the months when the Army was supposed to service the White House, and when it was the Navy's responsibility, Commander Kramer picked the "magics" which he thought might be of special interest to the President. He would then show them to Captain Beardall, who related those items to Mr. Roosevelt that stuck in his mind.

When, however, the situation sharpened and the intercepts became more explicit in their revelation of Japan's intentions, the President began to feel that he needed this intelligence in its original form. He therefore suggested that actual copies of the translated intercepts be presented to him instead of being merely briefed about them by Mr. Hull or getting only their "gist" from the memoranda Kramer was preparing and occasionally leaving with the naval aide for transmission to the President.

This created a crisis within the crisis. In some consternation Kramer took the matter up with the Director of Naval Intelligence, explaining that he needed G-2's approval before he could deliver any raw intercepts to the White House. The DNI told Kramer to "clear it" with Bratton, and Bratton then carried the problem to General Miles. After some wrangling and under pressure from Captain Beardall, G-2 granted the permission, as it was called, to show some of the intercepts to Mr. Roosevelt.

On November 1 it became the Army's turn again to service the White House, but Bratton chose to ignore the new arrangement. When no deliveries had been made by the 7th, the President instructed Captain Beardall to settle "this ridiculous thing" once and for all, by picking up "the original material" and presenting it to him each day.

Beardall reopened the controversy in ONI, but now Kramer balked. Using the argument that this was November, "the Army's month for dissemination," he told the naval aide there was nothing he could do to get the intercepts for the President. For three days the issue was debated in G-2 and ONI, without producing a solution. But when Beardall informed the President of this hassle, Mr. Roosevelt directed the naval aide "to pay no attention to those dunderheads in the Army and Navy" and bring him the intercepts each day as soon as they were processed. An emergency meeting was called in General Miles's office, and G-2 finally agreed to letting Beardall handle the *original* material for the President.[7]

It required no exceptional imagination, no reading between the lines to gauge the portent of these intercepts. Yet for all their clear understanding of the ominous message which the intercepts carried, both the President and Mr. Hull decided to bide their time. They undertook nothing to advise the nation of the utmost seriousness of the situation or to alert the Army and the Navy for the showdown. While the pall of war thus hung heavily over the Pacific, Mr. Hull preferred to continue the talks—"for the purpose," as he wrote on November 29, "of making a record."

His three major advisers—Hornbeck, Hamilton and Ballantine—were caught in the forms rather than the substance of crisis diplomacy, and paid but passing attention to the feverish "magics." They were too busy drafting a note in which the United States would answer the Japanese "proposals" (that Nomura and Kurusu had got around to submitting only on November 20). It was to set forth the "principles" on which Washington would be willing to agree to a "truce."

They worked under enormous pressure. The Chinese objected vehemently to a modus vivendi. The British and the Dutch beseeched Mr. Hull to make the occasion of his note a demonstration of American determination. Mr. Churchill voiced his opposition from behind Chinese backs. "What about Chiang Kai-shek?" he wrote to the President. "Is he not having a very thin diet?"

If the dispatches passing between Togo and Nomura made it unmistakably clear that Japan was accelerating its move to war, the Ogawa–Yoshikawa exchange of telegrams pinpointed Pearl Harbor as an objective in the coming conflict. And since they were sent through the facilities of the Foreign Ministry in a diplomatic code which the Americans had cracked, "Magic" had them completely covered. It

---

[7] It was, therefore, only from November 12 on (when "Magic" had already been operating for about fourteen months) that the President was allowed to see the intercepts—but even then only those which Commander Kramer chose to give to Beardall for delivery to the White House. The President was thus granted the privilege of seeing the actual "magics" for only twenty-five days immediately prior to Pearl Harbor. The total number of intercepts he was finally permitted to read between November 12 (when the originals started going to him) and December 7 (up to two hours before the attack) totaled sixty-four out of some eighteen hundred processed during this same period.

had become more than just a source of diplomatic intelligence. Suddenly it began to carry at least some of the information the United States Navy had lost with the collapse of its traffic analysis and change of the FLAG OFFICERS code.

Most of Ogawa's telegrams to Honolulu and Yoshikawa's reports to the Third Bureau were intercepted by at least three of the "Magic" monitoring stations—by the Navy's Station S in Puget Sound or by the Army's MS-2 in San Francisco and MS-5 in Hawaii. Moreover, Ogawa's telegram of November 15 and Yoshikawa's report three days later had been fully processed by December 3 and 6, respectively. Three other Ogawa dispatches—those of November 18, 20 and 29— were also translated before December 7. But this particular coverage went no further. At this stage of "Magic," the operation was startlingly similar to Yardley's activities, especially during the Washington Conference when the War Department conducted the venture not to satisfy its own intelligence requirements but solely for the benefit of the State Department.

The "magics" were, of course, avidly read in the War and Navy departments by the handful of Ultras who had access to them. But as they saw it, "Magic" was merely a collection of broken *diplomatic* codes—important to the White House and the State Department, to be sure, but yielding only a trickle of hard intelligence of any "operational or tactical value" to the Army and the Navy.

In the preoccupation with "Magic's" importance as a source of diplomatic intelligence it was overlooked that now it also carried information of inestimable military and naval significance. The consular traffic between Honolulu and Tokyo was still deprecated as reflecting merely the haphazard intelligence effort of a band of amateurs. It was left, now as before, in the "deferred" category of intercepts that deserved no special consideration and whose processing required no particular haste. The sudden increase of Yoshikawa's reports, and the tone and urgency of Ogawa's telegrams to Honolulu, did not impress any of the men who processed these "magics" as being unduly significant.

Most of these intercepts were decrypted by SIS and Op-20-G as soon as they arrived in Washington from the interception stations. There, however, their processing ended. They were sent to Commander Kramer for translation and distribution, but his section was now overburdened with the more important "magics" it had to handle.

The PURPLE messages of high-priority rating were flowing in a steady stream as the Tokyo–Washington traffic was reaching peak volume.

Yoshikawa's espionage messages piled up in the incoming baskets of the translators in Op-20-GZ. They were left there, unattended, to await their turn—until it was too late. . . .

On November 30, 1941, despite Hull's and Stimson's warnings that relations with Japan had left the bounds of diplomacy, F.D.R. still persisted in the belief that he was gaining the time the Army and the Navy were pleading for. And he was confident that the State Department's note of November 26—conspicuously marked "tentative" to indicate that it was still leaving the door ajar—would bring an answering note through normal diplomatic channels, and not war.[8]

It was, therefore, with a light heart and in a buoyant spirit that the President sat down with the patients in Warm Springs for a belated Thanksgiving dinner. But in the midst of it Lieutenant Commander George Fox, his physical therapist, had to wheel him out to answer a call from Washington. Mr. Hull was calling to tell the President that Premier Tojo had proclaimed in a "belicose speech" that Japan was "morally bound for the honor and pride of mankind" to "purge" Great Britain and the United States "from all of East Asia with a vengeance." Hull construed the statement as "a last straw" and decided to call the President about it. He now advised Mr. Roosevelt to return to Washington immediately because a Japanese attack seemed imminent.

The President left at once and arrived back in Washington in the morning of December 1, only to find that what had threatened to develop into an explosive incident had blown out meekly. Alarmed over Tojo's intemperate remarks, and more anxious than ever to lull the Americans a little longer, the Japanese went to some lengths to disavow their Premier.

On December 1 Ambassador Grew cabled from Tokyo that he had received what amounted to an apology for Tojo's statements and that "several prominent Japanese" with whom he had discussed the incident "all appear to desire continuance of the Washington conversations."

There would have been ample reason for the President to remain

---

[8] Ambassador Nomura, omitted to transmit to Tokyo the conspicuous reference to the "tentative" character of the American proposals and thus created the impression that they represented the definitive and final terms of the United States.

uneasy despite Mr. Grew's reassuring cable. The "magics" (which he was now seeing in the full text of the intercepts) continued to carry their disturbing message. Three which awaited him on his return in particular seemed to bear out Hull's apprehension over Tojo's speech rather than Grew's optimistic interpretation.

One intercept showed that the Japanese were transferring First Secretary Terasaki from their embassy in the United States to Argentina. Since he was, according to Kramer, "head of Japanese espionage in Western Hemisphere," this seemed to indicate, as Kramer indeed pointed out in a footnote, that Tokyo was dismantling its intelligence service in the United States and establishing it in a neutral American country, presumably because rupture of relations or war would make it impossible for Terasaki to continue to function in Washington.

The second was the set of telegrams from Kameyama to the various Japanese missions abroad arranging for the gradual destruction of their code material and confidential papers.

The third was a dispatch from Foreign Minister Togo instructing Ambassador Oshima in Berlin to see Hitler and Ribbentrop and tell them "very secretly . . . that there is extreme danger that war may suddenly break out between the Anglo-Saxon nations and Japan through some clash of arms," and that "the time of the breaking out of this war may come quicker than anyone dreams."

When Captain Beardall showed the Togo telegram to Mr. Roosevelt, the President spent some time studying it. The next day he asked the naval aide to bring it back from the files, for he wanted to read It again. It made an enormous impression on him. Even much later it stuck in his mind as the one intercept he had seen that convinced him of the seriousness of the Japanese threat. On this December 2 the President seemed to be sure that some warlike action was imminent and that the United States might not be as immune as he had thought. He sent for Stimson, Knox and Sumner Welles (the latter substituting for Secretary Hull, who went to bed for a day to recoup his strength that was beginning to crumble under the strain of the crisis). This was virtually the only time during this period that the President showed vigor, determination and initiative to counter the Japanese moves with a number of American arrangements.

A flurry of action ensued in the Navy Department, as reflected in a number of OPNAV signals sent during the day to Admiral Hart of the

Asiatic Fleet, Admiral Kimmel in Pearl Harbor, and the commandants of the 14th and 16th Naval districts. They were told that the Japanese missions at Hong Kong, Singapore, Batavia, Manila, Washington and London had been ordered to "destroy most of their codes and ciphers, and to burn all other important confidential and secret documents." An "action dispatch" to Hart and the commandant of the 16th Naval District went so far as to actually mention a "magic"—the one in which Kameyama had ordered Washington to destroy the B machine and had instructed the consul general in Batavia "to return [his] machine to Tokyo at once." . . .

On the day Captain Mayfield managed to gain access to the Japanese consulate's confidential dispatches at their source, an unusual amount of first-hand data became available about Japanese moves toward war and, in fact, about their plan to attack Pearl Harbor.

In Honolulu the telegram containing Kühn's scheme of signaling was filed with and transmitted by RCA, and was intercepted by no fewer than three separate operations: by Captain Mayfield, who was given a copy of the original by Manager Street of RCA; by the Army's MS-7 at Fort Hunt, Virginia; and by the Navy's Station M in Cheltenham, Maryland. MS-5, the mystery station at Fort Shafter, picked up Captain Ogawa's telegram to Kita with the order that the consulate report daily henceforth the movements of ships (instead of twice a week as heretofore) and asking details of the anti-torpedo nets and barrage balloons at Pearl Harbor.

Neither intercept was processed when picked up. But in Washington a "strictly secret" telegram of December 2 from Tokyo—ordering the embassy to "destroy all codes except one, one of the cipher machines, and all confidential documents"—became available in translation. The message was the classic order usually issued on the eve of war, and Colonel Bratton immediately recognized it as such. But he now found himself in an awkward position. He had lost face badly with his prediction that war with Japan would break out on November 30, and was ridiculed as a "worry-bird" in the War Plans Division. He felt deeply the humiliation of his debacle and hardly dared to show himself at the "front offices" in the Munitions Building.

But now the code-destruction telegram propelled him back into action. He sent Lieutenant Schindel from his Section up Massachusetts Avenue to ascertain whether the embassy was complying with the order. Judging from the grayish-white smoke escaping through one of the chimneys of the quaint embassy building, Schindel concluded that they were and so reported back to Bratton, who took the intercept and the lieutenant's report to General Miles. At Miles's suggestion he then went to War Plans, gave his opinion that this was "the culmination of the complete revelation of Japanese intentions" and said that it was construed by G-2 as meaning "immediate war." He suggested that War Plans send another warning to the overseas commands, but Gerow turned him down. "I think they have had plenty of notification," he said and told Bratton rather curtly that he did not wish to discuss the matter any further.

As was his practice when he could not make any headway with his fellow officers in the War Department, Bratton went over to the Navy Department to review the situation with Commander McCollum, his opposite number in ONI. The problem of further warnings, especially to Hawaii, was explored in an impromptu conference attended by Admiral Noyes of Naval Communications, Captain Wilkinson, the Director of Naval Intelligence, McCollum and Bratton. The evidence was impressive. Aside from the latest code-destruction message, the "winds" code was haunting the scene. Wilkinson was, therefore, all in favor of another warning signal to Kimmel. Noyes, however, objected on the ground that it would be "an insult to the intelligence of the admiral."

"I do not agree with you," Wilkinson said. "Admiral Kimmel is a very busy man." But Noyes persisted in his objection and refused to transmit any further warnings.

Bratton returned to Miles with an idea to circumvent Noyes's objections. McCollum had revealed to Bratton the existence of Rochefort's organization and that Rochefort himself was aware of the "winds" message inasmuch as his interception stations had orders to monitor for "the implementing message." McCollum had suggested that as a way out of their difficulty Miles send a message to Colonel Kendall J. Fielder, General Short's G-2 at Fort Shafter, "to see Rochefort at once." It was assumed that Rochefort would then warn Fielder and somehow the warning would reach Kimmel in the end.

Miles agreed to send a message and Bratton then composed one that read: "Commander Rochefort, who can be located through the 14th Naval District, has some information on Japanese broadcasts in which weather reports are mentioned that you must obtain. Contact him at once."

The message went out as "Secret Cablegram No. 519" a few minutes before noon on December 5, but it evaporated as soon as it reached Fort Shafter. Fielder chose to ignore it when he found that Commander Rochefort was the officer in charge of a *combat* intelligence unit. On the principle that "there is no combat intelligence unless there is combat," he decided not to contact Rochefort or, for that matter, probe the obscure meaning of the message. The next-to-last chance to alert Short and Kimmel to the acuteness of the danger, even if only in an indirect way, was thus missed. . . .

Whatever excitement there was in the "Magic" circle the day before seems to have diminished considerably by the morning of December 6 when the staffs of SIS and Op-20-G assembled at their desks. It was Saturday. Work at both places would cease around noon except for Commander Safford's watch in his decrypting section, operating the PURPLE machine day and night.

Safford himself was relaxed. He was planning to go home early and take the rest of the weekend off. Kramer was making his rounds as usual, delivering a few intercepts (none of which seemed urgent or important) at the White House and calling at his stations in the Navy Department.

In Kramer's absence his confidential yeoman, Chief Ships Clerk H. L. Bryant, presided over the Cryptographic Section's six translators, who for the first time in weeks had no top priority messages before them requiring their immediate attention. After the hectic traffic of the previous days, PURPLE calmed down. There were hardly any telegrams going out from Nomura or coming in from Togo—apparently they had told each other everything that needed to be said.

One of the translators was a novice. She had been with the Section for a little over two weeks, still tense and exhilarated as outsiders usually are when suddenly they find themselves inside an intelligence organization. She was a plain woman of thirty-eight, Dorothy Edgers by name, married, a schoolteacher by profession. She had lived in Japan for more than thirty years and held a diploma to teach Japanese to Japanese pupils up to the high school level. Her command of the language was perfect, and her eagerness to work hard and do her best at this mystery-shrouded, scintillating job was usually not in evidence among Kramer's regular crew of translators.

Neither Commander Kramer nor Chief Bryant had assigned any special work to her, although she had a number of decrypted intercepts before her in the incoming basket awaiting translation. However, they were all in the "deferred" category, and "magics" of this kind would be left in the baskets for weeks at times before having their processing completed with the translation.

Both eager and bored, and loath just to sit there doing nothing, Mrs. Edgers pulled up the basket and began to scan the intercepts. The more she read them, the more engrossed and intrigued she became. To her mind these were important messages, and it seemed most urgent not to leave them gathering dust in the crisis. One of the "magics" she glanced at was dated December 2 and intercepted on the same day by the Army monitoring station in Hawaii. It was Ogawa's telegram to Kita instructing the consulate to file its ship-movement reports daily henceforth and inquiring about the torpedo nets and balloons at Pearl Harbor.

Another telegram was considerably older—dated November 24, when it was also intercepted by the Army station at the Presidio. A long dispatch sent in two parts, it seemed to be a most detailed report on "the manner in which the American fleet moves"—the battleships, aricraft carriers and cruisers, down to the lowliest mine sweepers. She found a third, dating back to November 28, that had been intercepted by the Army station at Fort Hunt just outside of Washington. It spoke of eight B-17 planes stationed at Midway and of the range of the anti-aircraft guns that Americans had on the island. It was labeled "Military Report," though it seemed to have originated at the consulate in Hawaii.

Mrs. Edgers then pulled out what appeared to be the longest intercept in the basket, its Japanese-language transcript covering sheet after sheet. It was one of the more recent "magics," only three days old, and had been routed to her that very morning. Its markings showed that it had been picked up by both Fort Hunt and the Navy's own Station M at Cheltenham.

As Mrs. Edgers began reading it—actually devouring it word for word instead of just glancing at it as she did with the other intercepts—she felt galvanized by what she read. As she remembered the dispatch even four years later, it was "a message saying how they were going to communicate from Honolulu to the parties interested information on our fleet movements from Honolulu, and apparently it was something which they had had previous arrangements but they had changed some of the minor details of how to go about it."

She went on to say: "I think there was something to do with lights, a window of a certain house, and there was also something about newspaper advertising."

It was Consul General Kita's telegram of December 3 to Tokyo, transmitting Otto Kühn's scheme of signals to Japanese ships lurking off shore. Mrs. Edgers was completely unfamiliar with any such things as strategy or espionage or the ruses of war. But she now sensed intuitively that the intercept she was holding in her hand had some bearing on every one of them. And she concluded that this special arrangement prepared for Pearl Harbor indicated rather unmistakably that the Japanese had something in store for the base and that the fleet at Pearl appeared to be in jeopardy.

She showed the intercept to one of her colleagues, senior translater Fred C. Woodrough, Jr., who felt that she was absolutely justified in her apprehension. Then she called it to the attention of Chief Bryant, suggesting that he call back Commander Kramer and start the processing of the intercept at once. Bryant agreed that the intercept was "interesting" but he did not think that it warranted any special attention on a weekend. It was too long, he said. Dorothy could never finish the translation by noon. It would "keep" till Monday!

But she refused to put it aside. She returned to her desk and on her own initiative began translating the intercept for Kramer, who, she was positive, would recognize, even as she did, its grave significance and urgency. At twelve o'clock the other translators went home. Mrs. Edgers remained behind with Chief Bryant in the nearly deserted office, she working on the translation, the chief just waiting to be relieved by his superior officer so that he, too, could go home for the weekend.

Kramer showed up at three o'clock, just when Mrs. Edgers was completing the final paragraph of her translation: "If the above signals and wireless messages cannot be made from Oahu, then on Maui Island, 6 miles to the northward of Kula Sanatorium . . . at a point halfway between Lower Kula Road and Haleakala Road (latitude 20° 40′N., longitude 156° 19′W., visible from seaward to the southeast and southwest of Maui Island) the following signal bonfires will be made daily until your EXEX signal is received: from 7 to 8, Signal 3 or 6, from 8 to 9, Signal 4 or 7, from 9 to 10, Signal 5 or 8."

She rushed to Kramer with her copy and he read it through still standing up. But instead of becoming electrified by the message, as Mrs. Edgers was, he showed some irritation with her for staying after office hours to work on a "deferred" intercept. In his annoyance he started to criticize her translation and sat down to edit the copy, changing a word here or a phrase there, to make it sound more "professional." He worked at it for a few minutes, then said: "This needs a lot of work, Mrs. Edgers. Why don't you run along now? We'll finish the editing sometime next week."

Mrs. Edgers tried to protest. "But, Commander," she said, "don't you think that this intercept ought to be distributed right away?"

"You just go home, Mrs. Edgers," Kramer said. "We'll get back to this piece on Monday."

When Colonel Bratton found out about this incident after the war and had his first opportunity to read the old intercept, he summed up what must be history's own verdict in this strange case: "If we had gotten that message on [December 6] . . . the whole picture would have been different."[9]

As far as Hawaii was concerned, the President was never told that Pearl Harbor was in jeopardy. Although every American war plan made a provision for an attack on the Pacific Fleet's major base, such an attack was now neither expected nor anticipated. In a basic summary the Intelligence Branch of G-2 had prepared on November 27 for presentation to the President there was no mention of Pearl Harbor. When he was specifically queried by the President, Admiral Stark assured him that the base was in no danger and that the fleet was at sea.

The President was never shown any of the intercept espionage messages and was never apprised that such reports to Tokyo existed at all. In fact, he was left completely in the dark about any such Japanese activity in Hawaii, and was told only that some sabotage by local Japanese elements could be expected in the event of a Japanese-American war.

Even in the diplomatic sphere of "Magic," Mr. Roosevelt was inadequately serviced. The crucial last-minute messages of the 900-

[9] Testifying before the Joint Congressional Committee on February 11, 1946, Kramer described Mrs. Edgers as "still unfamiliar with the practices and procedures in my office" and was, therefore, not especially qualified to adjudge what was important and what was not among the intercepts. He dismissed the intercept itself as "containing information that was not materially different than information we already had." He persisted in criticizing Mrs. Edgers' translation, claiming that he had to spend "several days [December 8, 9 and 10, after the attack] cleaning garbles and working with this message before it was completed in the form you now see it." He went on to claim that he had had "no clue to the subject or importance of this message," and protested that anyway it was December 6, an even day, "a date of Army responsibility." Beyond that he had no clear recollection of the incident. Mrs. Edgers had been heard briefly by the Hewitt Inquiry on June 22, 1945, but was never called to testify in any of the other investigations.

Serial were taken to the White House only around ten in the morning on December 7, although several of them had been on hand since the 6th. Captain Beardall then chose only the last part of the long note for presentation to the President. Seven other intercepts which Commander Kramer had in the "book"—including the pilot message and the vital telegram instructing Ambassador Nomura to deliver the note at one o'clock—were never submitted to the President. . . .

December 6, 1941

. . . The room was dimly lit by the green-shaded lamp on the President's desk, casting shadows on the pastel walls, on the thick beige carpet, and on the sofa where Harry L. Hopkins sat, trying to stay awake. He had come out of the hospital only a few days before and was not feeling too well. But he was, as ever, the available man, sharing this lonely vigil with the President.

Mr. Roosevelt was toying with his stamp collection and chatting with Hopkins. He talked easily, in a low key, skipping from one topic to another as they came to his mind. He discussed a few more serious matters, like the indiscretion of the Chicago *Tribune,* and his new budget, which he had worked on that morning with Harold Smith, musing about the mayhem Congress was likely to do to it.

But mostly the conversation was in a lighter and even somewhat frivolous vein. He joked about Vincent Astor, his friend and Dutchess County neighbor who had visited him that afternoon, trying to "unload," as the President put it, his costly yacht on the United States Navy. And he brought up a favorite topic of his that recurred often in his nostalgic chats with his closest confidant—retirement to a cozy secluded spot in Florida. Even in the midst of the uncertainties and dangers of these days, Roosevelt remained preoccupied with his plans for a fishing retreat at Key West for Harry Hopkins and himself.

At nine-thirty the door opened quietly, and an usher announced a visitor: "Lieutenant Schulz, Mr. President." Behind the usher was a handsome lad in his twenties, flushed with the excitement of this nocturnal mission to his Commander-in-Chief. He was Lieutenant Robert Lester Schulz from Iowa, Annapolis class of 1934. A week before, he had been sent on temporary duty to the White House to act as assistant to the naval aide.

Captain Beardall had gone home at five-thirty, then on to the dinner party at Captain Wilkinson's house, leaving it to young Schulz to handle whatever urgent messages might still come over from the Office of Naval Intelligence. Thus Schulz had to take to the President a pouchful of dispatches that had just been brought in by Commander Kramer.

Schulz stood at attention at the President's desk, on which he had placed the locked pouch. Then he unlocked it quickly with a key Captain Beardall had entrusted to him, and laid the "book" before the President. There were six documents in it.

On top was a dispatch reporting on the Rostov front in Russia where the Red Army was going over to a promising counteroffensive. Next was a telegram with description of gains Field Marshal Erwin Rommel's Afrika Korps had scored at Tobruk. Another dispatch was the report of a conversation Admiral Nomura and Saburo Kurusu had had with Secretary Hull the day before.

Three brief telegrams involved a controversial First Secretary of the Japanese embassy and a cipher apparatus referred to as "the B-machine."

The President scanned the dispatches briefly, then picked up the telegram at the bottom of the pile. It consisted of some fifteen pages, fastened together in a sheaf with a paper clip, its text typed on the Navy Department's secret-message forms. Mr. Roosevelt read it avidly but quickly, at a rate of about three hundred words per minute, somewhat too fast to allow careful study of the long dispatch.

When he had finished he scooped up the sheets and handed them to Hopkins, who was now on his feet, pacing up and down. Mr. Roosevelt waited for about ten minutes while Hopkins read the document. Then, recovering it for another glance, he said:

"This means war."

He said it quietly, without any bathos, in a voice that betrayed no emotions but stated simply a seemingly inescapable fact. The President and Hopkins went on to discuss the document for another five minutes, in the presence of Lieutenant Schulz.

"Hopkins agreed," the lieutenant later said in recalling their conversation. "The substance of it was—I believe Mr. Hopkins mentioned it first—that since war was imminent, the Japanese intended to strike first, when they were ready, at a moment when all was opportune for them, when their forces were most properly deployed for their advantage. Indochina in particular was mentioned because the Japanese forces had landed there and there were indications of where they would move next. The President mentioned a message he had sent to the Japanese Emperor concerning the presence of Japanese troops in Indochina, in effect requesting their withdrawal.

"Mr. Hopkins then expressed the view," Schulz added, "that since war was undoubtedly going to come at the convenience of the Japanese, it was too bad that we could not strike the first blow and prevent any sort of surprise. The President nodded and said, 'No, we can't do that. We're a democracy and a peaceful people.' Then he raised his voice, and this much I remember definitely. He said, 'But we have a good record.' "

Lieutenant Schulz then picked up the papers and returned them to the pouch for delivery back to the Navy. Commander Kramer was waiting downstairs, drumming with nervous fingers on a long table at which he was sitting in the deserted mail room in the White House basement.

"One thing is abundantly clear," Robert E. Sherwood later wrote. "Roosevelt at that moment faced the most grievous dilemma of his entire career." . . .

Colonel Bratton arrived on Independence Avenue at nine o'clock, entering the Munitions Building with Lieutenant Colonel John R. Deane, one of the assistant secretaries of the General Staff who was to be the duty officer in General Marshall's outer office on this Sunday. Bratton found the fourteenth part of the Japanese note waiting for him—Colonel Dusenbury had come in earlier, taken a copy of the intercept to Marshall's office, left another copy in War Plans and carried the third copy to the State Department to complete the delivery to Mr. Hull.

Until this moment Bratton had not been inclined to make much of the fourteen-part note. In his opinion it was the long-awaited Japanese reply to the American note of November 26. "We just don't barge off to war whenever the spirit moves us" was his way of putting it later. "We have to go through certain formalities." This, then, seemed to be one of the formalities. "This was primarily of . . . immediate interest to the Secretary of State," he said, "not to the Secretary of War or the Chief of the General Staff, for it was not an ultimatum, it was not a declaration of war, nor was it a severance of diplomatic relations."

If anything, it had a reassuring undertone. As he viewed the note with its pilot message, it indicated that "we probably had a little bit more time before the shooting war started." "There was nothing [to it] even after the arrival of the fourteenth part," Bratton said. "There was no military significance to its presence in Washington as long as the Japanese ambassador kept the note locked up in his safe."

As he was reading the fourteenth part, however, Major Doud came in with the intercept of the one o'clock-delivery message. Now the whole crisis gained a different complexion. Immediately upon its receipt, Bratton later claimed, he "became convinced the Japanese were going to attack some American installation in the Pacific area." It stunned him, he said, into frenzied activity. He picked it up and literally ran with it next door looking for General Miles, then down the corridor to War Plans, finally to Deane in the front office asking for General Marshall. None of these officers was in, so Bratton dashed back to his own office, and on his own initiative and without going through channels, put in a call to General Marshall at his quarters in Fort Myer.

Sergeant Aguirre, one of Marshall's orderlies, answered the phone and told Bratton that the general had left the house about ten minutes before, to go horseback riding.

"Well," Bratton said, "you know generally where he goes. Do you think you could get ahold of him?"

"Yes, sir," Aguirre said, "I think I can find him."

"Please go out at once," Bratton said, "get assistance if necessary, and find General Marshall—tell him who I am and ask him to go to the nearest telephone, that it is vitally important that I communicate with him at the earliest practicable moment."

Sergeant Aguirre said he would do so.

Bratton then called General Miles at his home and told him what he had done. "You better come down at once," he said to Miles. "General Marshall may want to see you and talk with you." Then he called Gerow and advised him to come to his office as fast as he could make it.

With the intercept in hand Bratton returned to the front office to see if Deane had any word from the general. There was no word. He then went back to his own office again, to wait for the call from Marshall.

Walking up 16th street toward Pennsylvania Avenue, Commander Kramer pondered the portent of the one o'clock-delivery note. He was quite wrought up by the time he reached the White House, where Captain Beardall had just arrived to find that he was the only presidential aide to put in an appearance. He had come on his own initiative, perhaps because he was a bit uneasy about the night before, when he had left the presentation of the thirteen parts of the important Japanese note to a junior grade lieutenant. Now he wanted to be on hand to deliver the fourteenth part as soon as it came in.

Kramer found Beardall in General Watson's office and gave him the "book." He told him also that Nomura had orders to deliver the note to Mr. Hull at one o'clock, which could be the time set for the launching of some operations. Beardall then went upstairs to Mr. Roosevelt's quarters. The President was still in bed, reading the papers; he took the intercept from the naval aide and went through it quickly. "The Japanese government regrets," it read, "to have to notify hereby the American government that in view of the attitude of the American government that [*sic*] it cannot but consider that it is impossible to reach an agreement through further negotiations."

It was exactly what he had expected: notice that the talks would be terminated but not an announcement of a break in diplomatic relations, certainly not a declaration of war. The President remarked to Beardall: "It looks like the Japs are going to break off the negotiations."

During the meeting, which lasted only a few minutes, Beardall said little if anything. As far as he could later recall it, he did not tell President that Numura had received instructions to deliver the note at one o'clock or mention Kramer's remark that the timing could mean the beginning of military operations somewhere. Mr. Roosevelt did not seem perturbed. He thanked his naval aide, then returned the intercept. It did not strike him as something that needed further attention.

Beardall then left for the Navy Building while Kramer crossed to the State Department, where Mr. Knox was waiting for his copy of the intercept. Kramer handed the "book" to John F. Stone, Mr. Hull's personal assistant, with an oral message for Secretary Knox repeating what he had told Bryant and Beardall about the coincidence in the timing of the delivery note. In Mr. Hull's anteroom Kramer met Dr. Hornbeck, Hamilton and Ballantine, and informed them, too, of the peculiar significance of the one o'clock delivery. As Hamilton remembered the conversation, Kramer "remarked on that occasion, in reference to the matter of an appointment for the Japanese ambassador to see the Secretary of State at 1:00 p.m. on December 7 that the naming of the hour might mean that it was the hour for some

Japanese movement." But no mention was made of Pearl Harbor or Hawaii.

From the State Department, Kramer returned to his office, picked up the processed intercepts that had come over from SIS during his absence and set out on his delivery route within the Department. None of his clients was at his desk. They all were at a conference with the Chief of Naval Operations.

It was now past ten o'clock—around four-thirty in the morning at Pearl—and Marshall was still out, but his opposite number in strategic command and responsibility in the Navy, Admiral Harold R. Stark, was at his desk, an arm's length from the telephone over which this whole awesome problem could have been resolved with a three-minute call.

"Betty" Stark impressed the President as a keen strategic thinker and pleased him with his enthusiastic support of the British in the Atlantic in the "undeclared war." In fact, the CNO was a scholarly, wise and progressive-minded officer, free of the prejudices of a navy that, according to Secretary Stimson, "frequently seemed to retire from the realm of logic into a dim religious world in which Neptune was God, Mahan his prophet, and the United States Navy the only true Church."

His erudition, articulateness and modesty, however, concealed his shortcomings. He lacked the ability to make quick decisions and the ruthlessness to organize and run the Navy Department tightly and efficiently. His laissez-faire created rampant inadequacies that left the Navy floundering, both mentally and physically unprepared for war. If the General Staff was paralyzed by the fact that Marshall was incommunicado, the Navy could have acted, for Stark was there. Moreover, it was his fleets in Pearl and Manila that stood out in front of the crisis and could be expected to bear the brunt of the onslaught.

Stark knew that the thirteen parts of the note had come in. He was the only high commander with whom the President had discussed it the night before, around eleven-thirty, when the CNO returned to his house on the Naval Observatory grounds from the theater. The fourteenth part of the note had been brought to him shortly after nine o'clock this morning, as soon as he arrived at his desk, by Captain Wilkinson and Commander McCollum. They stayed with Stark to discuss its possible meaning. Shortly afterward the intercepts of the telegrams with the one o'clock deadline and the order to destroy the last remaining cipher machine were brought in by Commander Kramer.

By then Stark's office had crowded up. All his top associates (except Admiral Turner) were at his side. Noyes was there from Naval Communications, and Captain Schuirmann, the Navy's liaison officer to the State Department, as was Admiral Ingersoll, the "brain" of Operations. They were joined by Captain Beardall, who had come over from the White House, sensing the urgency of the hour and eager to be closer to the rapidly developing events.

None of these men expected that the Japanese would "dare" to strike at Pearl Harbor. McCollum persisted in his assumption that the fleet was at sea. Wilkinson and the others had their apprehension focused on the Gulf of Siam, Singapore and the East Indies. But they knew of Japanese concentrations in the Marshalls and regarded them, intuitively rather than rationally, as a probable threat to Oahu. They suggested to the CNO, in the deferential manner of their relationship, that he do something. "Why don't you pick up the telephone," Wilkinson asked, "and call Admiral Kimmel?"[10]

Stark reached for the phone to put in the call. But then he thought it over. It was ten thirty-five in Washington but only five minutes past five in Hawaii, an ungodly hour to disturb Admiral Kimmel in his sleep. For another thing, Stark was addicted to the Navy protocol by whose rules it was definitely *not* the function or duty of the high command in Washington to "direct and supervise the detailed administration of commanders in the field." It was, in fact, the fundamental policy in both the Navy and Army high commands "not to interfere unduly with commanders in the field whose records justified the assumption of great responsibilities." The idea of telling Kimmel what to do or not to do was "repugnant" to the Washington staffs. Last but not least, Stark did not think that Pearl Harbor was in danger. He held to the thought he had expressed in a letter to Kimmel as recently as October 17: "Personally I do not believe the Japs are going to sail into us."

---

[10] The intriguing question as to why the telephone was never used in the emergency was raised by the various Pearl Harbor investigations and was answered by General Marshall, who said: "The telephone was not considered as means of transmission because, in the nature of things, it would have been too time-consuming." The Chief of Staff testified further: "From our own experience, my own experience, even now [in 1944] our telephone is a long-time procedure. . . . We now find we do a little bit better by teletype than we do on the telephone." No teletype link with the Hawaiian Department existed prior to the Pearl Harbor attack.

As he was holding the telephone he shook his head and said no, he would rather call the President. He reached the White House switchboard promptly, only to be told that the President's line was busy. Stark replaced the receiver and left it at that. He called for Admiral Turner, who came over quickly, but Stark did not deem it necessary to tell him about the Japanese deadline or the order to destroy the B machine. Rather, he began to discuss with him a recent letter from Admiral Hart requesting clarification of the duties of the Asiatic Fleet in a war that would *not* involve the United States.

The conference in the CNO's office disbanded. The men Stark had dismissed when Turner came in went over to Room 2601, the office of the watch, banding together like a flock of apprehensive birds before a storm. They talked and talked, but their conversation was neither of substance nor consequence. Stark's "so what" attitude, as McCollum described the CNO's reaction to the latest intercepts, had rendered them totally impotent.

Nothing more was done by anybody in the Navy to act upon the alarm sounded by the morning's intercepts. "The basic trouble was," Admiral Ernest J. King, Stark's successor as CNO, told Admiral Zacharias, "that the Navy failed to appreciate what the Japanese could and did do."[11] And in his post-mortem on the disaster he wrote: "Even two hours' advance warning would have been of great value alerting planes and in augmenting the condition of readiness existing on board ship," concluding that "lack of efficiency in Admiral Stark's organization" was one of the major contributing factors in the disaster.

---

[11] The commander's conduct in a situation confronting Stark in Washington and Kimmel in Pearl Harbor is lucidly described in *Sound Military Decision*, by Admiral E. C. Kalbfus, who wrote: "In his estimate, however, the commander's interest is not confined to what the enemy will *probably do; probabilities are subject to change,* and do not, therefore, cover the whole field of capabilities. The commander is not exclusively interested in what the enemy *may intend to do,* or even in what the enemy may be known, at the time, to intend to do; such *intentions are also subject to change.* The commander is interested in *everything that the enemy can do* which may materially influence the commander's own course of action." And Secretary Stimsom said in this connection: "The outpost commander is like a sentinel on duty in face of the enemy. . . . He must assume that the enemy will attack at the time and in the way in which it will be most difficult to defeat him. . . . It is [the commander's duty] to meet him at his post at any time and to make the best possible fight that can be made against him with the weapons with which he has been supplied." Whatever the extenuating circumstances of Kimmel's conduct may have been, he did not meet the challenge of December 7 according to Kalbfus' concept of the commander's interest or Stimson's postulate of his duties.

Samuel Eliot Morison

WHO WAS RESPONSIBLE?

Samuel Eliot Morison, Rear Admiral, U.S.N.R., ret., and professor emeritus of history at Harvard University, has followed his monumental History of United States Naval Operations in World War II *with a concise one-volume work,* The Two-Ocean War, *in which he ranges more freely in discussion of the whys and wherefores. In the selection below, he reviews the question of responsibility, refuting the arguments that Roosevelt knowingly provoked the attack. Morison, author of one of the leading textbooks in American history, along with many other works, has been Harmsworth Professor at Oxford and has won Pulitzer and Bancroft prizes.*

The Pearl Harbor disaster made a tremendous emotional impact on the American people. The Japanese high command, by their idiotic act, had made a strategic present of the first order to the United States; they had united the country in grim determination to win victory in the Pacific. Isolationism and pacifism now ceased to be valid forces in American politics; but some of their exponents, and many well-meaning people too, became violent propagandists for the bizarre theory that the Roosevelt administration, with the connivance of leading generals and admirals in Washington, knew perfectly well that the attack was coming and deliberately withheld knowledge of it from Kimmel and Short in order, for their own foul purposes, to get us into the war.

Even if one can believe that the late President of the United States was capable of so horrible a gambit, a little reflection would indicate that he could not possibly have carried it off. He would have needed the connivance of Secretaries Hull, Stimson and Knox, Generals Marshall, Gerow and Miles, Admirals Stark, Turner and Wilkinson, and many of their subordinates, too—all loyal and honorable men who would never have lent themselves to such monstrous deception. More reflection might suggest that if Roosevelt and his cabinet ministers and armed service chiefs had schemed to get us into the war, their purpose would have been better served by warning the Hawaiian commanders in time to get the Fleet to sea and the planes airborne. Even a frustrated attempt to strike Pearl Harbor would have been sufficient *casus belli* to satisfy the most isolationist congressman. Actually, the administration and the heads of the armed forces, as we have seen, were doing their best to prevent or postpone a war with Japan. Roosevelt even sent a personal appeal to Hirohito on the evening of 6 December.

After any overwhelming disaster there is a search for the culprit; and this search is still being pursued, for partisan purposes, after two Navy and two Army investigations and a lengthy congressional one have combed every phase of omission and commission. No military event in our or any other country's history, not even the Battles of Gettysburg and Jutland, has been the subject of such exhaustive research as the air assault on Pearl Harbor.

A principal reason why Washington and Pearl Harbor were caught unawares was their inability to imagine that Japan would do anything so stupid and suicidal. But Joseph Grew in Tokyo—one of the most alert and perceptive ambassadors in United States history—warned Washington on 3 November 1941 against any possible misconception "of the capacity of Japan to rush head-long into a suicidal conflict with the United States. National sanity would dictate against such an event, but Japanese sanity cannot be measured by our own standards of logic. . . . Japan's resort to [war] measures . . . may come with dramatic and dangerous suddenness." Grew's warning fell on deaf ears.

Three weeks later almost everyone in a responsible position in Washington expected Japan to make an aggressive move on the weekend of 29 November; but not on Pearl Harbor. And the curious lethargy into which official Washington seemed to fall after the "war warning" is partly explained by the decrypting of a whole series of dispatches from Tokyo to its ambassadors, to the effect that the deadline was approaching, time was running out, etc. There were no fewer than 19 such messages between 2 and 26 November, yet nothing had happened.

The Army and Navy cryptographers in Washington were experts, but grossly overworked. The stuff was coming in faster than they could deal with it, and one could not tell which dispatch was important and which was not until all were decrypted.[1] A message from the

---

[1] In the subsequent "conspiracy" theory of the surprise, much is made of one of the decoding machines being given to the British instead of to Kimmel. It was actually exchanged for machines that the British invented, and Washington wanted, for decrypt-

Japanese consulate at Honolulu dated 6 December, which ended, "There is a considerable opportunity . . . to take advantage for a surprise attack against these places" (Pearl Harbor and vicinity), was not decrypted until after the attack. The "berthing plan" message and Honolulu's replies were not assigned their proper significance at Washington, because they were mixed in with hundreds of messages, which had to be decrypted and translated, from all parts of the world. Observers in China, for instance, were sending as many as fifty messages a week, warning of forthcoming Japanese attacks on Siberia, Peru, and other unlikely places.

Army and Navy Intelligence officers in Washington were somewhat in the position of a woman with a sick child trying to take instructions from a doctor over the telephone while the neighbors are shouting contrary advice in her ear, dogs are barking, children screaming, and trucks roaring by the house. The noise overwhelmed the message. Personalities also entered into it. Rear Admiral Turner, Navy War Plans officer, was highly opinionated and difficult to work with. He actually forbade the Japanese language officers who did the decrypting and translating, to make estimates from the dispatches, insisting on doing that himself. And Turner, until late November, was obsessed by the idea that Japan was going to attack Russia, not American or British possessions.

Intelligence data received in Washington were handled in a manner that dissipated their impact. Copies of all decrypted messages that the translators thought significant, sometimes running to 130 a day, were placed in locked briefcases and carried by special messengers to the President, the Secretaries of State, War, and Navy, and about six top-ranking members of the armed forces. The recipient, without taking notes, had to read these signals in the presence of the messenger, who returned them to Army or Navy Intelligence office, where all copies but one were burned. This system, devised for security, denied to all these important people the opportunity to digest data and draw conclusions. It was nobody's particular and exclusive business to study all intelligence material and come up with an estimate. Nobody got anything but excerpts and dribblets.

It must also be remembered that in the late months of 1941 all

---

ing certain German ciphers; and since Britain had interests in the Far East at least equal to ours, the exchange was natural and proper. Another machine destined for Pearl Harbor was being constructed when war began. Admiral Hart already had one at Cavite.

high Army, Navy and State Department officials in Washington were deeply concerned with the "short of war" conflict in the Atlantic, and with Europe, where it then seemed probable that Hitler would gobble up Russia as he had France, order American merchantmen to be sunk, and step up his subversive activities in Central and South America.

Every one of the Japanese messages deorypted and translated before 7 December was ambiguous. None mentioned Pearl Harbor. None even pointed clearly at Japanese intent to attack the United States anywhere. Thus, no clear warnings were sent to Hawaii because Washington saw no reason to anticipate an attack on Hawaii. Washington, moreover, was determined not to begin a war with Japan. That was the meaning of the passage in the diary of War Secretary Stimson, recording the cabinet meeting of 25 November, after one of Tojo's deadline messages had been decrypted and translated. "The President predicted that we were likely to be attacked perhaps next Monday. . . . The question was how we should maneuver them into the position of firing the first shot." This quotation has been made much of by those trying to prove conspiracy between F.D.R. and his cabinet to get us into war. Mr. Stimson's use of the verb "maneuver" was unfortunate, but his intent is clear—we were not going to provoke the Japanese by an overt act; peace would continue until and unless they chose to strike. This was exactly the same attitude as President Lincoln's about Fort Sumter; or, to go further back, Colonel Parker's classic speech to the Minutemen at Lexington on 19 April 1775: "Don't fire unless fired upon, but if they mean to have a war, let it begin here."

Pearl Harbor, besides lacking the complete Intelligence picture, had the additional handicap of divided responsibility. General Short was charged with the defense of Oahu, including Pearl Harbor and antiaircraft batteries ashore; Admiral Bloch, commandant Fourteenth Naval District, was responsible for the defense of the Navy Yard, and Admiral Kimmel for that of the Fleet. Relations between them were friendly but inadequate; each one . . . assumed that the others were doing something that they didn't do.

A series of false assumptions, both at Washington and Oahu, added up to something as serious as the sins of omission. In Hawaii, the Navy assumed that the Army had gone on full alert, and that the radar warning net was completely operational. The Army assumed that the Navy was conducting an effective air reconnaissance around the island. Admiral Kimmel assumed that aërial torpedoes could not operate in the shoal waters of Pearl Harbor. Both Army and Navy Intelligence officers assumed that Japan was sending all her naval forces south, and that in any event Japan would not be so stupid as to attack Pearl Harbor. In Washington, Colonel Bratton of Army Intelligence assumed that the Pacific Fleet would go to sea after the 27 November "war warning," so to him the intercepted reports of ships' positions by the Japanese consulate registered waste effort; and Captain Wilkinson of Naval Intelligence assumed that these reports were simply evidence of the Japanese inordinate love for detail. Rear Admiral Turner of War Plans assumed that this and all other relevant intelligence was going to Admiral Kimmel, and General Gerow of Army War Plans assumed that Kimmel and Short were exchanging every scrap of what they did get, which was considerable. Washington was as vague and uncertain about what was going to happen on the first or second weekend after 27 November as Pearl Harbor itself. It was a case of the blind *not* leading the blind; false assumptions at both ends of the line.

The gravest charge against Admiral Kimmel and General Short is that they virtually ignored the "war warning" dispatch of 27 November from Washington. Admiral Kimmel . . . did send air reinforcement promptly to Wake and Midway Islands. He had already (with Admiral Bloch's cooperation) set up the surface and air patrol off the mouth of Pearl Harbor which encountered the midget submarines. He had, on 14 October, warned the Fleet against a submarine attack as a herald of something worse. Thus, the charge whittles down to this: that he did not repeat this warning and beef-up air patrol after 27 November. He thought that he had done everything that could reasonably be expected, in view of the intelligence received. Nevertheless, an "unwarranted feeling of immunity from attack" prevailed in Oahu at the crucial moment, as Admiral King observed; and it is not unfair to hold Kimmel and Short responsible.

Finally, we have to consider the "East Wind, Rain" dispatch which, by people bent on proving dastardly deception by Washington, has been blown up to a definite word from Tokyo that Pearl Harbor was about to be attacked. Actually, it was nothing of the sort. On 19 November, Tokyo notified the principal Japanese representatives abroad, in a dispatch that Washington decrypted, that if all other means of communication failed, they would be ordered to destroy codes in a plain-language weather broadcast. In this broadcast, "East

Wind, Rain" would mean, "Japanese-United States relations in danger"; "North Wind, Cloudy" would mean the same as to Russia; "West Wind, Clear" would mean the same as to England. There was no mention of Pearl Harbor, or any other target; not even a clear forecast of war. This "Winds" message, however, was taken seriously in Washington where a number of officers were alerted to watch Japanese broadcasts for the false weather forecast. Whether or not that was ever sent is disputed; but in no case would it have told Washington or Hawaii anything more than what they already knew, viz., that Japanese embassies had been ordered to destroy their codes.

Fundamentally, however, it was the system, the setup both at Washington and at Pearl, rather than individual stupidity or apathy, which muffled and confused what was going on. No one person knew the whole picture that the intelligence data disclosed; no one person was responsible for the defense of Pearl Harbor; too many people assumed that others were taking precautions that they did not take.

*   *   *

The Japanese war plan, brought together at a Supreme War Council on 6 September 1941, was as follows: First, prior to a declaration of war, destruction of the United States Pacific Fleet and the British and American air forces on the Malay Peninsula and Luzon. Second, while the British and American Navies were decimated and disorganized, a quick conquest of the Philippines, Guam, Wake, Hong Kong, Borneo, British Malaya (including Singapore), and Sumatra. Third, when these were secure, the converging of Japanese amphibious forces on the richest prize, Java, and a mop-up of the rest of the Dutch islands. Fourth, an intensive development of Malayan and Indonesian resources in oil, rubber, etc.; and, to secure these, establishment of a defensive perimeter running from the Kurile Islands through Wake, the Marshalls, and around the southern and western edges of the Malay Barrier to the Burmese-Indian border. With these bases the Japanese Navy and air forces could cut all lines of communication between Australia, New Zealand and the Anglo-American powers, which would then be forced to sue for peace. Fifth and finally, Japan would proceed completely to subjugate China.

Over half the world's population would then be under the economic, political and military control of the Emperor.

This scheme of conquest was the most enticing, ambitious and far-reaching in modern history, not excepting Hitler's. It almost worked, and might well have succeeded but for the United States Navy.

This being Japan's plan, it is astonishing to find her American apologists claiming that she was goaded, provoked and coerced into making war on us by the Roosevelt administration. . . .

Husband E. Kimmel
ADMIRAL KIMMEL'S STORY

The commander of the Pacific Fleet at the time of the surprise attack presents his own defense in this selection from Admiral Kimmel's Story *(1955). He cites deficiencies in the military establishment that stemmed from public neglect, political commitments of which he was not informed, and specifies those things known to various levels of the United States government of which he was left unaware, purposely or otherwise.*

Although the commanders at Hawaii were never supplied with the equipment and trained personnel to decode intercepted "magic" Japanese dispatches, I learned during the investigations in Washington that the commander-in-chief of our Asiatic Fleet was fully equipped to decode the "magic" intercepted Japanese dispatches as received; also that the Navy Department in Washington maintained a check system and supplied the Asiatic decoding unit with copies of important intercepts which the organization failed to obtain with their own facilities. I also learned that a fourth set of equipment destined for assignment to the commander-in-chief, U.S. Pacific Fleet, at Hawaii was diverted to the British in the summer of 1941. The Navy and War Departments in Washington were each supplied with equipment and personnel to decode their intercepts.

The care taken to keep the commander-in-chief of our Asiatic Fleet and the British in London informed of Japanese intentions while withholding this vital information from our commanders at Pearl Harbor has never been explained.

In the month of July 1941, the Chief of Naval Operations sent me at least seven dispatches which quoted intercepted Japanese diplomatic messages from Tokyo to Washington, Tokyo to Berlin, Berlin to Tokyo, Tokyo to Vichy, Canton to Tokyo. These dispatches identified by number the Japanese messages they quoted and gave their verbatim text.

I was never informed of any decision to the effect that intelligence from intercepted Japanese messages was not to be sent to me. In fact, dispatches sent to me by the Navy Department in the week before the attack contained intelligence from intercepted messages. On December 1, a dispatch from the Chief of Naval Operations, sent to me for information, quoted a report of November 29 from the Japanese ambassador in Bangkok to Tokyo which described a Japanese plan to entice the British to invade Thai, thereby permitting Japan to enter that country in the role of its defender. On December 3, a dispatch to me from the Chief of Naval Operations set forth an order from Japan to diplomatic agents and expressly referred to this order as "Circular Twenty Four Forty Four from Tokyo." Another dispatch from the Chief of Naval Operations on December 3 referred to certain "categoric and urgent instructions which were sent yesterday to Japanese diplomatic and consular posts."

The Navy Department thus engaged in a course of conduct which definitely gave me the impression that intelligence from important intercepted Japanese messages was being furnished to me. Under these circumstances a failure to send me important information of this character was not merely a withholding of intelligence. It amounted to an affirmative misrepresentation. I had asked for all vital information. I had been assured that I would have it. I appeared to be receiving it. My current estimate of the situation was formed on this basis. Yet, in fact, the most vital information from the intercepted Japanese messages was withheld from me. This failure not only deprived me of essential facts. It misled me.

I was not supplied with any information of the intercepted messages showing that the Japanese government had divided Pearl Harbor into five areas and was seeking minute information as to the berthing of ships of the fleet in those areas which were vitally significant. . . .

In the volume of intercepted Japanese dispatches eliciting and securing information about American military installations and naval movements, the dispatches concerning Pearl Harbor, on and after September 24, 1941, stand out, apart from the others. No other harbor or base in American territory or possessions was divided into sub-areas by Japan. In no other area was the Japanese government seeking information as to whether two or more vessels were alongside the same wharf. Prior to the dispatch of September 24, the information which the Japanese sought and obtained about Pearl Harbor followed the general pattern of their interest in American fleet movements in other localities. One might expect this type of conventional espionage.

With the dispatch of September 24, 1941, and those which followed, there was a significant and ominous change in the character of the information which the Japanese government sought and obtained. The espionage then directed was of an unusual character and outside the realm of reasonable suspicion. It was no longer merely directed to ascertaining the general whereabouts of ships of the fleet. It was directed to the presence of particular ships in particular areas; to such minute detail as what ships were double-docked at the same wharf.

In the period immediately preceding the attack, the Jap consul general in Hawaii was directed by Tokyo to report even when there were no movements of ships in and out of Pearl Harbor. These Japanese instructions and reports pointed to an attack by Japan upon the ships in Pearl Harbor. The information sought and obtained, with such painstaking detail, had no other conceivable usefulness from a military viewpoint. Its utility was in planning and executing an attack upon ships in port. Its effective value was lost completely when the ships left their reported berthings in Pearl Harbor.

No one had a more direct and immediate interest in the security of the fleet in Pearl Harbor than its commander-in-chief. No one had a greater right than I to know that Japan had carved up Pearl Harbor into sub-areas and was seeking and receiving reports as to the precise berthings in that harbor of the ships of the fleet. I had been sent Mr. Grew's report earlier in the year with positive advice from the Navy Department that no credence was to be placed in the rumored

Japanese plans for an attack on Pearl Harbor. I was told then, that no Japanese move against Pearl Harbor appeared "imminent or planned for in the foreseeable future." Certainly I was entitled to know when information in the Navy Department completely altered the information and advice previously given to me. Surely, I was entitled to know of the intercepted dispatches between Tokyo and Honolulu on and after September 24, 1941, which indicated that a Japanese move against Pearl Harbor was planned in Tokyo. . . .

The intercepted dispatches about the berthings of ships in Pearl Harbor also clarified the significance of other intercepted Japanese dispatches, decoded and translated by the Navy Department prior to the attack. I refer particularly to the intercepted dispatches which established a deadline date for agreement between Japan and the United States. When this date passed without agreement, these dispatches revealed that a Japanese plan automatically took effect. . . .

In at least six separate dispatches, on November 5, 11, 15, 16, 22, and 24, Japan specifically established and extended the deadline of November 25, later advanced to November 29. The dispatches made it plain that after the deadline date a Japanese plan was automatically going into operation. The plan was of such importance that, as the deadline approached, the government of Japan declared: "The fate of our Empire hangs by the slender thread of a few days."

When the deadline date of November 29 was reached with no agreement between the United States and Japan, there was no further extension. The intercepted dispatches indicated that the crisis deepened in its intensity after that day passed. On the first of December, Tokyo advised its ambassadors in Washington: "The date set in my message No. 812 has come and gone and the situation continues to be increasingly critical." This message was translated by the navy on the first of December. This information was never supplied to me.

An intercepted Japanese dispatch from Tokyo to Washington of November 28, 1941, made it clear that the American proposal of November 26 was completely unsatisfactory to Japan and that an actual rupture of negotiations would occur upon the receipt of the Japanese reply. A dispatch on November 28, decoded and translated on the same day, stated:

> *Well, you two ambassadors have exerted superhuman efforts but, in spite of this, the United States has gone ahead and presented this humiliating proposal. This was quite unexpected and extremely regrettable. The Impe-*

rial Government can by no means use it as a basis for negotiations. Therefore, with a report of the views of the Imperial Government on this American proposal which I will send you in two or three days, the negotiations will be de facto ruptured. This is inevitable. . . .

This information was never supplied to me.

The commanders at Pearl Harbor were not kept informed of the progress of negotiations with Japan. I was never supplied with the text of Mr. Hull's message of November 26, 1941 to the Japanese government which has frequently been referred to as an ultimatum. This was a most important document. It stated the policy of the United States that would be carried out by force, if necessary. Mr. Stimson referred to this message as Mr. Hull's decision "to kick the whole thing over. . . ."

The Japanese reply to this message was delivered in Washington within hours of the Japanese attack at Pearl Harbor. Nor were the commanders at Pearl Harbor supplied with the text of previous messages exchanged between the United States and Japanese governments. Their information on this subject was obtained from the radio and newspapers. I now believe that the Washington newspaper correspondents and the editors of our leading newspapers were much more accurately informed of the seriousness of the situation than were the commanders at Pearl Harbor. . . .

After November 27, there was a rising intensity in the crisis in Japanese–United States relations apparent in the intercepted dispatches. I was told on November 27 that negotiations had ceased and two days later that they appeared to be terminated with the barest possibilities of their resumption. Then I was left to read public accounts of further conversations between the State Department and the Japanese emissaries in Washington which indicated that negotiations had been resumed.

The Navy Department knew immediately of the reactions of Nomura and Kurusu to the American note of November 26—"Our failure and humiliation are complete."

The Navy Department knew immediately of the reactions of the Japanese government to the American note of November 26. Japan termed it:

[A] humiliating proposal. This was quite unexpected and extremely regrettable. The Imperial Government can by no means use it as a basis for negotiations. Therefore, with a report of the views of the Imperial Government on

*this American proposal which I will send you in two or three days, the
negotiations will be de facto ruptured. This is inevitable. . . .*

The Navy Department knew that Nomura and Kurusu suggested to
Japan on November 26 one way of saving the situation—a wire by the
President to the Emperor.

The Navy Department knew that the Japanese government advised
Nomura and Kurusu on November 28 that the suggested wire from
the President to the Emperor offered no hope: "What you suggest is
entirely unsuitable."

The Navy Department knew that on November 30, Japan gave
Germany a detailed version of the negotiations with the United
States. Japan stated that "a continuation of negotiations would inevitably be detrimental to our cause," and characterized certain features of the American proposal of November 26 as "insulting"—
"clearly a trick." Japan concluded that the United States had decided
to regard her as an enemy.

The Navy Department knew that Japan had instructed her ambassadors in Berlin on November 30 to inform Hitler:

*The conversations begun between Tokyo and Washington last April . . .
now stand ruptured—broken. Say very secretly to them [Hitler and Ribben-
trop] that there is extreme danger that war may suddenly break out between
the Anglo-Saxon nations and Japan through some clash of arms and add
that the time of the breaking out of this war may come quicker than anyone
dreams.*

All this vital information came from intercepted dispatches, decoded and translated in Washington, either on the day they were sent
or a day or two later. None of this information was supplied to
me. . . .

It is one thing to warn commanders at a particular base of the
probable outbreak of war in theaters thousands of miles away, knowing and expecting that they will continue their assigned tasks and
missions after the receipt of such warning, and that the very nature
of the warning emphasizes to them the necessity for continuing such
tasks and missions.

It is quite another thing to warn commanders at a particular base
of an attack to be expected in their own locality.

In 1941, we of the Pacific Fleet had a plethora of premonitions, of
generalized warnings and forebodings that Japan might embark on

aggressive action in the Far East at any one of the variously predicted dates. After receipt of such warnings, we were expected to continue with renewed intensity and zeal our own training program and preparations for war rather than to go on an all-out local alert against attack.

In the year 1941 the international situation was grave and, at times, tense. However, preparing the fleet for war through an intensive training program had to go on. There was a vital element of timing involved in determining when the fleet should curtail training for all-out war measures. Maximum security measures, consistent with the maintenance of the training program, were already in effect in the fleet. When would Japanese-American relations reach the point that all training should cease and all-out war dispositions should be made? This was what we needed to know in the Pacific in the year 1941.

The dispatch fixing the hour for the delivery of the Japanese ultimatum to the United States as 1:00 p.m., Washington time, was intercepted and decoded by the Navy Department by 7:00 on the morning of December 7—7:00 a.m., Washington time, 1:30 a.m., Hawaiian time—nearly six and a half hours before the attack. The translation of this short message from the Japanese was a two-minute job. Not later than 9:00 a.m., the Chief of Naval Operations was informed of it. This information was not supplied to me prior to the attack.

I cannot tell from the evidence that has been presented the precise hours on the morning of December 7, when various responsible officers of the Navy Department knew that 1:00 p.m., Washington time, was the hour fixed for the delivery of the Japanese ultimatum to this government. This much I know. There was ample time, at least an interval of approximately three and one-half hours, in which a message could have been dispatched to me. Regardless of what arguments there may be as to the evaluation of the dispatches that had been sent to me, I surely was entitled to know of the hour fixed by Japan for the probable outbreak of war against the United States. I cannot understand now—I have never understood—I may never understand—why I was deprived of the information available in the Navy Department in Washington on Saturday night and Sunday morning.

On November 28, 1941, the Navy Department could have informed me of the following vital facts:

1. Japan had set November 29 as an immovable deadline date for agreement with the United States.

2. The United States gave to Japan certain proposals for a solution of Japanese-American relations on November 26, which amounted to an ultimatum. I might remark parenthetically that an authoritative statement from my government as to the general nature of these proposals would have been most enlightening but it was not supplied.

3. Japan considered the United States proposals of November 26 as unacceptable and planned to rupture negotiations with the United States when her reply to them was delivered to this government.

4. Japan was keeping up a pretext of negotiations after November 26 to conceal a definite plan which went into effect on November 29th.

This was the type of information which I had stated in May I needed so urgently in making the difficult decisions with which I was confronted.

The question will arise in your minds, as it has in mine: Would the receipt of this information have made a difference in the events of December 7? No man can now state as a fact that he would have taken a certain course of action years ago had he known facts which were then unknown to him. All he can give is his present conviction, divorcing himself from hindsight as far as humanly possible, and re-creating the atmosphere of the past and the factors which then influenced him. I give you my views, formed in this manner.

Had I learned these vital facts and the "ships in harbor" messages on *November 28th,* it is my present conviction that I would have rejected the Navy Department's suggestion to send carriers to Wake and Midway. I would have ordered the third carrier, the *Saratoga,* back from the West Coast. I would have gone to sea with the fleet and endeavored to keep it in an intercepting position at sea. This would have permitted the disposal of the striking power of the fleet to meet an attack in the Hawaiian area. The requirements of keeping the fleet fueled, however, would have made necessary the presence in Pearl Harbor from time to time of detachments of various units of the main body of the fleet.

On December 4, ample time remained for the Navy Department to forward to me the information which I have outlined, and in addition the following significant facts, which the Navy Department learned between November 27 and that date:

1. Japan had informed Hitler that war with the Anglo-Saxon powers would break out sooner than anyone dreamt;
2. Japan had broadcast her winds code signal using the words "east wind rain," meaning war or a rupture of diplomatic relations with the United States.

Assuming that for the first time *on December 5* I had all the important information then available in the Navy Department, it is my present conviction that I would have gone to sea with the fleet, including the carrier *Lexington* and arranged a rendezvous at sea with Halsey's carrier force, and been in a good position to intercept the Japanese attack.

At some time prior to December 6, 1941, the commanders of Hawaii could have been informed of the promise of armed support as detailed by the War Department in London to Air Marshal Brooke Popham in Singapore. This vital information was denied to them.

On December 6, fifteen hours before the attack, ample time still remained for the Navy Department to give me all the significant facts which I have outlined and which were not available to me in Hawaii. In addition, the Navy Department could then have advised me that thirteen parts of the Japanese reply to the American proposals had been received, that the tone and temper of this message indicated a break in diplomatic relations or war with the United States, and that the Japanese reply was to be formally presented to this government at a special hour soon to be fixed. Had I received this information on the *afternoon of December 6,* it is my present conviction that I would have ordered all fleet units in Pearl Harbor to sea, arranged a rendezvous with Halsey's task force returning from Wake, and been ready to intercept the Japanese force by the time fixed for the outbreak of war.

Even on the morning of December 7, four or five hours before the attack, had the Navy Department for the first time seen fit to send me all this significant information, and the additional fact that 1:00 p.m., Washington time, had been fixed for the delivery of the Japanese ultimatum to the United States, my light forces could have moved out of Pearl Harbor, all ships in the harbor would have been at general quarters, and all resources of the fleet in instant readiness to repel an attack.

The Pacific Fleet deserved a fighting chance. It was entitled to receive from the Navy Department the best information available.

Such information had been urgently requested. I had been assured that it would be furnished me. We faced our problems in the Pacific confident that such assurance would be faithfully carried out. . . .

Roberta Wohlstetter

SIGNALS AND NOISE: THE INTELLIGENCE PICTURE

Mrs. Wohlstetter analyzes the information available on the eve of the Pearl Harbor attack from the standpoint of an intelligence expert and argues that evidence which appears clearcut in hindsight to critics of the Administration did by no means lead to such obvious conclusions for those who had to evaluate it at the time. This selection is the summary from her Pearl Harbor: Warning and Decision *(1962), a detailed and careful survey of the problems of intelligence and defense in the months before war came.*

If our intelligence system and all our other channels of information failed to produce an accurate image of Japanese intentions and capabilities, it was not for want of the relevant materials. Never before have we had so complete an intelligence picture of the enemy. And perhaps never again will we have such a magnificent collection of sources at our disposal.

Retrospect

To review these sources briefly, an American cryptanalyst, Col. William F. Friedman, had broken the top-priority Japanese diplomatic code, which enabled us to listen to a large proportion of the privileged communications between Tokyo and the major Japanese embassies throughout the world. Not only did we know in advance how the Japanese ambassadors in Washington were advised, and how much they were instructed to say, but we also were listening to

Reprinted from *Pearl Harbor: Warning and Decision* by Roberta Wohlstetter, pp. 382–96, with the permission of the publishers, Stanford University Press. © 1962 by the Board of Trustees of the Leland Stanford Junior University.

top-secret messages on the Tokyo-Berlin and Tokyo-Rome circuits, which gave us information vital for conduct of the war in the Atlantic and Europe. In the Far East this source provided minute details on movements connected with the Japanese program of expansion into Southeast Asia.

Besides the strictly diplomatic codes, our cryptanalysts also had some success in reading codes used by Japanese agents in major American and foreign ports. Those who were on the distribution list for Magic had access to much of what these agents were reporting to Tokyo and what Tokyo was demanding of them in the Panama Canal Zone, in cities along the East and West Coasts of the Americas from northern Canada as far south as Brazil, and in ports throughout the Far East, including the Philippines and the Hawaiian Islands. They could determine what installations, what troop and ship movements, and what alert and defense measures were of interest to Tokyo at these points on the globe, as well as approximately how much correct information her agents were sending her.

Our naval leaders also had at their disposal the results of radio traffic analysis. While before the war our naval radio experts could not read the content of any Japanese naval or military coded messages, they were able to deduce from a study of intercepted ship call signs the composition and location of the Japanese Fleet units. After a change in call signs, they might lose sight of some units, and units that went into port in home waters were also lost because the ships in port used frequencies that our radios were unable to intercept. Most of the time, however, our traffic analysts had the various Japanese Fleet units accurately pinpointed on our naval maps.

Extremely competent on-the-spot economic and political analysis was furnished by Ambassador Grew and his staff in Tokyo. Ambassador Grew was himself a most sensitive and accurate observer, as evidenced by his dispatches to the State Department. His observations were supported and supplemented with military detail by frequent reports from American naval attachés and observers in key Far Eastern ports. Navy Intelligence had men with radio equipment located along the coast of China, for example, who reported the convoy movements toward Indochina. There were also naval observers stationed in various high-tension areas in Thailand and Indochina who could fill in the local outlines of Japanese political intrigue and military planning. In Tokyo and other Japanese cities, it is true, Japanese censorship grew more and more rigid during 1941, until

Ambassador Grew felt it necessary to disclaim any responsibility for noting or reporting overt military evidence of an imminent outbreak of war. This careful Japanese censorship naturally cut down visual confirmation of the decoded information but very probably never achieved the opaqueness of Russia's Iron Curtain.

During this period the data and interpretations of British intelligence were also available to American officers in Washington and the Far East, though the British and Americans tended to distrust each other's privileged information.

In addition to secret sources, there were some excellent public ones. Foreign correspondents for the *New York Times,* the *Herald Tribune,* and the *Washington Post* were stationed in Tokyo and Shanghai and in Canberra, Australia. Their reporting as well as their predictions on the Japanese political scene were on a very high level. Frequently their access to news was more rapid and their judgment of its significance as reliable as that of our Intelligence officers. This was certainly the case for 1940 and most of 1941. For the last few weeks before the Pearl Harbor strike, however, the public newspaper accounts were not very useful. It was necessary to have secret information in order to know what was happening. Both Tokyo and Washington exercised very tight control over leaks during this crucial period, and the newsmen accordingly had to limit their accounts to speculation and notices of diplomatic meetings with no exact indication of the content of the diplomatic exchanges.

The Japanese press was another important public source. During 1941 it proclaimed with increasing shrillness the Japanese government's determination to pursue its program of expansion into Southeast Asia and the desire of the military to clear the Far East of British and American colonial exploitation. This particular source was rife with explicit signals of aggressive intent.

Finally, an essential part of the intelligence picture for 1941 was both public and privileged information on American policy and activities in the Far East. During the year the pattern of action and interaction between the Japanese and American governments grew more and more complex. At the last, it became especially important for anyone charged with the responsibility of ordering an alert to know what moves the American government was going to make with respect to Japan, as well as to try to guess what Japan's next move would be, since Japan's next move would respond in part to ours. Unfortunately our military leaders, and especially our Intelligence officers, were sometimes as surprised as the Japanese at the moves of the White House and the State Department. They usually had more orderly anticipations about Japanese policy and conduct than they had about America's. On the other hand, it was also true that State Department and White House officials were handicapped in judging Japanese intentions and estimates of risk by an inadequate picture of our own military vulnerability.

All of the public and private sources of information mentioned were available to America's political and military leaders in 1941. It is only fair to remark, however, that no single person or agency ever had at any given moment all the signals existing in this vast information network. The signals lay scattered in a number of different agencies; some were decoded, some were not; some traveled through rapid channels of communication, some were blocked by technical or procedural delays; some never reached a center of decision. But it is legitimate to review again the general sort of picture that emerged during the first week of December from the signals readily at hand. Anyone close to President Roosevelt was likely to have before him the following significant fragments.

There was first of all a picture of gathering troop and ship movements down the China coast and into Indochina. The large dimensions of this movement to the south were established publicly and visually as well as by analysis of ship call signs. Two changes in Japanese naval call signs—one on November 1 and another on December 1—had also been evaluated by Naval Intelligence as extremely unusual and as signs of major preparations for some sort of Japanese offensive. The two changes had interfered with the speed of American radio traffic analysis. Thousands of interceptions after December 1 were necessary before the new call signs could be read. Partly for this reason American radio analysts disagreed about the locations of the Japanese carriers. One group held that all the carriers were near Japan because they had not been able to identify a carrier call sign since the middle of November. Another group believed that they had located one carrier division in the Marshalls. The probability seemed to be that the carriers, wherever they were, had gone into radio silence; and past experience led the analysts to believe that they were therefore in waters near the Japanese homeland, where they could communicate with each other on wavelengths that we could not intercept. However, our inability to locate the carriers exactly, combined with the two changes in call signs, was itself a danger signal.

Our best secret source, Magic, was confirming the aggressive intention of the new military cabinet in Tokyo, which had replaced the last moderate cabinet on October 17. In particular, Magic provided details of some of the preparations for the move into Southeast Asia. Running counter to this were increased troop shipments to the Manchurian border in October. (The intelligence picture is never clearcut.) But withdrawals had begun toward the end of that month. Magic also carried explicit instructions to the Japanese ambassadors in Washington to pursue diplomatic negotiations with the United States with increasing energy, but at the same time it announced a deadline for the favorable conclusion of the negotiations, first for November 25, later postponed until November 29. In case of diplomatic failure by that date, the Japanese ambassadors were told, Japanese patience would be exhausted, Japan was determined to pursue her Greater East Asia policy, and on November 29 "things" would automatically begin to happen.

On November 26 Secretary Hull rejected Japan's latest bid for American approval of her policies in China and Indochina. Magic had repeatedly characterized this Japanese overture as the "last," and it now revealed the ambassadors' reaction of consternation and despair over the American refusal and also their country's characterization of the American Ten Point Note as an "ultimatum."

On the basis of this collection of signals, Army and Navy Intelligence experts in Washington tentatively placed D-day *for the Japanese Southeastern campaign* during the weekend of November 30, and when this failed to materialize, during the weekend of December 7. They also compiled an accurate list of probable British and Dutch targets and included the Philippines and Guam as possible American targets.

Also available in this mass of information, but long forgotten, was a rumor reported by Ambassador Grew in January 1941. It came from what was regarded as a not-very-reliable source, the Peruvian embassy, and stated that the Japanese were preparing a surprise air attack on Pearl Harbor. Curiously the date of the report is coincident roughly with what we now know to have been the date of inception of Yamamoto's plan; but the rumor was labeled by everyone, including Ambassador Grew, as quite fantastic and the plan as absurdly impossible. American judgment was consistent with Japanese judgment at this time, since Yamamoto's plan was in direct contradiction to Japanese naval tactical doctrine.

Perspective

On the basis of this rapid recapitulation of the highlights in the signal picture, it is apparent that our decision-makers had at hand an impressive amount of information on the enemy. They did not have the complete list of targets, since none of the last-minute estimates included Pearl Harbor. They did not know the exact hour and date for opening the attack. They did not have an accurate knowledge of Japanese capabilities or of Japanese ability to accept very high risks. The crucial question then, we repeat, is, If we could enumerate accurately the British and Dutch targets and give credence to a Japanese attack against them either on November 30 or December 7, why were we not expecting a specific danger to *ourselves*? And by the word "expecting," we mean expecting in the sense of taking specific alert actions to meet the contingencies of attack by land, sea, or air.

There are several answers to this question that have become apparent in the course of this study. First of all, it is much easier *after* the event to sort the relevant from the irrelevant signals. After the event, of course, a signal is always crystal clear; we can now see what disaster it was signaling, since the disaster has occurred. But before the event it is obscure and pregnant with conflicting meanings. It comes to the observer embedded in an atmosphere of "noise," i.e., in the company of all sorts of information that is useless and irrelevant for predicting the particular disaster. For example, in Washington, Pearl Harbor signals were competing with a vast number of signals from the European theater. These European signals announced danger more frequently and more specifically than any coming from the Far East. The Far Eastern signals were also arriving at a center of decision where they had to compete with the prevailing belief that an unprotected offensive force acts as a deterrent rather than a target. In Honolulu they were competing *not* with signals from the European theater, but rather with a large number of signals announcing Japanese intentions and preparations to attack Soviet Russia rather than to move southward; here they were also competing with expectations of local sabotage prepared by previous alert situations.

In short, we failed to anticipate Pearl Harbor not for want of the relevant materials, but because of a plethora of irrelevant ones. Much of the appearance of wanton neglect that emerged in various investigations of the disaster resulted from the unconscious suppression of vast congeries of signs pointing in every direction except Pearl Harbor. It was difficult later to recall these signs since they had led nowhere. Signals that are characterized today as absolutely unequivocal warnings of surprise air attack on Pearl Harbor become, on analysis in the context of December 1941, not merely ambiguous but occasionally inconsistent with such an attack. To recall one of the most controversial and publicized examples, the winds code, both General Short and Admiral Kimmel testified that if they had had this information, they would have been prepared on the morning of December 7 for an air attack from without. The messages establishing the winds code are often described in the Pearl Harbor literature as Tokyo's declaration of war against America. If they indeed amounted to such a declaration, obviously the failure to inform Honolulu of this vital news would have been criminal negligence. On examination, however, the messages proved to be instructions for code communication after normal commercial channels had been cut. In one message the recipient was instructed on receipt of an execute to destroy all remaining codes in his possession. In another version the recipient was warned that the execute would be sent out "when relations are becoming dangerous" between Japan and three other countries. There was a different code term for each country: England, America, and the Soviet Union.

There is no evidence that an authentic execute of either message was ever intercepted by the United States before December 7. The message ordering code destruction was in any case superseded by a much more explicit code-destruction order from Tokyo that was intercepted on December 2 and translated on December 3. After December 2, the receipt of a winds-code execute for code destruction would therefore have added nothing new to our information, and code destruction in itself cannot be taken as an unambiguous substitute for a formal declaration of war. During the first week of December the United States ordered all American consulates in the Far East to destroy all American codes, yet no one has attempted to prove that this order was equivalent to an American declaration of war against Japan. As for the other winds-code message, provided an execute had been received warning that relations were dangerous between Japan and the United States, there would still have been no way on the basis of this signal alone to determine whether Tokyo was signaling Japanese intent to attack the United States, or Japanese fear of an American surprise attack (in reprisal for Japanese aggressive moves against American allies in the Far East). It was only after the event that "dangerous relations" could be interpreted as "surprise air attack on Pearl Harbor."

There is a difference, then, between having a signal available somewhere in the heap of irrelevancies, and perceiving it as a warning; and there is also a difference between perceiving it as a warning, and acting or getting action on it. These distinctions, simple as they are, illuminate the obscurity shrouding this moment in history.

Many instances of these distinctions have been examined in the course of this study. We shall recall a few of the most dramatic now. To illustrate the difference between having and perceiving a signal, let us turn to Colonel Fielder. . . . Though he was an untrained and inexperienced Intelligence officer, he headed Army Intelligence at Pearl Harbor at the time of the attack. He had been on the job for only four months, and he regarded as quite satisfactory his sources of information and his contacts with the Navy locally and with Army Intelligence in Washington. Evidently he was unaware that Army Intelligence in Washington was not allowed to send him any "action" or policy information, and he was therefore not especially concerned about trying to read beyond the obvious meaning of any given communication that came under his eyes. Colonel Bratton, head of Army Far Eastern Intelligence in Washington, however, had a somewhat more realistic view of the extent of Colonel Fielder's knowledge. At the end of November, Colonel Bratton had learned about the winds-code setup and was also apprised that the naval traffic analysis unit under Commander Rochefort in Honolulu was monitoring 24 hours a day for an execute. He was understandably worried about the lack of communication between this unit and Colonel Fielder's office, and by December 5 he finally felt that the matter was urgent enough to warrant sending a message directly to Colonel Fielder about the winds code. Now any information on the winds code, since it belonged to the highest classification of secret information, and since it was therefore automatically evaluated as "action" information, could not be sent through normal G-2 channels. Colonel Bratton had to figure out another way to get the information to Colonel Fielder. He sent this message: "Contact Commander Rochefort immediately thru Commandant Fourteenth Naval District regarding broadcasts from Tokyo reference weather." Signal Corps records establish that Colonel Fielder received this message. How did he react to it? He filed it. According to his testimony in 1945, it made no impression on him and he did not attempt to see Rochefort. He could not sense any urgency behind the lines because he was not expecting immediate trouble, and his expectations determined what he read. A warning signal was available to him, but he did not perceive it.

Colonel Fielder's lack of experience may make this example seem to be an exception. So let us recall the performance of Captain Wilkinson, the naval officer who headed the Office of Naval Intelligence in Washington in the fall of 1941 and who is unanimously acclaimed for a distinguished and brilliant career. His treatment of a now-famous Pearl Harbor signal does not sound much different in the telling. After the event, the signal in question was labeled "the bomb-plot message." It originated in Tokyo on September 24 and was sent to an agent in Honolulu. It requested the agent to divide Pearl Harbor into five areas and to make his future reports on ships in harbor with reference to those areas. Tokyo was especially interested in the locations of battleships, destroyers, and carriers, and also in any information on the anchoring of more than one ship at a single dock.

This message was decoded and translated on October 9 and shortly thereafter distributed to Army, Navy, and State Department recipients of Magic. Commander Kramer, a naval expert on Magic, had marked the message with an asterisk, signifying that he thought it to be of particular interest. But what was its interest? Both he and Wilkinson agreed that it illustrated the "nicety" of Japanese intelligence, the incredible zeal and efficiency with which they collected detail. The division into areas was interpreted as a device for shortening the reports. Admiral Stark was similarly impressed with Japanese efficiency, and no one felt it necessary to forward the message to Admiral Kimmel. No one read into it a specific danger to ships anchored in Pearl Harbor. At the time, this was a reasonable estimate, since somewhat similar requests for information were going to Japanese agents in Panama, Vancouver, Portland, San Diego, San Francisco, and other places. It should be observed, however, that the estimate was reasonable only on the basis of a very rough check on the quantity of espionage messages passing between Tokyo and these American ports. No one in Far Eastern Intelligence had subjected the messages to any more refined analysis. An observer assigned to such a job would have been able to record an increase in the frequency and specificity of Tokyo's requests concerning Manila and Pearl Harbor in the last weeks before the outbreak of war, and he would have noted that Tokyo was not displaying the same interest in other American ports. These observations, while not significant in isolation, might have been useful in the general signal picture.

There is no need, however, to confine our examples to Intelligence personnel. Indeed, the crucial areas where the signals failed to communicate a warning were in the operational branches of the armed services. Let us take Admiral Kimmel and his reaction to the information that the Japanese were destroying most of their codes in major Far Eastern consulates and also in London and Washington. Since the Pearl Harbor attack, this information has frequently been characterized by military experts who were not stationed in Honolulu as an "unmistakable tip-off." As Admiral Ingersoll explained at the congressional hearings with the lucidity characteristic of statements after the event:

> If you rupture diplomatic negotiations you do not necessarily have to burn your codes. The diplomats go home and they can pack up their codes with their dolls and take them home. Also, when you rupture diplomatic negotiations, you do not rupture consular relations. The consuls stay on.
>
> Now, in this particular set of dispatches that did not mean a rupture of diplomatic negotiations, it meant war, and that information was sent out to the fleets as soon as we got it. . . .[1]

The phrase "it meant war" was, of course, pretty vague; war in Manila, Hong Kong, Singapore, and Batavia is not war 5000 miles away in Pearl Harbor. Before the event, for Admiral Kimmel, code burning in major Japanese consulates in the Far East may have "meant war," but it did not signal danger of an air attack on Pearl Harbor. In the first place, the information that he received was not the original Magic. He learned from Washington that Japanese consulates were burning "almost all" of their codes, not all of them, and

[1] *Hearings,* Part 9, p. 4226.

Honolulu was not included on the list. He knew from a local source that the Japanese consulate in Honolulu was burning secret papers (not necessarily codes), and this back yard burning had happened three or four times during the year. In July 1941, Kimmel had been informed that the Japanese consulates in lands neighboring Indochina had destroyed codes, and he interpreted the code burning in December as a similar attempt to protect codes in case the Americans or their British and Dutch allies tried to seize the consulates in reprisal for the southern advance. This also was a reasonable interpretation at the time, though not an especially keen one.

Indeed, at the time there was a good deal of evidence available to support all the wrong interpretations of last-minute signals, and the interpretations appeared wrong only *after* the event. There was, for example, a good deal of evidence to support the hypothesis that Japan would attack the Soviet Union from the east while the Russian Army was heavily engaged in the west. Admiral Turner, head of Navy War Plans in Washington, was an enthusiastic adherent of this view and argued the high probability of a Japanese attack on Russia up until the last week in November, when he had to concede that most of Japan's men and supplies were moving south. Richard Sorge, the expert Soviet spy who had direct access to the Japanese Cabinet, had correctly predicted the southern move as early as July 1941, but even he was deeply alarmed during September and early October by the large number of troop movements to the Manchurian border. He feared that his July advice to the Soviet Union had been in error, and his alarm ultimately led to his capture on October 14. For at this time he increased his radio messages to Moscow to the point where it was possible for the Japanese police to pinpoint the source of the broadcasts.

It is important to emphasize here that most of the men that we have cited in our examples, such as Captain Wilkinson and Admirals Turner and Kimmel—these men and their colleagues who were involved in the Pearl Harbor disaster—were as efficient and loyal a group of men as one could find. Some of them were exceptionally able and dedicated. The fact of surprise at Pearl Harbor has never been persuasively explained by accusing the participants, individually or in groups, of conspiracy or negligence or stupidity. What these examples illustrate is rather the very human tendency to pay attention to the signals that support current expectations about enemy behavior. If no one is listening for signals of an attack against a highly improbable target, then it is very difficult for the signals to be heard.

For every signal that came into the information net in 1941 there were usually several plausible alternative explanations, and it is not surprising that our observers and analysts were inclined to select the explanations that fitted the popular hypotheses. They sometimes set down new contradictory evidence side-by-side with existing hypotheses, and they also sometimes held two contradictory beliefs at the same time. We have seen this happen in G-2 estimates for the fall of 1941. Apparently human beings have a stubborn attachment to old beliefs and an equally stubborn resistance to new materials that will upset them.

Besides the tendency to select whatever was in accord with one's expectations, there were many other blocks to perception that prevented our analysts from making the correct interpretation. We have just mentioned the masses of conflicting evidence that supported alternative and equally reasonable hypotheses. This is the phenomenon of noise in which signal is embedded. Even at its normal level, noise presents problems in distraction; but in addition to the natural clatter of useless information and competing signals, in 1941 a number of factors combined to raise the usual noise level. First of all, it had been raised, especially in Honolulu, by the background of previous alert situations and false alarms. Earlier alerts, as we have seen, had centered attention on local sabotage and on signals supporting the hypothesis of a probable Japanese attack on Russia. Second, in both Honolulu and Washington, individual reactions to danger had been numbed, or at least dulled, by the continuous international tension.

A third factor that served to increase the natural noise level was the positive effort made by the enemy to keep the relevant signals quiet. The Japanese security system was an important and successful block to perception. It was able to keep the strictest cloak of secrecy around the Pearl Harbor attack and to limit knowledge only to those clearly associated with the details of military and naval planning. In the Japanese Cabinet only the Navy Minister and the Army Minister (who was also Prime Minister) knew of the plan before the task force left its final port of departure.

In addition to keeping certain signals quiet, the enemy tried to create noise, and sent false signals into our information system by carrying on elaborate "spoofs." False radio traffic made us believe that certain ships were maneuvering near the mainland of Japan. The Japanese also sent to individual commanders false war plans for Chinese targets, which were changed only at the last moment to bring them into line with the Southeastern movement.

A fifth barrier to accurate perception was the fact that the relevant signals were subject to change, often very sudden change. This was true even of the so-called static intelligence, which included data on capabilities and the composition of military forces. In the case of our 1941 estimates of the infeasibility of torpedo attacks in the shallow waters of Pearl Harbor, or the underestimation of the range and performance of the Japanese Zero, the changes happened too quickly to appear in an intelligence estimate.

Sixth, our own security system sometimes prevented the communication of signals. It confronted our officers with the problem of trying to keep information from the enemy without keeping it from each other, and, as in the case of Magic, they were not always successful. As we have seen, only a very few key individuals saw these secret messages, and they saw them only briefly. They had no opportunity or time to make a critical review of the material, and each one assumed that others who had seen it would arrive at identical interpretations. Exactly who those "others" were was not quite clear to any recipient. Admiral Stark, for example, thought Admiral Kimmel was reading all of Magic. Those who were not on the list of recipients, but who had learned somehow of the existence of the decodes, were sure that they contained military as well as diplomatic information and believed that the contents were much fuller and more precise than they actually were. The effect of carefully limiting the reading and discussion of Magic, which was certainly necessary to safeguard the secret of our knowledge of the code, was thus to reduce this group of signals to the point where they were scarcely heard.

To these barriers of noise and security we must add the fact that the necessarily precarious character of intelligence information and predictions was reflected in the wording of instructions to take action. The warning messages were somewhat vague and ambiguous. Enemy moves are often subject to reversal on short notice, and this was true for the Japanese. They had plans for canceling their attacks on American possessions in the Pacific up to 24 hours before the time set for attack. A full alert in the Hawaiian Islands, for example, was one condition that might have caused the Pearl Harbor task force to return to Japan on December 5 or 6. The fact that intelligence predictions must be based on moves that are almost always reversible makes understandable the reluctance of the intelligence analyst to make bold assertions. Even if he is willing to risk his reputation on a firm prediction of attack at a definite time and place, no commander will in turn lightly risk the penalties and costs of a full alert. In December 1941, a full alert required shooting down any unidentified aircraft sighted over the Hawaiian Islands. Yet this might have been interpreted by Japan as the first overt act. At least that was one consideration that influenced General Short to order his lowest degree of alert. While the cautious phrasing in the messages to the theater is certainly understandable, it nevertheless constituted another block on the road to perception. The sentences in the final theater warnings—"A surprise aggressive move in any direction is a possibility" and "Japanese future action unpredictable but hostile action possible at any moment"—could scarcely have been expected to inform the theater commanders of any change in their strategic situation.

Last but not least we must also mention the blocks to perception and communication inherent in any large bureaucratic organization, and those that stemmed from intraservice and interservice rivalries. The most glaring example of rivalry in the Pearl Harbor case was that between Naval War Plans and Naval Intelligence. A general prejudice against intellectuals and specialists, not confined to the military but unfortunately widely held in America, also made it difficult for intelligence experts to be heard. McCollum, Bratton, Sadtler, and a few others who felt that the signal picture was ominous enough to warrant more urgent warnings had no power to influence decision. The Far Eastern code analysts, for example, were believed to be too immersed in the "Oriental point of view." Low budgets for American Intelligence departments reflected the low prestige of this activity, whereas in England, Germany, and Japan, 1941 budgets reached a height that was regarded by the American Congress as quite beyond reason.

*   *   *

In view of all these limitations to perception and communication, is the fact of surprise at Pearl Harbor, then, really so surprising? Even with these limitations explicitly recognized, there remains the step between perception and action. Let us assume that the first hurdle has been crossed: An available signal has been perceived as an indication of imminent danger. Then how do we resolve the next questions: What specific danger is the signal trying to communicate, and what specific action or preparation should follow?

On November 27, General MacArthur had received a war warning very similar to the one received by General Short in Honolulu. MacArthur's response had been promptly translated into orders designed to protect his bombers from possible air attack from Formosan land bases. But the orders were carried out very slowly. By December 8, Philippine time, only half of the bombers ordered to the south had left the Manila area, and reconnaissance over Formosa had not been undertaken. There was no sense of urgency in preparing for a Japanese air attack, partly because our intelligence estimates had calculated that the Japanese aircraft did not have sufficient range to bomb Manila from Formosa.

The information that Pearl Harbor had been attacked arrived at Manila early in the morning of December 8, giving the Philippine forces some 9 or 10 hours to prepare for an attack. But did an air attack on Pearl Harbor necessarily mean that the Japanese would strike from the air at the Philippines? Did they have enough equipment to mount both air attacks successfully? Would they come from Formosa or from carriers? Intelligence had indicated that they would have to come from carriers, yet the carriers were evidently off Hawaii. MacArthur's headquarters also pointed out that there had been no formal declaration of war against Japan by the United States. Therefore approval could not be granted for a counterattack on Formosan bases. Furthermore there were technical disagreements among airmen as to whether a counterattack should be mounted without advance photographic reconnaissance. While Brereton was arranging permission to undertake photographic reconnaissance, there was further disagreement about what to do with the aircraft in the meantime. Should they be sent aloft or should they be dispersed to avoid destruction in case the Japanese reached the airfields? When the Japanese bombers arrived shortly after noon, they found all the American aircraft wingtip-to-wingtip on the ground. Even the signal of an actual attack on Pearl Harbor was not an unambiguous signal of an attack on the Philippines, and it did not make clear what response was best.

Suggestions for Additional Reading

As official archives have been opened, the records of the combatants made available, and the diaries and memoirs of those concerned with America's foreign relations published, historians in generous numbers have developed their interpretations of what happened. The student in search of facts or opinions will find no dearth of material. The selections included in the foregoing readings are centered for the most part directly on two issues, the relations of the United States and Japan and the blame for the surprise attack. Limitations of space make it necessary to omit much pertinent detail in the arguments of the authors. Consequently, further reading in the books from which selections have been taken is recommended.

In addition, a balanced account of Roosevelt in the months leading to war may be found in the second volume of James MacGregor Burns's excellent biography, *Roosevelt: The Soldier of Freedom* (New York, 1970) or the somewhat less critical *Roosevelt and Pearl Harbor* (New York, 1970) by Leonard Baker. An able journalistic work from an early period is Forrest Davis and Ernest K. Lindley, *How War Came* (New York, 1942) and the readable Walter Millis, *This is Pearl* (New York, 1947). Popular treatment of the attack in books by Walter Lord, *Day of Infamy* (New York, 1957) and A. A. Hoehling, *The Week before Pearl Harbor* (New York, 1963) provide many details.

General works on American diplomatic efforts include the standard study by William L. Langer and S. Everett Gleason, *The Undeclared War, 1940–1941* (New York, 1953), George F. Kennan's brief but stimulating *American Diplomacy, 1900–1950* (Chicago, 1951), and the critical view of U.S. policy toward China by A. Whitney Griswold, *The Far Eastern Policy of the United States* (New York, 1938). British views may be found in Sir Llewellyn Woodward, *British Foreign Policy in the Second World War* (London, 1962) and Winston Churchill's *The Grand Alliance* (Boston, 1950), volume three of his personal history of the war.

Both political and military aspects are in Samuel Eliot Morison's *The Rising Sun in the Pacific* (Boston, 1948), a volume in Morison's history of the United States Navy in World War II; in the volume by Mark S. Watson, *Chief of Staff: Prewar Plans and Preparations* (Washington, 1950), from the official *United States Army in World War II*.

Japanese viewpoints are expressed in John Toland's best seller, *Rising Sun: The Decline and Fall of the Japanese Empire, 1936–1945* (New York, 1970); David J. Lu, *From the Marco Polo Bridge to Pearl Harbor: Japan's Entry into World War II* (New York, 1961); Robert J. C. Butow's examination of policymaking in the upper levels of Japan's diplomatic establishment, *Tojo and the Coming of the War* (Princeton, 1961); and Toshikazu Kase, *Journey to the Missouri* (New Haven, 1950).

Diplomatic histories both favorable and unfavorable toward Roosevelt's policies are, respectively, Robert A. Divine, *The Reluctant Belligerent: American Entry into World War II* (New York, 1965), and William A. Williams, *The Tragedy of American Diplomacy* (New York, 1962).

The hot controversy that raged between Roosevelt's defenders and detractors may be followed in a number of books and articles. Attacking the President were Charles A. Beard, *President Roosevelt and the Coming of the War, 1941* (New Haven, 1948); Charles Callan Tansill, *Back Door to War: The Roosevelt Foreign Policy, 1933–1941* (Chicago, 1952); William Henry Chamberlin, *America's Second Crusade* (Chicago, 1950); George Morgenstern, *Pearl Harbor: The Story of the Secret War* (New York, 1947); Frederick C. Sanborn, *Design for War: A Study of Secret Power Politics* (New York, 1951); John T. Flynn, *The Roosevelt Myth* (New York, 1948); and Harry Elmer Barnes, ed., *Perpetual War for Perpetual Peace* (Caldwell, Idaho, 1953), especially the article by William L. Neumann, "How American Policy toward Japan Contributed to War in the Pacific." See also Neumann's *America Encounters Japan—From Perry to McArthur* (Baltimore, 1963). A fellow officer in the Navy, Robert A. Theobald came to Admiral Kimmel's defense in *The Final Secret of Pearl Harbor* (New York, 1954). See also Francis C. Jones, *Japan's New Order In East Asia: Its Rise and Fall, 1937–1945* (New York, 1954), and Bruce M. Russett, *No Clear and Present Danger: A Skeptical View of the U.S. Entry into World War II* (New York, 1972), which are more balanced and credible books.

An early defender of Roosevelt was Basil Rauch, who attacked Beard in *Roosevelt from Munich to Pearl Harbor* (New York, 1950). Feis, from whom a selection is printed herein, and the aforementioned work by Langer and Gleason were more substantial works justifying the policies of the Roosevelt administration. A number of historians came to the defense of the government in articles such as

Robert H. Ferrell, "Pearl Harbor and the Revisionists," *The Historian* 17 (Spring 1955); Samuel Eliot Morison, "Did Roosevelt Start the War—History through a Beard," *Atlantic Monthly,* August 1948; Arthur M. Schlesinger, Jr., "Roosevelt and his Detractors," *Harpers Magazine,* June 1950; Col. T. N. Dupuy, "Pearl Harbor: Who Blundered?" *American Heritage* 13 (February 1962); and General Sherman Miles, "Pearl Harbor in Retrospect," *Atlantic Monthly,* July 1948.

Influences on American policy are traced in a number of the articles in Dorothy Borg and Shumpai Okamoto, eds., *Pearl Harbor as History* (New York, 1973), along with a number of essays analyzing Japanese forces influential in that country. For American isolationists the best general introduction is Wayne S. Cole, *American First: The Battle against Intervention, 1940–1941* (Madison, Wis., 1953). Mark L. Chadwin, *Hawks of World War II* (Chapel Hill, N.C., 1968) is limited to examining one group of interventionists.

Accounts by participants in policymaking must be read with regard for personal viewpoints. Among the most useful are *The Public Papers and Addresses of Franklin D. Roosevelt,* edited by Samuel I. Rosenman, volume X (New York, 1950); Cordell Hull, *The Memoirs of Cordell Hull* (New York, 1948); Henry L. Stimson and McGeorge Bundy, *On Active Service* (New York, 1948); Joseph C. Grew, *Ten Years in Japan* (New York, 1944) and his papers published by Walter Johnson in two volumes, *Turbulent Era* (Boston, 1952). See also the article by Joseph W. Ballantine, "Mukden to Pearl Harbor," *Foreign Affairs* (July 1941).

Biographies of American leaders include Robert E. Sherwood, *Roosevelt and Hopkins* (New York, 1948; rev. ed., 1950) utilizing Harry Hopkins' papers; Elting S. Morison, *Turmoil and Tradition: A Study of the Life and Times of Henry L. Stimson* (New York, 1964); Waldo Heinrichs, Jr., *American Ambassador: Joseph C. Grew and the Development of the United States Diplomatic Tradition* (Boston, 1966); Julius W. Pratt, *Cordell Hull, 1933–1944,* 2 volumes (New York, 1964) in the series *American Secretaries of State and Their Diplomacy;* Forrest C. Pogue, *George C. Marshall: Ordeal and Hope, 1939–1942* (New York, 1965–66); and John Deane Potter, *Admiral of the Pacific: The Life of Yamamoto* (London, 1965). The essay by Edward M. Bennett, "Joseph C. Grew, Diplomacy of Pacification," in Richard Dean Burns and Edward M. Bennett, eds., *Diplomats in Crisis: United States, Chinese, Japanese Relations, 1919–1941* (Santa Barbara, 1974) provides a penetrating analysis.

For an accurate, readable account of the technical aspects of the vital and impressive work done by American cryptanalysts in providing intelligence of Japanese measures, especially the cracking of the Purple code, see chapter one of David Kahn, *The Codebreakers* (New York and London, 1967).

For additional historiographical and bibliographical comment and listings, see Robert A. Divine, ed., *Causes and Consequences of World War II* (Chicago, 1969), the first two sections; John E. Wiltz's extended essay, *From Isolation to War, 1931–1941* (New York, 1968); Wayne Cole, "American Entry into World War II: A Historiographical Appraisal," *Mississippi Valley Historical Review* 43 (March 1957); and Ernest R. May, *American Intervention, 1917 and 1941* (Washington, 1967).